Which of these

ha...

chance for su...ss?

1. The husband is a youngest child; his wife is an oldest child.

2. The husband and wife are both eldest in their families.

3. The husband has older sister(s) and the wife has younger brother(s).

4. The husband and wife are both youngest in their families.

5. The husband has older and younger sisters and the wife has older brother(s).

6. The husband has younger sister(s) and the wife has older brother(s).

7. The husband has older sister(s) and the wife has older and younger brothers.

The Birth Order Factor answers many more relationship questions, and suggests the best way of handling your special personality traits to make your life richer and more rewarding.

ANSWERS: Numbers 1, 3, and 6.

The
BIRTH ORDER
FACTOR

HOW YOUR PERSONALITY IS INFLUENCED BY YOUR PLACE IN THE FAMILY

by

LUCILLE K. FORER, Ph.D.

WITH HENRY STILL

A KANGAROO BOOK
PUBLISHED BY POCKET BOOKS NEW YORK

THE BIRTH ORDER FACTOR

McKay edition published 1976

POCKET BOOK edition published July, 1977

This POCKET BOOK edition includes every word contained in
the original, higher-priced edition. It is printed from brand-
new plates made from completely reset, clear, easy-to-read type.
POCKET BOOK editions are published by
POCKET BOOKS,
a Simon & Schuster Division of
GULF & WESTERN CORPORATION
1230 Avenue of the Americas,
New York, N.Y. 10020.
Trademarks registered in the United States
and other countries.

ISBN: 0-671-80871-0.

Printed in the U.S.A.

ACKNOWLEDGMENTS

I am indebted to hundreds of researchers who have studied birth-order effects and supplied substantive results which I integrated with my own clinical observations.

My one regret is that private clinical practice did not offer me the resources for individual research on the grand scale of college, university, and government facilities. However, I have drawn upon small-scale studies of my own to describe observed birth-order effects in situations hardly ever examined by more conventional investigators. (Attitudes of persons toward becoming parents, as discussed in Chapter 14, "Parenthood: I," is one example of this. Another one is the material on marital relationships between persons of various birth orders.)

Both Henry Still and I wish to acknowledge the expert assistance of Dr. Bertram R. Forer, who read the manuscript and made valuable contributions and suggestions. His creative ideas and clinical observations have been so helpful that he should be considered a major contributor to this book.

AUTHOR'S NOTE REGARDING
CASE STUDIES

It is common for readers of psychological works to "find themselves" in a book. Some readers, including former clients of mine or their relatives, may think they recognize themselves in various case studies cited in this book. Actually, they will only be identifying with common patterns of behavior, since all of us have experiences and personalities which are similar to those of many others.

A great deal of care has been taken in every case study to change all identifying details. In many instances, an individual case is representative of many persons with the same birth order. Occasionally material reported by other therapists has been integrated into the case histories. Accounts of treatment have been simplified, with an emphasis on therapeutic attention to the specific problems associated with birth-order effects.

—LUCILLE K. FORER, PH.D.

Contents

INTRODUCTION   xiii

SECTION I   BIRTH BOUND
Chapter 1   A Place in the Family   3
Chapter 2   Why Birth-Order Effects Occur   15
Chapter 3   Special Circumstances   26

SECTION II   THE GROWTH OF A PERSON
Chapter 4   Personality Patterns: I   39
Chapter 5   Personality Patterns: II   47
Chapter 6   Achievement   60

SECTION III   THE WORLD OF WORK
Chapter 7   Vocations and Creativity   75
Chapter 8   Women Who Achieve   87
Chapter 9   Power and Politics   100

SECTION IV   SEXUAL DEVELOPMENT AND
             SOCIAL RELATIONSHIPS
    Chapter 10   The Social Network   115
    Chapter 11   Developing Sex Roles   133
    Chapter 12   Sexual Adequacy   151

SECTION V   MARRIAGE AND PARENTHOOD
    Chapter 13   Marriage   165
    Chapter 14   Parenthood: I   186
    Chapter 15   Parenthood: II   201

SECTION VI   A LOOK INTO THE FUTURE
    Chapter 16   Using the Information   227
    Chapter 17   Which Birth Position Is
                  Best?   231
    Chapter 18   Implications for the
                  Future   236

NOTES   250

BIBLIOGRAPHY   257

INDEX   261

Introduction

One of the most serious and rewarding activities of life is that of trying to discover who we are, why we are that way, and—if we don't like what we see—what we can do about it. The process begins at birth (and possibly at conception), and does not end until we die.

Psychology is probably the most pervasive of the sciences, because of its search into human thought and motivation. It is also the most nebulous science, because it deals with myriad variables.

A newborn child is bound by the pattern of germ plasm brought by its parents to conception, and remains linked to the changing environment into which it is born. No two human beings are born completely equal or the same —not even identical twins—and it is impossible for two people to live identical lives from birth to death. Every experience changes the course and texture of one's life.

Genetic inheritance greatly influences a child, whether a boy or a girl, light or dark, large or small, intelligent or dull, a genius or retarded, healthy or unhealthy, well formed or malformed, with countless gradations of difference between each pair of extremes. The infant's environment may be loving or hostile, harsh or benign, rich or poor, hot or cold, rural or urban—again, a myriad number of variables comes into play.

Scientific study requires observation and experiment to establish general rules under which known conditions lead to predictable results. An astronomer can predict the moment when a solar eclipse will occur, and the proper combination of hydrogen and oxygen always produces water. But psychology yields no precise formulae by which a human being may be neatly classified and expected to remain within that particular category.

As a result, psychology is a continuing labor of trying to identify the major influences upon the life and behavior of human beings, relating these to similar experiences, and approaching rules which are generally applicable. The word *approaching* is critical, because absolute precision is impossible. A century of study, however, has evolved guidelines which are partially applicable to nearly everyone. We know that genetic inheritance leaves indelible marks, and that sexual development and gratification are important. Whether parents are loving or non-loving affects a person struggling to maintain, actualize, and enhance his or her personality. Being male or female makes a great difference. Family wealth or poverty also plays an important role. These are a few of the variables which impinge on the lifelong development of an individual.

One such variable—an important one—is *birth order*, the position into which a child is born within the framework of the family: the first, second, third, fifth, eighth, last, or only child.

Researchers have found that there are specific strengths, as well as weaknesses, inherent in each birth-order position. They vary widely, depending not only upon the order of birth but also on the sex of each child. My primary purpose is to explain what is known about the significance of birth order, and then to help you understand why you are as you are, so you can maximize your strengths and modify your weaknesses.

We are concerned basically with examining how family organization and attitudes influence human beings, and their effects on individual adjustment in adult years: personal relationships, love affairs, marriages, parental behavior, work attitudes, and success or failure. Overall, we seek to learn what happens in the childhood home that enables a person to meet what Alfred Adler [1] calls the three requirements of satisfactory adjustment to social relationships: vocation, sex, and affection.

We care about individual adjustment, but we also care about the effects of childhood relationships on the way human beings carry on the larger affairs of living together in the world: politics and economics, business, national and international affairs. We tend to depersonalize our leaders, but the leaders of nations, like all of us, were once members of childhood families, with problems of adjustment to parents and to siblings. National and international leaders, like the rest of us, were influenced by their birth-order roles. A President's interaction with his parents and brothers and sisters—influenced by the ordinal position to which he was born—thus must play some part in the way he conducts the nation's business. It has been suggested that relationships developed during childhood may form the psychological basis of war and peace. As we go along, I will touch on some world leaders and other prominent men and women to illustrate my points. I hope to contribute not only to your understanding of self and motivation, but also to understanding what family influences are necessary to develop men and women who can promote world affairs in a manner most conducive to wholeness of those living in it.

If this goal seems ambitious, it is only because I am convinced that childhood relationships with parents and brothers and sisters are major factors in personal development.

Most research into birth order has dealt only with the single child and with families of up to three children. It has been difficult to delineate birth-order differences when dealing with child positions in large families—those in which four or more are born. From my clinical studies, however, I have learned that it *is* possible to distinguish birth-order differences among those children in families larger than three. Those whose place is between second and youngest I designate the "later middles." While building my foundation on studies relating to birth order, it is my clinical experience which has enabled me to refine the data and approach greater explicitness in identifying personal trends and traits related to birth order, whether the family is large or small.

The knowledge of birth-order effects is potentially useful to everyone. If you become aware of the tendencies growing out of each birth position, you can make use of the information in daily living.

First, as you learn that each position offers the possibility of developing special strengths, you become more aware of those strengths. You also become more aware of your limitations, how to cope with them, and how to be more tolerant of yourself.

Second, this knowledge provides understanding of your tendencies to behave in accordance with personality and relationships which grew out of your birth order. You may come to see how you automatically force yourself and others into unrealistic patterns of behavior by acting according to your accustomed and comfortable sibling role.

Third, you also learn how birth-order effects may cause you to interact with others in terms of *their* birth orders as well as yours. You may harbor certain attitudes toward people and expectations of their reactions because of your birth order and theirs. They too have such attitudes and expectations of you. If you understand your own tendencies and theirs, you can react with tolerance and avoid much discomfort in personal relations.

If problems arise because of birth-order effects, it is often because you are not conscious of how you are re-living the role learned from your place in the family. As you become conscious of its effects, you can work to change anything which does not please you. Then you do not need to force yourself and others to repeat childhood patterns which are sometimes not constructive. You will then know how to appraise situations and other people more accurately, so that you can behave more constructively and efficiently. That is my major goal in studying this phenomenon.

We will explore the foundations of current opinions concerning birth-order influences and relate them to personality development, work experience, love, marital relationships, and parenting children who may profit more from *their* birth positions because you learned something about the subject. Also, if the order of birth seems to have locked you into unpleasant patterns, I hope to show you how the lock can be broken. I hope you will find a sentence, a paragraph, or a page here which will help you to live in greater harmony and fulfillment.

SECTION

I

Birth Bound

CHAPTER 1

A Place in the Family

Your place in the family strongly influences how you cope with people and the world. You may recognize that your life was affected by being a first- or lastborn, or preceded by a more powerful brother or mothering sister, but you probably have assumed that your experience was unique. You *are* unique, of course, as an individual, but it may surprise you to know that the personality development of millions of other people has been influenced in a similar manner.

"I have five children," a mother says with a sigh. "I thought my experience with the first one would help me with the others, but they're all so *different!*"

Or a man complains:

"I was second in the family. My dad always favored my older brother—because he was first, I suppose. He was bigger and stronger, and could grind me into the dirt. I felt like nobody. I thought up all sorts of sneaky ways to get around him and have some fun."

Or another man says:

"I had three sisters, and my dad was away from home most of the time. I grew up with dolls and tea parties. It seemed like women were precious and the only important people in the world. I didn't know what it meant to be a boy for a long time."

Or this response from a woman:

"My brother was older and bigger and stronger, and got his kicks telling me that girls couldn't do this or that. I felt inferior in almost every way while I was growing up."

In twenty-five years of clinical practice, my husband (also a clinical psychologist) and I have come to realize not only that the ordinal position of birth exerts a profound influence upon personality development, but also that the effects are predictable within general limits and within similar societies. Almost without exception, when we try to sort out the puzzle pieces of a troubled person, we learn something important by looking back at the birth position in the family.

LETTING PARENTS OFF THE HOOK

Ever since Sigmund Freud opened the Pandora's box of parental influence on children, this relationship has been carefully studied by social scientists and psychologists. Every facet of parental behavior, from eating to loving, has been assigned responsibility for various emotional and personality characteristics of children. This trend has become so exaggerated in recent years that whatever a youngster does, his behavior is attributed to some parental idiosyncrasy. As a result, we now have a generation of parents frightened to live normal lives for fear of injuring Junior's psyche, or burdened with guilt for already having done so. Children are quick to grasp the cop-out of blaming parents for their own failure to accept responsibility.

Now it's time to let Mom and Dad off the hook, at least a little. Our parents usually are not the only people with whom we grow from childhood to adulthood. Nearly two-thirds of us are born into homes where there are children already. We live as long with these brothers and sisters as we do with our parents. Most of the other third, born as first children, generally acquire one or more siblings early in their lifetimes. For many the interaction with these brothers and sisters may be more frequent and intimate than it is with their parents; this is often the case where both parents work. Therefore, much of a child's development depends on interactions with siblings. Ultimately, children also influence their parents' life styles as well as those of their brothers and sisters.

HISTORY

Interest in the effects of birth order on personal development and achievement is not new. More than a century ago a British scientist, Sir Francis Galton,[1] concluded that the disproportionately large number of only and firstborn sons he found among eminent English scientists was due in part to the fact that parents often treated an only or firstborn child differently from laterborn children. He believed that this was especially true of sons. Galton pointed out that there was a close parental relationship with the first child because he was the only child, at least for a time, and that the first one was given more responsibility.

There was more to it than that in Galton's Victorian England. At that time, England (and most other major nations) still followed the custom of primogeniture, under which the firstborn son inherited the family fortune and in turn accepted responsibility for the welfare of other members of the family after the father died. Primogeniture was rooted in the even older need to have a son to carry on the family name or bloodline. Such considerations were important for practical reasons of economics, honor, and prestige when a dukedom, lordship, or family fortune was at stake.

It was not surprising, then, that Galton found a high proportion of firstborn sons among eminent English scientists. Oldest sons of upper-class families—those affluent enough to afford their sons' education—were expected and urged to achieve higher education and greater distinction than their brothers and sisters.

Even in a family with one or more older girls, the first son held the favored position. Higher education for women was an exception rather than the rule, although occasionally a doting father might favor a bright daughter with such an advantage. The attitude was similar among upper classes in America during the same period, although girls did sometimes go to college and become career women. It was not until after World War I and the achievement of women's suffrage, however, that the gradual movement toward today's liberated women gained momentum.

Since Galton, many researchers have studied birth order, seeking parameters of relationship to developing and crystallized life styles. First to hypothesize that birth order impresses characteristic stamps upon life style was Dr. Alfred Adler, physician, psychiatrist, and psychologist. He presented information concerning birth-order effects in numerous papers and books. Adler concluded that although primogeniture has declined in Western civilization, the family position still exerts a strong influence on development. The interaction of a child with his parents and/or brothers and sisters tends to develop certain traits and characteristics which would not be present if his birth order had been different. Adler wrote:

> Wherever I have studied adults, I have found impressions left on them from their early childhood and lasting forever. The position in the family leaves an indelible stamp upon the style of life. Every difficulty of development is caused by rivalry and lack of cooperation in the family.
>
> If we look around at our social life and ask why rivalry and competition is its most obvious aspect. . . . then we must recognize that people are everywhere pursuing the goal of being conqueror, of overcoming and surpassing others. This goal is the result of training in early childhood, of the rivalries and competitive striving of children who have not felt themselves an equal part of their whole family. We can get rid of these disadvantages only by training children better in cooperation.[2]

I concur with Adler, after long clinical experience, which repeatedly has revealed the importance of birth order among the forces which shaped a person's development. However, I must emphasize two points:

First, birth order is only one of many environmental factors important in developing and maintaining life roles.

Second, it is not the *position* of birth that is important but rather your experiences with other members of your family as a *result* of being the oldest, middle, youngest, or only child.

You may have grown up with brothers and sisters; you may have been an only child. You may be the older or younger of two. You may be the first, last, or middle of three. You may be the first, last, or one of several middle children in a larger family. You may be an only girl among boys, or an only boy among girls in one of these situations.

Whatever your position, it has determined to a large degree how you attempt to meet the goals you set for yourself, or that have been assigned to you. All members of a family force on one another certain patterns of behavior as they interact in meeting their needs. Included in these patterns of behavior are attitudes—ways of coping with situations and with others—which are related to the position the person holds in the family. Together they make up the role which the individual assumes later in life whenever he is placed in a situation similar to one encountered in his childhood family. It is in this way, as Alfred Adler believed, that the position in the family leaves an indelible stamp on a person's life style.

LIFE STYLES AND ROLES

Clothing and music are not the only areas in which styles become fads. People adopt certain verbal phrases and use them for a while, only to drop them and take up something else—or make them part of the continually evolving language. One current phrase used in this faddish way is "life style."

The popular use of the term obscures the meaning originally intended by Dr. Adler when he emphasized "style of life" in describing human personality development. One young woman, for instance, said: "So what if I want to have a child without marriage? And if I like drugs and living in a commune, that's my style of life. You want to do something else, that's your style of life."

Adler used the term to refer to the psychological functioning of an individual in attempting to reach life goals. He believed that the most important influences in forming a life style were problems encountered in significant developmental areas, such as formulating a sex role, position in birth order, and experiencing childhood disorders. Children's life styles reveal the results of their attempts to adapt to particular circumstances, and family position, like the sex role, is inescapable.

Remember, however, that nothing absolute or irreversible results from your birth position. Your development may or may not conform to that experienced by others with the same birth position. Also—through understanding birth order as one among many factors which have made you what you are—it is possible to change your viewpoint, attitudes, and life style. That's what counseling and the information contained in following chapters may do to help touch up or change the role cast for you by your parents and brothers and sisters.

THE MAJOR PATTERNS

First and only children may appear to have the best of all possible worlds in terms of parental love and attention, but the blessings are mixed. Because of the close relationship with the parents, the first child receives in full force their love, standards, attitudes, and values. He (or she) also receives the full force of their discipline and protectiveness. Since the first child is likely to be disciplined more strictly than later children are, firstborns tend to develop stringent consciences. This child may well become a strong, upright citizen of the community, but he is also likely to be rigid and intolerant toward those who do not meet his standards.

For the only child, the parental relationship remains close and intense even into adulthood. For the oldest child this relationship becomes more attenuated when a second child is born. From then on, each new child has another person between him and his parents; thus, laterborns have more than one model to copy—brothers and sisters as well as parents.

A child learns to grow increasingly confident in competing with family members so long as the relationships are fairly easygoing. When competition is strong, the inabilities of the less capable may give rise to feelings of inadequacy.

ONLY CHILD

For the only child, particularly if a boy, the absence of competition seems to increase self-confidence. The world is his oyster, and he recognizes no competition which he cannot meet satisfactorily.

If you were an only child, you're likely to be dominant, verbal, and a perfectionist—but not jealous, because your position in the family has never been threatened. You may occasionally suffer loneliness. This fact often requires you to make major adjustments in marriage to keep one close relationship that fulfills you. Only children learn to do things by themselves. They keep busy following solitary projects, and solve problems by themselves. Yet they always are eager to please the authority figure, whether it be Mother, a boss, or a military commander.

Of the first twenty-three American astronauts, twenty-one were only children or the oldest in their families. Other only children who have reached positions of eminence include President Franklin D. Roosevelt; George Gamov, nuclear physicist, teacher, and writer; entertainer Sammy Davis, Jr.; Leonardo da Vinci; Emile Zola; Oscar Wilde; Charles Lindbergh; and Albert Einstein. Women in this category have included the Duchess of Windsor, Mary Astor, and Indira Gandhi.

FIRST FOLLOWED BY OTHERS

Each child contributes in his own way to the development of every other in the family. Once a second child is born, the first is likely to shift allegiance from Mother to Father. This may be because the firstborn unconsciously realizes that Mother was responsible for producing the competition for love and attention once reserved solely for him; in a sense, the firstborn rejects her. When the first is a boy, the move toward Father presents few problems. When the first is a girl, however, she may develop a desire for intellectual achievement rather than the domestic pursuits associated with her mother. A conflict may result from this shift.

For example, a thirty-two-year-old woman named Julia complained of feeling inadequate in her work. She felt that she was under pressure and not accomplishing enough. She had never married, and now admitted that she regretted it and still hoped to find the "right" man. She had enjoyed intimate relationships with men, but complained that they always turned out to be too dependent upon her.

Julia was the older of two sisters, and during childhood they had been intense rivals. Julia admitted that she had tried to be close to her father as she was growing up.

"I tried to show him that I could do things as well as boys might," she said, "but it didn't seem to impress him much."

True to form as a firstborn, Julia excelled in school and completed college with honors. Her sister did not go to college but married at twenty-one and worked for a few years before becoming pregnant. She had three children.

As I counseled Julia, she came to understand that her intellectual interests were basically neither strong nor personally expressive. She had used this ability primarily as a way to compete with her sister. She also realized that in her relations with men she needed to dominate and force them into dependent situations. She interpreted men's actions as dependent whether or not they actually were. With them she exercised the dominance she wanted to wield over her sister. She began to recognize that she had literally trained men to be dependent on her.

Eventually Julia began to realize her own dependency needs and to take interest in noncompetitive activities, such as gourmet cooking and needlepoint. The drive to compete with her sister subsided, and they began to enjoy each other's company. Later Julia's life took a storybook turn: Her sister's husband introduced her to the man she later married.

Firstborn children (who of course are onlies until the next baby comes along) tend to be more conscientious, achieve higher scholastically, and go to school longer than laterborns. They also are more apt to become scientists or eminent in their chosen careers than are later children in the family. But the firstborn also may be jealous and angrier than a middle or youngest brother or sister. He may be tense and driven because of parents who no longer provided exclusive attention after the next baby was born. Parents also expect a higher level of achievement from their first child than from later children.

Eminent firstborns include Pablo Picasso, Norman Mailer, George Washington, Lyndon Johnson, Alexander Hamilton, Harry Truman, Leonard Bernstein, and Henry Ford. Among firstborn women of note are Katharine Hepburn, Angela Davis, Gloria Steinem, and Rose Kennedy.

THE SECOND CHILD AND OTHER MIDDLE CHILDREN

If you are a second child, you are likely to be diplomatic and a good negotiator, because you've been forced to work your way around an older, stronger sibling. You may be more friendly and able to maintain better relationships in life than the firstborn. You learned from infancy how to get your way with a more powerful brother or sister. You had an easier time with your parents, because they became more relaxed and less demanding (if you were not followed by other children). If you're the second of three or more, you learned in childhood to adjust to both adults and children, as do other middle children in large families.

Theodore Roosevelt was the younger of two children, and so were Charlie Chaplin, Jane Fonda, Barbara Walters, Jennie Churchill, and Joan Crawford.

Richard Nixon was second among five sons. Other second-borns in large families include Hubert Humphrey, Benjamin Disraeli, John Kennedy, John Q. Adams, Bernard Baruch, Herbert Hoover, Susan B. Anthony, and Joan Baez.

Middle children in large families have included Robert Kennedy, Woodrow Wilson, Dwight Eisenhower, Benjamin Franklin, and the writer Charlotte Brontë.

THE YOUNGEST

If you are the youngest child you are likely to be charming, a good companion, playful and lighthearted. You may have strong expectations that there always will be someone to take care of you, since you were the baby of the family and there always was one or more older persons around to help you. Examples of youngest children include Ted Kennedy, Anna Freud, Lady Bird Johnson,

Beverly Sills, and the poet Gertrude Stein, who was the youngest of five children, with three older brothers and a sister. Gertrude Stein was very concerned with identity, and in childhood she connected much of her sense of self with her brother Leo, two years her senior. Later she wrote:

> I was the youngest member of my family and there were five of us and this my brother was only two years older. Naturally everyone always took care of me and naturally he always took care of me and I had a great deal of care taken of me and that left me with a great deal of time altogether.
>
> . . . It is better if you are the youngest girl in a family to have a brother two years older, because that makes everything a pleasure to you, you go everywhere and do everything while he does it all for you and with you which is a pleasant way to have everything happen to you.[3]

Obviously, Gertrude Stein enjoyed her position as the baby of the family, and later it became her life style to be "taken care of" by Alice B. Toklas.

BEING MALE OR FEMALE

There will be more to say about women's liberation further on, but at this point it is worth emphasizing that your gender and that of your siblings is also important in predicting birth-order effects. An example of this is Margaret Mead, noted anthropologist and sociologist, who wrote:

> I was a first child, wanted and loved. Before my birth my mother kept a little notebook in which she jotted down: "When I knew baby was coming, I was anxious to do the best for it." . . . My father called me, very affectionately, "Punk." Then when my brother was born two years later, I was called the "original punk" and Dick was known as "the Boy punk," a reversal of the usual pattern according to which the girl is only a female version of the true human being, the boy.
>
> Before Dick was born, my parents made the com-

mon mistake of promising me a playmate in the new baby. As a result, I found his newborn ineptitude very exasperating. I have been told that I once got him, as a toddler, behind a door and furiously demanded: "Can't you say anything but da, da, da all the time?" [4]

This is a typical reaction of an intelligent girl to the birth of a younger brother. She finds him inept and rubs it in. She believes him to be a bother to their parents, and thinks of him as weaker than she. Such attitudes have their effect upon little brother as well, and the pressure may cause him to withdraw from competition. Sometimes this withdrawal may be severe, as with several of my clients who resisted school and are still resisting competition in the adult world.

One facet of the complex importance of sex roles in birth order and sibling interaction is demonstrated by a twenty-eight-year-old professional man who complained of feelings of unreality and depression and inability to assert himself with his colleagues. George explained that since early childhood he had always felt unable to meet the standards of his parents and school authorities.

He had a sister who was four years his senior. She was intellectually precocious as well as physically strong, and arrogantly asserted that he was "just a baby who can't do anything."

For a boy in such a situation there is much to overcome, particularly if the attitudes of parents *and* the other sibling are unfavorable toward him. Girls develop more quickly than boys, both physically and mentally, so the effect can be demoralizing to the brother who is not only younger and weaker but also slower to develop.

In his early years George had abandoned attempts to excel intellectually, because he felt competition with his sister was futile. During therapy he was able to understand that the pattern had perpetuated itself in his later life. Now his position in a professional field has improved considerably and is in keeping with his potential.

The reverse situation was suffered by a twelve-year-old boy, a firstborn followed only ten months later by a sister.

Carl was intensely jealous from the day his mother came back from the hospital with the new baby. His feelings were compounded by the fact that the baby sister developed physical dexterity and cleverness more quickly than he. When the children were small, his parents were forced to watch him closely to prevent him from harming the baby.

When the two children reached school age, they were scheduled to enter first grade together, because of their birthdates. Recognizing a potential emotional disaster, the parents decided to hold the daughter back a year in order to give Carl a chance to develop self-confidence without facing his sister's direct competition in school. In spite of this, Carl's sister was brighter and performed her schoolwork better than he did. Also, by now she had learned devious ways to "get his goat" by using various stratagems such as taunting him and then running to father for protection. This drove Carl to the point of violence. He vented his hatred toward her, often physically, even though he knew his actions would lead to severe punishment.

The situation did not improve until Carl found outside interests, such as Boy Scouts and Little League baseball, from which his sister was barred. She, in turn, was wise enough not to try to compete with him in his own arena, found her own circle of friends, and by age eleven was living a satisfactory life which seldom brought her into conflict with her brother.

Although Carl's sister seemed to adjust to the life role thrust upon her, it would require many exclusive triumphs before he would rid himself of the feelings of inadequacy he had suffered in competition with a "mere" girl, and the guilt accumulated from the times he had been punished for venting his rage.

Again, it is important to consider the position of your birth, your sex, and the sex of brothers and sisters in evaluating birth-order effects.

CHAPTER 2

Why Birth-Order Effects Occur

In primitive societies a high percentage of babies died at birth or shortly thereafter. Men were cast in the life role of hunters and foragers, because a pregnant woman's strength and agility are limited. A mother nursed her first-born and carried him on her hip only until the second child came along; then the first was dropped to toddle at her side, with only an adult hand now and then to help him keep up with the tribe. While not understanding the reason for his rejection, the first youngster learned competitive skills to obtain his share of the family food—either that or he died. The oldest child developed food-gathering skills and had a head start in physical strength, and therefore continued to hold a competitive advantage over his siblings whenever hunters brought in the meat. Other things being equal, he retained this dominant position in the family, no matter how many brothers and sisters came along.

The "why" of birth-order differences begins here, but it cannot end here, because we have done little more than construct a sketch of the dominance or "pecking" order, which pertains to so many other living creatures. While the pecking order certainly exists, development of life roles in modern society depends more on the *pattern* of the human family.

Most children spend the first five years of life within the close family circle. During these years indelible marks of dominance and birth-order differences are stamped on the developing child which carry on to adulthood, but we must not assume these differences begin only at birth. As one investigator pointed out: "The two-way relationship between an individual and his physical environment, which does so much to determine his life pattern, begins not at his birth but at conception." [1]

LIFE BEFORE BIRTH

We shall not attempt to analyze the complexities of genetic inheritance, except to note that nature has established a system for almost infinite variety of physical and mental attributes. This variety, however, is limited for each individual to the combination of genes and chromosomes in the parents' germ plasm. Genetic influences are important in determining one's intelligence, temperament, and physiology; the offspring, with certain variations, will reflect parents and grandparents. Conception and possibly some intrauterine and other environmental conditions determine if a child will be male or female.

Does the genetic inheritance from a set of parents remain identical from one child to the next? There are indications that as a person grows older, changes may occur in individual germ cells. Physical or chemical forces, such as nuclear radiation and drugs, may alter the machinery of cell development. Therefore, the germ cells which create a later child may be different from those that existed when an earlier child was conceived.

Genetic defects may also occur. One of many possibilities is Down's syndrome, commonly known as Mongolism, a genetic defect which causes mental retardation. A child's chances of being born Mongoloid increase as the mother approaches the age of thirty-five and go up more sharply after forty. Up to age twenty-five, a mother's chances of producing a Mongoloid child are only 1 in 3,000. By age thirty the odds have grown to 1 in 1,500. Over age thirty-five, the risk approaches 1 in 100, and over forty the odds are 1 in 50 or higher. [2]

This information is not meant to frighten prospective parents, but to show that, because the mother's age increases with each pregnancy, later children in large families are more likely to suffer this particular genetic error. (It follows, incidentally, that if the current trend toward small families should continue, prospects are good for a reduction of the number of Mongoloid children born.) Down's syndrome and a number of other defects now can be diagnosed before birth.

Some potential handicaps for unborn children also exist at the beginning of pregnancy. The second child of a woman at a given age is more likely to be healthy than the first child of a woman of *the same age.* One reason is that the placenta of a firstborn fetus is smaller than those of later fetuses, and this reduces nourishment and oxygen available, which affects growth and development.

A second reason is that the first child usually experiences a longer labor. It takes him longer than a laterborn to travel the four-inch journey from the womb to the world. A first labor averages fourteen hours, compared to a later one of about eight hours. Laterborns also experience few labor complications than first babies do. They are more often spontaneously delivered, and show a higher percentage of normal births.[3]

A woman carrying her first child often feels differently than she would during a later pregnancy, and her emotions may influence the child both before and after birth. Thus, there is a web of sometimes contradictory conditions which can determine the physical and mental health of early and later children.

PARENTAL ATTITUDES

If you are a prospective parent, your attitudes toward the birth of a new child are subject to change through the years, ranging perhaps from delight with the firstborn to "a cross which must be borne" feeling with later children. The change in parental attitudes is most obvious in Western society, where no longer are many sons and daughters needed to help with the family work. Such attitude changes were demonstrated by a fifty-year-old woman who had five children over twenty years.

Mrs. Clay was married to a moderately successful businessman. They lived comfortably, and their children were conceived under religious constraints which prohibited

artificial birth control. Mrs. Clay accepted the duty of
bearing children, and felt helpless about controlling their
number.

"I remember the first one very well," Mrs. Clay said.
"My husband was still in college, and we lived in an up-
stairs apartment. Near the end of pregnancy it was difficult getting up and down stairs, but we were happy with
the prospect of our first youngster.

"My husband wanted a boy, I could tell, although he
said he didn't care which it might be. I didn't really care,
but I guess I hoped for a boy—to make him happy and
carry on the name. It was a good time, although we didn't
have much money. I had a long labor, but he was born
naturally.

"Yes, it was a boy. I was proud because I had delivered what my husband wanted. We did the normal
things, I suppose, counting fingers and toes to see if he
was all there in the right places." Mrs. Clay smiled.

"When we got him home I found out what it meant to
have a baby. I was the oldest of four children, and was
familiar with taking care of brothers and sisters, but this
was different. This was mine. I worried when he cried,
and he cried a lot those first several weeks. We were delighted every time he smiled or did something new like
learning to crawl. We imagined he said words long before he did. I think we always expected more of him than
we did of any of the later children. We pressed him hard
in school, and in behavior.

"Our second one, almost four years later, was a girl.
She probably would have come sooner except that my
husband was on sea duty during the war. I did not enjoy
that pregnancy, because I was alone in a big city and had
to ride a bus to get to the hospital. My husband came
home on leave in time to help me when she was born. I
was happy to have a daughter.

"This was a hard time, because my son had had me all
to himself for three years. He was jealous of his father
and he was jealous of his new sister. I was a little disappointed as my daughter started growing out of baby-
hood," Mrs. Clay continued. "I hoped she would play with
dolls and girl things, but she spent most of her time trail-
ing after her big brother. They gradually learned to play
together, but she was a tomboy all the way.

"After that I was never really happy to find myself

pregnant again. After another three years we had another boy, and two years later another. I loved them all, but I guess I paid less attention to the two later boys than I did to the first children. We lived in a large place then, and the two younger brothers played a lot together. They were close, but also rivals in everything. The younger one wanted to be able to do everything his brother could. That rivalry continued, really, until they were old enough to leave home.

"It was a struggle, trying to take care of all four. My husband had a night job, so that most of the discipline and chauffeuring to school and things were left to me. I was tired of children. It seemed like my whole life was absorbed, that I never had any time to do the things I wanted." Mrs. Clay sighed.

"The house was usually a mess, although I loved to keep it neat and clean. I yelled at the kids a lot to get them to take care of their own things. My daughter and I were surrounded by males. I didn't want any more babies, but each time we had a new one I longed for another girl. She never came.

"We moved, and my husband took a new job. I breathed a little easier as each year passed without another baby. Finally the diapers were all down off the line, and all four youngsters were in school.

"Then, eight years after our last child was born, I became pregnant again. I must confess I hated it from the beginning—not the child himself but everything the pregnancy represented—another trip to the hospital, more diapers, more crying and baby puke, and now I knew I would be an old woman before the last of my kids left home. I was deeply depressed, but finally reconciled myself to it. I was forty-one, but he was a healthy baby.

"Sometimes I've been just too tired and sick to give this last boy the attention he needs, but the other children helped make up for that. In some ways this last boy—now that the other kids have mostly gone—is like having an only child, like starting a new family all over again. It's fortunate that my husband is home more of the time now, and he pays more attention to this boy than he did to the others.

"The thing is, though, we're just plain tired of having kids and their problems. It's a tense kind of tiredness, as though we're always anticipating problems and trouble.

We love this last boy very much, but wish we didn't have to go through the struggles with teen-agers and everything we've had before."

Mrs. Clay's reactions and attitudes are not unique. As she talked about her children, it seemed that she fit the patterns we have found in many families. Her tiredness is more than physical. Since having a hysterectomy her physical health is fairly good, but her experiences point up the psychological and emotional differences which affect the way younger and older mothers relate to their children.

Mothers probably react differently to laterborn children because they have accumulated experience, and parents differ in their own behavior from one child to the next. There may be a psychological aging, apart from physical aging, which takes place, and this will make a great difference in the way later children see their parents. It may also be that once the novelty of the first child has passed, parents pay less attention to the needs and achievements of later children. Many mothers have described their delight with first words of the firstborn child, but less pleasure when a later child learns to talk. Later children may be seen as a burden and given less attention (because the parents' workload has increased), and thus personality development depends more on interaction with brothers and sisters than with parents. On the other hand, the experienced mother, with less anxiety than she felt with her first, may be more relaxed and show more warmth toward second- and laterborn children. A great deal also depends upon the personality and health of the parents, as well as the nature of brother-sister relations.

PATTERNS OF NEED

It is important to think of families as composed of individuals interacting *with* one another, acting *on* one another, and reacting to the *presence* of one another. These are human beings, each intent on maintaining and actualizing himself. Father's needs may be different from those felt by Mother or children. He may need solitude and quiet—in a home full of growing youngsters. Mother has her special needs. Perhaps she gave up a career as an interior decorator to give herself more fully to her small children. Rearing them may be one of her needs, but another may be to have a lovely home. Relations with her children may be strained because these needs are contradictory. Each child has his own needs, and will use every tool at his disposal to see that those needs are met.

The parents have a relationship in which each tries to satisfy the other's needs for affection, acceptance, and security. The children also need things from one another, like companionship, as well as affection, acceptance, and security.

A child quickly learns to use the means at hand to enhance and maintain himself. In this new environment outside the womb there are other human beings to fetch and carry, but the baby is oblivious to Mother's schedule or other duties. Baby cries when hungry or wet, and soon learns to associate crying with fetching Mother to provide what he needs. The infant begins to use his senses, his muscles, and the cortical level of intelligence to deal with discomfort, to bring pleasure to himself. Gradually the human organism begins to perceive that "*I* am bringing this about for *me*." Thus, both I and Me are brought together as the total of Self: *myself*, which is both object and that which initiates action.

As needs become more complicated, the child learns to meet these as well: the need to be valued and be cared *about* as well as cared *for*. Personality and behavior express a striving for superiority, utilizing the energy at one's disposal to bring relaxation and comfort, to actualize, maintain, and enhance one's position from one day to the next in a changing environment.

Interweaving needs and ways of satisfying them change as the family changes. Parents and one child interact in ways that must change when another child is born. In fact, the conditions of family life change so much as children are added that the development of each in a large family may be strikingly different, according to birth order, from the development of each child in a small family. In large families, for instance, the oldest child may be limited in achievement and the youngest more apt to achieve—a reversal of what happens in small families. Many people are puzzled about radical differences among their siblings because "we all had the same environment."

Genetic differences aside, the environments are *not* the same for different children in the same family.

As children emerge from total family absorption during preschool days, they begin to use their resources to establish positions and grow in relation to boys and girls in the wider arena of school and neighborhood. Their methods and success will depend greatly on what they learned at home. Individual behavior may change, but it still exhibits a birth-order effect different for firstborns than for laterborns. For example, first children tend to be less physically aggressive than later children during preschool years, but after they enter first grade they show an increase in aggression, while laterborns exhibit less.

THE POWER STRUGGLE

A major factor in birth-order effects is the power struggle between parents and among children of a family. This struggle is basic to each person's need to maintain, actualize, and enhance himself, no less for Mother and Father than for the children.

The tug and pull between parents, however, is not limited to their interaction with each other, as they may believe, and cannot fail to have an effect upon the children, because it involves matters of discipline, imposed values, and determination of family activities. Each child feels this parental struggle in a different way, and the first receives the greatest intensity of feeling.

Equally important is the power struggle between parent and child. This is what discipline is about: parental attempts to impose values, beliefs, and wishes on their child. The reason is usually benign: a desire to mold their son or daughter into what they see as a useful member of society. The child has no concept of what society will require, but does know what he wants from one moment to the next, whether it be food or love, and he tries in whatever ways are available (such as crying or whining) to impose his will on the parents.

For each child the disciplinary relationship is different. First children usually receive the strictest discipline, the greatest number of admonitions and punishment. This is why firstborns often become serious adults with strong self-discipline. The first youngster is inclined to be compliant, but hostile domination by either parent may impel him toward rebellion, especially during adolescence.

A later child may try to get what he wants in some way other than direct confrontation. Having witnessed the altercation between older sibling and parents, the younger child may become sweet and good, in contrast to a verbal and demanding older brother or sister. The child may learn to be satisfied with very little, or learn devious means to obtain what he needs. This is probably the basis for the observed manipulative tendency of laterborns (as shown in later chapters) in contrast to first children.

The third phase of the power struggle takes place among the children, but it also contains elements and extensions of the other conflicts. The first child is prince (or princess) of the family. If he is an only, he will live that role for life. If a second child is born, the first suddenly loses power over the parents, who have turned their attention to the more helpless baby. This is traumatic for the firstborn, who struggles to regain his former power, but never fully succeeds, because he must now share what the parents have to give.

By simple logic, the first child turns his power guns on the younger brother or sister who usurped his position. He cannot understand that there is enough love to share, so if impulses were reduced to raw desire, he would like to destroy the new baby. As the two grow together, the first (especially if a boy) remains physically stronger, and may use this strength to suppress the new sibling. The newborn, unable to match power with the first, is thus likely to develop more devious ways to get what he wants, both from the parents and from the older brother or sister.

The main goal of this power struggle is to gain parental indulgence. In early years it is sought mainly from the mother, and only when this fails does the child turn to the father. To the child, his mother appears to be the source of most good things, particularly affection and approval.

When the second child arrives, the first usually becomes jealous and the stage is set for the firstborn to utilize any method of dominance which seems to offer successful competition with the new rival. The sibling hierarchy is a little social system in which dominance is exercised by the more powerful. Older children are usually physically stronger, and play a parent-surrogate role. As adults they are often bossy, as in childhood, especially if they were the oldest among a number of children. While young, later children may shout and cry to overcome the verbal bossiness of an older brother or sister. Thus, laterborns may seem more physically aggressive, but by adulthood they often have developed clever, indirect ways of obtaining power. All children in a family are rivals of one another, and use all means at their disposal to maintain and enhance their status.

A second child followed by one or more brothers and sisters may be competitive and ambitious to outstrip the older sibling as well as the younger children. Second children often emerge from the "sandwich" power struggle as highly competitive adults. They may manifest their competitiveness in high professional productivity, or, if the person was consistently thwarted in self-realization, he may follow destructive pathways, as happened to one young man who sought counseling.

Rance was the middle child of three, with an older sister, who was favored by their parents, and a younger brother, who was coddled as the baby of the family.

"From childhood," Rance said, "I've been afraid that someone will find out that I am not adequate, that I'm not as big as I want them to think I am."

As a teen-ager he turned to vandalism and other scrapes with the law in his lower-class neighborhood.

"I think my destructiveness is to show how much guts I have," he said. "It's important to me to do something risky and not get caught. I like to be known as the meanest kid on the block."

Both Rance's sister and brother did well in school, so it seemed that the dangerous physical things he did were the only way he thought he could compete with them.

Rance did not seek psychological help of his own volition. His wife asked him to enter counseling along with her because she was afraid his continuing violence would get them into serious legal difficulties. Unfortunately, Rance was not willing to look deeply into himself for areas of possible change, and his wife was finally forced to divorce him.

A later-middle or youngest child may find that a dependency role pays off. If the youngest waits for things to be done, older children or parents will do them for him because he is the baby. The youngest may also find that doing clever things earns praise, which may teach him to make efforts to achieve.

MODELING AND PUNISHMENT

Later children often use older siblings as models—if they are the same sex—finding them a source of sex-role identification. If they are of opposite sexes, there may be a tendency to develop opposite-sex characteristics. Sisters with brothers seem more influenced toward adoption of opposite-sex characteristics than are brothers with sisters. If brothers have sisters close in age, their own male characteristics may be intensified, while the sisters often adopt male interests and attitudes. This may occur in the girls because male attributes still seem more prestigious in our society.

Not only do the punishments and rewards of parents determine how a child feels and behaves in each place in the family, but children themselves reward and punish one another for behavior that agrees with or opposes their own needs. The oldest may reward younger children if they behave in ways that allow him to enjoy the rights and prerogatives of his seniority. If a younger sister allows older sister to show how responsible and able she is, the older sister will be nice to the younger one. If the younger sister asserts herself, the older one is likely to punish her, in ways ranging from verbal complaints to physical blows. The younger sister may appear subservient to a stronger authority figure, but she also learns to punish the older sister by cajoling an even higher authority figure: the parent.

Thus, it is the interaction among members of the family which trains each of them to take on certain patterns of behavior and life roles. Each child has certain potentials for enhancing and maintaining himself. One grows to associate those possibilities—in feelings, behavior, and attitudes—with one's role or place in the family. These roles form the basis for personality development and the basis for adult behavior patterns—the "why" of birth-order effects.

CHAPTER 3

Special Circumstances

It seems easy enough to count one, two, three, etc., and establish your place as only, oldest, middle, or youngest child. However, it may not be as simple as that. Special circumstances, such as the number of years between children, disability or illness, adopted or stepchildren, or multiple births (such as twins), can make a difference in the way birth order is experienced. For instance, even though you have brothers and sisters, you may be an only child so far as birth-order effects are concerned.

THE YEARS BETWEEN

The reason you may be an "only child" even though you have brothers and sisters is that the number of years between you and a sibling ahead of or after you may isolate you in a way that makes you experience your birth order as though you are an only child. The span of years between siblings also may make other differences in the way you experience your place in the family.

Gertrude Stein commented that her friend, Alice B. Toklas, "had a tendency to think that anyone is an only child because she was one, that is to say she had a brother, but he came so much later that she was an only child." [1]

The number of years between siblings that seems to shift their experienced place in the family may be as little as four or five.

Evidence that spacing causes different birth-order effects was shown by infants as young as thirty-eight to fifty-six weeks who were observed reacting to a stranger and then to a novel toy. In both situations, the greatest fear was shown by children who were either firstborn or who had been born three or more years after the previous sibling. [2] These laterborns showed fewer positive social responses than laterborns closer in age to their older brothers and sisters.

The explanation for this seems to be that both the first-born and the widely spaced laterborn are protected by older persons in the family from contact with peers, and hence do not learn as quickly as laterborns with siblings closer in age to them to feel comfortable in new situations. In adult life the difference in reaction to fear-provoking stimuli is carried over. This was demonstrated in a study of Navy recruits in which lastborns at least five years younger than their next older siblings reacted more like only children than "small-gap" laterborns. [3]

An example of a firstborn who was really an only child because of the age gap between her and younger siblings, was Jasmine. She was seven when her next younger sister was born; another sister followed two years later. As a young woman Jasmine came to see me because she felt lonely and unloved by her parents, her sister, and her boy friends.

"I've never felt that I was part of the family," she said. "I've felt like an outsider."

For the first seven years of her life Jasmine was reared by parents who were both working in the family business and were distracted by constantly being on the edge of business failure and poverty. By the time her sisters arrived, Jasmine's parents had achieved some security, and her mother stayed home to supervise the younger sisters. But Jasmine attended school and was left much to herself by her mother, who saw her as more independent than the younger girls.

Jasmine struggled through school, hating it and getting by only "by the skin of my teeth." Adolescence meant that she could have boy friends, but even then she found that she never maintained the relationships for long. At twenty-two she hated herself and felt that she was disliked by everyone. She felt, as she said, "like someone always looking on while others have fun."

As we examined her relationships with parents and sisters, it became evident that Jasmine *had* been an "outsider." The two younger girls were close friends, and their interests didn't coincide with hers. She carried her feelings of rejection into her relationships with men, which caused her to cling so closely to them that they soon felt stifled and lost interest in her.

Another woman who was so much older than her younger sisters might have attempted to mother the boy friends, but Jasmine had not been mothered herself even before her sisters were born. She did not know how to develop closeness at any level.

When Jasmine became aware of the extent to which she had been acting like an only child rather than a member of a family, she began to develop a relationship with her sisters. They, in turn, seemed happy to have her more mature advice and guidance, especially as they moved into adolescence and began dating.

Jasmine later married an only child who, like herself, had experienced loneliness and rejection by parents who were involved with other commitments. These two "only" children give each other the constancy and security each needed during childhood.

A common example of the years between is the "caboose baby," the child born many years later than the next oldest brother or sister. This child often seems to have it pretty good, with many adult figures in the house who may be indulgent and willing to give guidance and any kind of help, including financial assistance. This child combines many characteristics of the only child and the youngest child.

Bossard, in his study of large families, found that "younger siblings . . . may be looked upon as one's own children, especially if the age difference is great." [4] Thus, the youngest child who follows his previous brother or sister after a wide gap of years is likely to be regarded by the others as their child. In many ways he will also experience his position as though he were an only child with a large number of parents.

Thus, when determining your birth order, you must take into account the number of years between you and your next siblings. If you are five or more years older than the next younger child, consider that spacing in determining your place in the family. If you are a firstborn, you are also an only child in many of your characteristics. If you are not a firstborn, you may have to think of yourself as the second of two in a two-child family (especially if there are *more* than five years between you and the next child) or the youngest of several children. If you are the child who follows by five or more years, you will have to take that into account. If you are not followed by any other children, you may consider yourself an only child. If you are followed by one or more other children, you may have many characteristics of an oldest child.

ILLNESS OR DISABILITY

Another circumstance that will make a difference in the way you experience your birth order is chronic illness or physical or mental disability in your family. It also makes a difference if you or a sibling are absent from the family during the early years of childhood. If a child is severely disabled or otherwise unable to take an active part in family activities, the next sibling in line is likely to assume the role of that child instead of his own.

A middle-aged woman, for example, consulted me about relations with her married son and his wife. She said it was the only flaw in her life, but was causing her great unhappiness.

Elizabeth's son had been married for ten years, and though she tried to be friendly, her daughter-in-law had completely shut her out of the relationship with her and her husband. Now a grandchild was to be born, and Elizabeth was afraid she would not be allowed to see the baby.

The daughter-in-law was the second of two children, with a brother two years older than she. Her husband was the older of two, with a sister two years younger than he. Elizabeth's son was a successful lawyer, dedicated to his profession and apparently happy with his wife. Outsiders, however, thought he was dominated by her. The daughter-in-law had alienated most of her own and her husband's relatives through her domineering manner.

"She seems to think no one knows how to do anything but her," complained Elizabeth, who herself was a subdued, passive, and compliant person.

In searching the daughter-in-law's background, I learned that although she was the second of two children, her older brother had been critically ill most of his life and had died at age eighteen. Their mother also had been sick most of the time, which had compounded the problem for Elizabeth's daughter-in-law. At an early age she had been forced into a position as boss of the household, much like a firstborn child. Everyone had depended on her, and she had become authoritarian and embittered by the heavy burdens placed on her. As an adult she transferred this bitterness to relatives and in-laws in a repetition of her childhood pattern of behavior.

I explained this situation to Elizabeth and advised her to be as compliant as possible to her daughter-in-law's wishes, giving help only when asked and expressing enthusiasm when invited to visit. By the time her grandchild was six months old, Elizabeth again was a happy woman. The relationship with her daughter-in-law had improved, and finally Elizabeth was asked to supervise the household and her grandchild while her daughter-in-law went to work outside the home.

Intellectual disability is likely to alter the usual status of a child even more than physical disability. With physical illness, the older child may still assume his role as he guides and directs his younger sibling(s). Richard Nixon's older brother, for instance, apparently participated in the family despite a chronic illness. Serious mental retardation, however, hampers the child in assuming the role of the oldest, and to all intents and purposes this child might become the youngest in the family.

Absence of a sibling, through death or otherwise, may shift birth-order patterns. Margaret Mead tells how the death of a sister changed the pattern in her family:

"Katherine's death made a gap in the family. Instead of our being five stair-step children, we fell into two pairs. The younger girls, born two and four years later, were treated almost like a second family and for years they were called 'the babies.'" [5]

STEPBROTHERS AND SISTERS

When it becomes a question of "yours, mine, and ours"—when children from a previous marriage are brought into a new marriage—they will bring with them the roles they have already learned with their original parents and siblings.

The stepchild who is older than three years may bring to the new home ways he or she has learned previously of relating to other children. If he was the only child in the preceding family and now must fit the role of older or younger brother, he will require some time to adapt. It also will take time for the child to adjust to the requirement of sharing his own mother or father with a stepbrother or sister. Children brought into a new marriage by the mother often seem to have an easier time adjusting than do children brought into the marriage by the father. The new stepmother must be aware of this and of the necessity for helping her new children adjust to her position as mother. It is often easier if the new stepmother has no children of her own, because the father's children then see no serious rivals invading the home.

When children are born after the second marriage, as frequently happens with a woman who has no children and marries a man with several, the children of the second marriage may line up much as children do in any family. This is especially true if there is a large age gap between the children of the father's first marriage and his children by the new wife. The first of these children may resemble an oldest child. Examples of this are George Washington and Sigmund Freud.

ADOPTED CHILDREN

The fact, per se, that children are adopted should make no difference in the birth-order effects for those children. Birth-order effects are no more than the result of parents' relating to their children in terms of their wishes, attitudes, and needs, and the children's relating to the parents and to one another in similar terms. If we take a hypothetical situation in which neither parents nor children were aware of their adoptive relationship, no difference in birth-order effects might be expected. Any genetic differences, such as appearance or intellectual level, would be handled in the same way any parents and children adjust to differences among themselves. There is no reason to believe any mysterious differences would exist.

Most adopted families are formed in sequence like any other family, i.e., there is a first child and perhaps later ones. Even though adoptive parents may have some concerns that biological parents do not (and do not share in some of those held by biological parents, such as: "Is he going to have my father-in-law's ears?"), adoptive parents have the task of parenting with the same dreams, the same hopes, and the same attitudes as do other parents.

Adoptive mothers relate to their first and later children in the same manner as biological mothers. They are generally more apprehensive and demanding with a first child and more relaxed and comfortable with second and later children. Thus, an infant adopted as the first child assumes the same attitudes and behavior any first child does. If other children are adopted as infants, they move into place as would natural children.

There are some conditions in adoptive families, however, which may deviate from the usual pattern of biological families. One has to do with socioeconomic status of adoptive parents, who tend to be of higher than average intellect, educational background, and economic level.

Adoptive parents may feel somewhat "on stage" as parents. They may believe they are being watched by the agency which placed the child with them, as well as by neighbors and relatives, challenging them to demonstate their prowess as parents. Thus, they may be more tense and anxious than they would be otherwise, and communicate some of this anxiety to their child, especially the first child. If they adopt others, they are likely to be more sure of themselves with the later children. Their first, however, may be even more driven to achieve competence and approval than the natural first child would.

The fact that adoptive parents usually are above average in education, intellect, and economic level can make them even more uneasy about the prowess of their adopted child. They may not know the specific background of their child, but they may expect it to be different from theirs and doubt the child's ability to live up to their expectations. This seems to be the source of the severe conflict that sometimes occurs between achieving parents, such as the famous or wealthy, and their adopted children. These parents do not realize that biological children do not often achieve at the level of their exceptional parents, and are disappointed if their adopted children do not meet their standards of competence. The weight of this pressure may be particularly great for their first adopted child. Like any other parent, adoptive parents must accept the fact that their children will gradually achieve their own identities out of their own resources and the personalities they develop in their childhood homes.

Other conditions are sometimes different for adopted than for biological families, and some of these are similar to situations experienced by families with stepchildren. There are times when the adopted child is not an infant. If so, the earlier surroundings of the adopted child will determine his reaction to his new home, as would be the case if he were a stepchild. If he is an only child and is older than five or six, he may always maintain some of the characteristics of an only child, just as a biological child does who is that old when a younger brother or sister is born.

Another differentiating condition exists where there are both natural and adopted children in a family. We can best understand what may happen then if we keep in mind the original premise: that any human being uses his own resources and those of the environment to maintain, actualize, and enhance himself. A parent cannot ignore the fact that one child is biological and one is adopted, but adjustment to this need not depreciate either child. In fact, such families are often the best-planned: A biological only girl can be followed by an adopted boy, whereas in biological families the sex of the second child cannot be so determined. Four biological children can be followed by a much-desired youngest of another race or color who is admired and loved by the other children in the family because they had a part in choosing their little brother or sister. If the adopted child is the only one of his sex in the family, he may hold a highly favored position.

How does the adopted child take his place among natural children in the family? Birth-order information takes on special importance in understanding such situations. Parents can be saved anxiety and concern if they know what to expect of first and later children, whether adopted or biological.

If the adopted child is first in the family, he will show emotional and intellectual reactions to parental pressures usually placed on a first child. If a biological child follows, parents need not be alarmed if he shows the usual tendencies of second children to be less achievement-oriented than the first. If the first is natural and the second adopted, parents need not feel that the different behavior of the second child is due to inherited deficiencies from his biological parents. Behavioral tendencies are the usual birth-order effects, and can be alleviated by parental efforts to fully develop the potential of their children—adopted or natural, firstborn or laterborn.

Parents do need to adjust to the facts of their situation when one (or more) is a natural and one (or more) an adopted child. A mother usually puts special pressures on her first natural child. Hence, an adopted child followed by a biological child may observe his mother giving special attention to that second child. Any child wants love, attention, and approval from his parents. If he doesn't get this, that child will react in a direction that, hopefully, will change the parents' response. If Mother or Father gives special attention to the second child, the adopted one may become more competitive with the natural child. Feelings of hopelessness and rejection may result if those efforts are unsuccessful. If parents are aware of these birth-order tendencies, they can recognize adverse symptoms and deal with them before larger problems arise.

In a mix of biological and adopted brothers and sisters, the usual differences of age, strength, and intellect at any one time will promote the usual birth-order effects of sibling rivalry. Older brother (biological) may "parent" little brother (adopted). Their interaction may be tinged with rivalry, using natural or adopted status as weapons against each other. Older brother may taunt the younger with "not really being part of the family" or with "not really having a mother and father."

The best prevention parents can offer for such hostile interaction among biological, adopted, or stepchildren is for themselves to be happy and comfortable with all their children and treat them all with equal affection, concern, and respect.

One couple with an eight-year-old daughter decided to

adopt a twelve-year-old girl because they believed their child should not grow up alone. (The parents were too advanced in age to adopt a child younger than their daughter. Both were in their late forties, and their only child had been born after the mother lost several earlier conceptions.)

At first their natural daughter, who had been an only child, did not take kindly to the advent of an older sister. She complained that she did not like being bossed by the older girl.

The father, who had been a younger member of a large family, sympathized with her and told her that he too had not liked being pushed around by his older brothers and sisters. The father's attitude apparently relieved some of his daughter's tension.

WHAT ABOUT TWINS?

Twins and other multiples have a birth order, even though they may be separated from each other only by a few minutes or hours. The fact that this separation is important to their parents and to them is indicated by the haste with which they inform others about who was born first.

The Biblical twins Jacob and Esau are long-standing examples of the giving of the inheritance to the firstborn, and the Machiavellian means used by the laterborn to obtain it. At one time in Eastern societies a different approach was taken in designating the one to receive the family property: The infant born second was considered to have shown his quality by being courteous enough to allow the other to go first.

In Western society the firstborn of twins or multiples often is accorded respect by the laterborn. Dan and Milt are an example of this. At age thirty-seven, both men had some years of successful teaching experience. Dan decided he needed assistance in becoming more assertive after Milt was made principal of his school. Dan, in another school, was passed over in favor of an older man.

Milt was born three minutes before Dan. All through their childhood Milt made this difference very clear to Dan, indicating that he was older and wiser.

This in itself might not have made Dan feel inadequate,

but Milt also was an inch taller and a few pounds heavier throughout most of their childhood.

"Fortunately," Dan said, "Milt didn't seem as interested as I was in athletics, so I was able to do better than he at sports. But then we went off to college together, and I quickly found that he was able to make better grades than I could. I felt more and more uncomfortable about competing with him.

"But we both got teaching jobs after we finished college. Then I began to see how much more assertive he was than I could be. He felt better about himself. He had always ordered me around, and now he began to tell me how to teach my classes, even though we were at different schools.

"Somehow it seemed that I had completely lost out when he was made a principal and I wasn't. I had heard about assertiveness training, and it seemed to me that it might be just what I needed."

It wasn't all that he needed. Dan also needed considerable assistance in developing inner comfort and self-esteem. In an unexpected development, he found he did not really wish to pursue an administrative role in his school. Although he and Milt were twins, Dan, as the second-born, had reacted to Milt's emphasis on educational achievement by stressing his own athletic prowess. He decided he would follow that course, and finally seemed more likely to become a college coach than a high-school principal.

If twins are not identical, the birth-order effects may be accentuated. Jane and Priscilla were non-identical twins. They looked so different, even at birth, that their mother decided to ignore their twin status as much as possible.

Jane, born first, was long, thin, and dark. Priscilla was shorter, chubby, very pink-and-white-skinned.

"Jane was always the quiet one, the thinker," said their mother. "Priscilla was cute and sweet and we all babied her. She was never as interested in school as Jane was."

Now, in adulthood, Jane is a college teacher, while Priscilla is administrator of a bank—a pattern of occupational differences that, as we shall see, fits in with expected birth-order results.

SECTION

II

The Growth
of
a Person

CHAPTER 4

Personality Patterns: I

Madeline, an only child, was a young married woman who sought counseling because she found it difficult adjusting to her husband and coping with two small children.

Madeline was immature. Her parents had never given her a chance to grow up, and her mother had done everything for her. As we talked I noticed signs of loneliness and protective isolation, which so often characterize the only child. She said her mother was domineering, while her father was "mild as toast."

"Mother and father always seemed to be together in their own separate worlds, and it never seemed to have anything to do with me," Madeline said. "Mother told me nothing about the world or its problems. I've had to learn it all since I grew up."

This young woman had not developed an identity separate from that of being the child of her parents. She said nothing except what she believed others wished to hear, and had nothing to give of herself. At the time she sought counseling, Madeline had an immature relationship with her two children. She screamed at her baby, and if problems overwhelmed her she simply left the children with her husband or a baby sitter and went away by herself.

"She's like a little girl playing house," her husband said. "She doesn't like sex, and she doesn't like having friends visit us because she wants me all to herself."

"I feel insecure," Madeline said. "I just don't know how to handle things as an adult."

After explaining to her that many of the characteristics of her personality are common among only children, I was able to support her ability to make needed personality changes. After some weeks of psychological counseling she commented: "I feel like an adult and capable of coping with my life."

The only child, such as Madeline, is a special case in the family hierarchy, because he or she goes through life without experiencing interpersonal relationships with brothers and sisters. The contrast with those who have grown up with siblings will become more apparent further along.

If you are encouraged and complimented for what you do, you are likely to try even harder and develop a high level of self-confidence. All through life the only child may take the attitude "I'm Number One because I try harder," and look with disdain upon other people who appear not to strive so hard for what they want.

On the other hand, because of the isolation with two adults who provide everything that's needed, the only child may be pampered and spoiled—as Madeline was— so that he is not prepared to make decisions or take the actions necessary to compete and pursue life goals.

During a child's early years the parents are strong models for sex-role identification, especially for only children. Male onlies tend to be more feminine than other males in interests and attitudes, while female onlies tend to be more masculine. The close association between an only boy and his mother, largely because she holds him as a precious possession, often causes him to be like her in everyday attitudes and interests. This can lead to heterosexual disturbance such as impotence or homosexuality in adulthood if the father is either physically or emotionally absent.

An only girl may identify with her father because she admires him, but she may also want the conventional feminine role of wife and mother. She is more likely than other girls to become a lesbian, but that outcome seems related to extremely disturbed parent-child relations. A hostile mother may force her into a close relationship and identification with her father, or into assuming an overprotective role toward her mother if the father is absent.

The only child generally enjoys high self-esteem and confidence, although this is more true of boys than girls— only girls crave approval for their actions more strongly than the boys do. The only child also tends to be optimistic, because he or she has been the beneficiary of everything a family has to offer, including undivided love, affection, and expression of approval and guidance. Onlies of both sexes develop a strong sense of their right to attention. They usually appear mature and self-sufficient, but there also may be an internal dependency conflict concerning their parents.

Birth-order characteristics again emerge clearly when we consider the firstborn child followed by others.

THE FIRSTBORN

If you are firstborn in a large family, you are, of course, an only child for a little while, and during that period will develop the personality attributes of an only child.

Until then the first boy or girl most often enjoys a warm and close relationship with the mother. Studies have shown that the mother is the parent who spends the most time with the firstborn child, whereas the father is the principal disciplinarian. The father tends to play a less important role in disciplining later children because he has learned from the first one to be more tolerant of child behavior. He is also generally more preoccupied with making a living for the growing family.

Thus, he may appear harsh to the oldest child but more benevolent to younger brothers and sisters.

The big shock for the firstborn comes when Mother goes to the hospital, leaving her child alone, and then returns with a new baby. The older child abruptly loses Mother's exclusive attention as she devotes time to the new infant. The first strives to regain the apparently lost ground, unable to understand that there is enough love to share with both children, and is jealous. If his actions lead to punishment, he is further convinced that Mother doesn't love him any more. Then he will try even harder, often with unpleasant tactics, to draw attention back to himself. If the firstborn can turn to Father for acceptance and approval while Mother's treasured love is focused elsewhere, the child will probably continue to develop a healthy personality. However, the father remains the chief disciplinarian for the firstborn—and more attention-demanding actions call for discipline, so that the firstborn may feel rejected by Father as well.

This was true of a middle-aged man named Harold, the older of two brothers, who came to me for therapy. Harold's mother was passive and submitted to her husband's wishes, while his father was angry and always punishing. After her second child was born the mother was bewildered when Harold developed the usual aggressiveness and assertion evidenced by a two-year-old child. She left his direction and punishment to his father. Her younger son, by contrast, was calm and quiet. Her relationship with him was warm and protective, while Harold was left much to himself and his father's harsh discipline.

As a result, Harold rebelled as soon as he could find an arena in which he could gain attention—principally in school. He resisted direction and conformity and frequently got into trouble. Not only did he get poor grades, but he was also physically aggressive and disrupted his class.

Because his brother had no problem with rebellion or conformity, the younger boy performed well in school and achieved better grades than his older brother did. After graduation from high school, Harold's brother obtained a position which was secure and paid well. He lived a comfortable, conforming existence.

In the meantime, Harold shifted from rebellion to competing with his father and brother. He even went to college and obtained a degree. After this, however, his basic rebellion again gained the upper hand, and by resisting authority he lost one job after another.

Now, in middle age, Harold is trying through therapy to gain a perspective on the father-brother relationships which affected him so strongly, and to resolve his conflict with authority which has caused him repeated failure. In time he may yet achieve what he needs: successful work utilizing his education.

In personality development, the oldest child is usually conservative, reflecting the mores and attitudes of the parents and of obedient self-control. Whether man or woman, the oldest is likely to be the member of the family who carries the patterns of an older generation into the new one. He is often jealous or anxious as a result of being superseded in the family nest, and often dissatisfied with himself because so much was expected of him as a child.

Oldest children need approval. They are susceptible to social pressure, and have a tendency to change opinions to agree with others. Confronted by authority, firstborns generally are more conforming and responsive to accepted standards than other children are. Where parental treatment has been fair, they are more respectful than children born in other ordinal positions.

General moods range from sensitive seriousness to depression in firstborns. Social attitudes usually include acceptance of religious training, social awareness, and a strong sense of responsibility. Firstborns often do not empathize with disadvantaged people. They may say, "We should care for the helpless," but their real feeling is: "They could do better if they would work harder."

Oldest children generally prefer to avoid conflict, but also regard themselves as able to change situations. However, if a situation arises which they cannot control (or believe they can't), their anxiety rises, and they seek reassurance from other people. In disaster situations firstborns tend to be more afraid than others, and seek out other people for support.

Firstborns are often considered most fortunate of all children in the family, because they were favored by parents and achieve more distinction in professional life. They are often high achievers, it is true, but not necessarily happier, whether they achieve or not. One research study found that firstborn girls of families of six or more children were outspoken about their adult discomfort, and they were the ones least envied by other children in their families. While being oldest confers many advantages, it does not guarantee better social or emotional adjustment. A case in point is Lorna, the oldest of three sisters.

At age thirty-five, Lorna was a very angry woman. Her anger was accompanied by depression, and she often found herself either screaming at her husband or in tears.

As we explored her problem together, it seemed to center around competition with the elder of her two sisters, who was close to Lorna in age. She described how much cuter her sister had been while they were growing up, and how her sister had developed more rapidly and outgrown Lorna, who was short and thin. This added to her problems because "I was afraid to fight back against her because she was very aggressive."

In the typical behavior pattern of an oldest or older sister, Lorna became the "good girl," hoping to regain favor with her mother. The younger sister was rebellious and fought back against her parents, always able to vent her feelings and express herself. Despite this, Lorna's mother always took the sister's side in any conflict between the two girls. Lorna also was troubled by her father's attitude, but she was more compliant. "I would do anything for Father when he called me his girl, as he always did when he wanted me to do something for him."

Her sister developed what Lorna considered an unfair tactic. When denied something, she cried until she became ill so that Father either gave in to her or, if the tantrum went too far, cuddled his favorite, cute little daughter.

"I gave up too quickly," Lorna said, "but it was because I thought I wouldn't get what I wanted or I would just make Mother or Father angry with me. I was always afraid to fight back against my sister, even when she was little, because I might hurt her and then I'd get into trouble."

Like many older sisters of sisters and older brothers of brothers, Lorna began developing her intellectual abilities as a way to compete with her sisters. Both parents were college-educated and expected their daughters to follow the pattern.

"I thought I had made it," Lorna said. "I didn't envy either of my sisters until they had kids. They married early and quickly had several children, but until that time I thought my better education gave me status with my parents."

Despite all the evidence of competition, envy, and anger, Lorna did not fully accept the depth and bitterness of her feelings until she dreamed about the sister with whom she had competed in childhood. In this dream she was safely inside her own house, but down in the street she could see her sister being attacked by thugs. The beating was vicious and cruel. Lorna could see her sister helpless, terrified, and bleeding, and tried to call the police, but was unable to get through. Then she awoke.

Lorna had some familiarity with dream analysis, and I

was able to make her see that *she* was the one who had dreamed this, *she* was the one who had seen to it in her dream that her sister was attacked, and *she* had not gotten the police to help her sister.

Lorna now could accept the dream violence as her own true feelings. She was also now able to see the frustration and resentment she felt at being unable to compete with her sisters' childbearing. As with many older sisters of sisters, the intellectual prowess she achieved became less important when the basic functions of marriage and childbearing entered into the competition with a younger sister.

Lorna then became pregnant. This desired condition, coupled with a better understanding of her anger, frustration, and wish to have her husband recognize her needs without her telling him about them, now made Lorna very comfortable. She withdrew from therapy for about one and a half years, until she started having another struggle —this time with her own baby.

Lorna's son was a strong, heavy child, and as assertive as an eighteen-month-old child is likely to be. Lorna worried about everything the baby did, and everything she did in rearing him. It was easy to see that her infant's demanding aggressiveness had reawakened her feelings about her sisters. She was afraid to be assertive with the baby, as she had been afraid with her sisters. When the child cried and she did not know what to do, she became angry. Then, not wishing to vent her anger on the infant, she ended up frustrated and in tears.

Lorna needed deeply to be a better mother than her sisters were. I was able to help her by corroborating the rightness of her judgments about mothering her child. She was an intelligent, warm, and loving woman, and her basic impulses were in the right direction. She was simply afraid to be assertive, or to accept her own ideas and impose them on her child, her husband, or anyone else. Defenses against her own rage at her sisters made her unable to express natural emotions.

Our working together helped Lorna become assertive and express what she wanted without being overcome by gut reactions like anger and tears. Such reactions previously had made it impossible for her to evaluate any uncomfortable situation. She had complained that she was never able to see what was going on, which she couldn't while blinded by rage and tears.

When she learned to control these reactions, simply because they just didn't occur, Lorna was able to evaluate situations with her husband, her child, or anyone else, and adapt her behavior according to realistic circumstances.*

---

* For more detailed information concerning the effect of the gender of the second child on the personality development of the first, see Lucille K. Forer, *Birth Order and Life Roles* (Springfield, Ill.: Charles C Thomas, 1969), pp. 55–65.

CHAPTER 5

Personality Patterns: II

If you are a second child, your way of life will depend upon whether you are the second of two or the second followed by one or more brothers and sisters.

SECOND OF TWO

Two conditions emerge with fair consistency in the two-child family:

1. The younger is placed at a competitive disadvantage with the older, more powerful sibling.

2. The younger boy or girl becomes the parents' favorite, because he or she adopts different tactics from the more demanding older child.

The secondborn quickly learns several adaptive techniques. One of these is to take advantage, as the baby, of parental protection against aggression from the older brother or sister. Another is learning the art of compromise. Third is the development of more devious ways to satisfy needs. Whereas the older brother or sister may exert direct force to reach a competitive goal, the younger child learns to run plays around end instead of bucking the line. This often includes the use of parental strength to curb the older sibling's aggression. **Your** life style as the second of two will depend on your gender and whether you have a brother or sister.

YOUNGER BROTHER OF A SISTER

If the younger brother of a sister is permitted to be assertive, he will probably become self-reliant and non-conforming, and care little about what others think of him. He is likely to have high self-esteem, but may retain characteristics like tenderness and the ability to communicate, because he had two "mothers." He also may become domineering with women.

As an adult a younger brother may continue to depend on his older sister. The wife of such a man once complained to me that instead of her going home to Mother when they quarreled, her husband would "pack up and run to his older sister's home."

Fairly typical of a younger brother who had not been permitted to be assertive was a young man who came to me with marital problems. Bill resented domination by his wife, who was the older of two girls. (It is a fairly common occurrence for a man who had an older sister to choose a firstborn wife.) Bill had grown up uncertain of his relationship with his father.

"I always wanted his company," Bill said, "but he only used me when he needed me. I felt he did not like me."

He felt his mother, on the other hand, "tried to stifle me," and the same pattern had developed with his older sister, so that his personality conflict was compounded. He was repeating his childhood history in his current relationship, unaware that he had chosen his wife to fit into this pattern and trained her to relive it with him.

As we explored his problem, Bill came to see how, as a child, he had internally fought against the domination of his mother and sister. He and his sister had quarreled, but she had overwhelmed him both verbally and physically. The distance from his father did not allow Bill to develop a strong male sex role, and he felt smothered by females. Thus, his strong-willed wife made him uncomfortable and rebellious. Once he was able to see the relationship with his sister in clearer perspective, Bill developed a degree of masculine assertiveness and his marriage improved. His ability to establish a rewarding, growing relationship with his wife meant he had to disengage her from the role of older sister.

GIRL WITH OLDER SISTER

A secondborn girl may be dominated by an older sister who rationalizes the domination as "mothering." The role of being dominated may be accepted freely by the younger sister, as it was by an eighty-year-old woman who said proudly:

"I've always been babied, first by my father, then by my sister, and then by my husband." Both girls married, but neither had children. For many years after their husbands died they lived together in a mother-child relationship.

The older sister's mothering also may be rejected by the younger.

"My older sister wants to live with me," one woman said. "I resent the fact that even though I'm forty-five years old and have been married twice, she still thinks she can tell me what to do." This younger sister solved her problem, at least temporarily, by moving to Hawaii, far from her home town and her sister.

A younger sister tends to adjust more comfortably in personal relationships, marries earlier, has children earlier, and is a more competent mother than her older sister. One reason may be the more relaxed relationship with parents enjoyed by the secondborn. Parents do not push as hard for achievement with the second child, and unintentionally may show favoritism toward him or her because *they* now feel more comfortable in their role as parents.

BOY WITH OLDER BROTHER

The younger son in a two-boy family is likely to develop physical skills and engage in body-contact sports, because it is difficult to compete intellectually with his brother. The younger is likely to be gregarious and fond of people of his own age. He is mentally flexible, with tolerance for novelty and variation, but once a notion is set he tends to be dogmatic. He sees the environment as outside his control, but shows less need than firstborns do for comfort and reassurance in a situation of fear and anxiety.

One study of eminent secondborns in two-child families indicated that they conform to peer values rather than to an inner conscience (internalized parents), as firstborns typically do. Thus, secondborn men tend to form opinions around current norms and are less easily influenced by established authority. They are therefore more likely to initiate or accept social change.

Personality development of a boy with an older brother is linked strongly to the quality of identification with their father. One of my clients, the second of two sons, had marital problems centered in a need to relate to older women.

Gary's father fancied himself an intellectual, but often was away from home gambling and drinking, contributing little to support his wife and sons. Gary's mother had been only sixteen when his older brother was born, out of wedlock, and eighteen at the time of Gary's birth.

In spite of her youth, the mother was the dominant force in the family. She operated a neighborhood grocery store to support the family, and Gary helped her, thereby strengthening their bond. His older brother was a "straight-A student who had his nose in books all the time." Their father, the self-styled intellectual, showered praise on the elder son.

During his childhood, Gary's behavior was contradictory. His mother considered him gentle and pleasant, yet he was aggressive with other youngsters. He explained his behavior as "fighting to show who had guts." His brother's opposite behavior apparently resulted from the father's excessive approval of the scholarly older son. Gary, however, received what he considered more important: the attention, affection, and approval of his mother.

Eventually his parents divorced and his mother remarried. This change in family structure enabled Gary to leave home and begin a new life independent of all the other family members. He married a woman six years his senior, and lived with her much as he had with his mother. At first his wife accepted the dominant role in supporting him, but when she tired of this role the marriage ended in divorce.

Gary still needed the security of a close relationship with an accepting and capable mother figure, so he remarried, this time to a woman four years older than he was. She quickly saw that he needed her more as a mother than as a wife, and that his aggressive competition with other men would continue to get him into trouble. She persuaded him to seek therapy.

During treatment Gary discussed and faced up to his childhood tendencies to use women for both emotional and financial security and to be overly aggressive with males. His insight into the way in which he was super-imposing the past on the present eventually helped him to relate to his wife in a more objective way and to retain the job he had nearly lost due to constant physical aggression.

THE MIDDLE SECOND

Second place in a family of three is often considered the most difficult of all birth positions. The second of two children generally is not openly competitive, but the second of three is wedged in a situation which stimulates maximum competitive potential. This forced struggle may lead to high success in the business and commercial world.

The middle child has special difficulties to overcome. He or she is second to a more powerful older child but senior to the third, who may receive more parental attention for a longer time than the middle does.

Middle children frequently complain of hardship in growing up between two others, and several studies verify the validity of this complaint. In a survey of three-child families, children and their teachers agree that the middle child seems most vulnerable to maladjustment, even though the parents of these children did not favor one sibling over another. Among nursery-school children from three-child families, secondborns rated highest on verbal aggression toward peers and on seeking help from adults.[1] One might suspect that they were unpopular with their peers. Generally speaking, secondborns of three are likely to have more social problems with teachers and with other boys and girls.

The middle child often is more excitable, demanding, attention-getting, and undependable than the older and younger children are. The middle one also may be more active and vigorous in most situations.

The center birth position seems to affect girls more strongly than boys. For instance, a middle boy among three boys usually is less anxious than either of his siblings, while the middle among three girls may be more serious, depressed, self-reproachful, and anxious than either of her sisters. For either a boy or girl middle child, being the only one of that sex in the family helps to build self-esteem. The middle girl with two brothers is likely to be more relaxed than her siblings, more emotionally mature than her older brother, and more gentle than the younger one.

In adulthood, the middle of three girls is likely to reflect her lifelong attempt to gain attention and the dissatisfaction shown by her parents because she was not a boy. (The parents' favorite child is *least* likely to be a daughter both preceded and followed by a girl.)

Both Joan Baez and Kate Millett were middle girls of three. Millett, the angry philosopher of women's liberation and author of *Sexual Politics,* states: "We were constantly reminded that we weren't sons, that we were mistakes."[2] Bonnie Parker, of Bonnie and Clyde, also was a middle among three girls.

As adults it may be difficult for middle children to control competitive tendencies in order to achieve comfortable relationships.

When a fourth child is born, however, the second shifts to a more advantageous position. There is no longer such a clear-cut difference between the second and the first or third children. In fact, when a fourth is born the second child inherits some of the advantages of the first. Parents now see him as more mature, and tend to delegate more responsibility to him.

If things go well in the family, the middle child may do *very* well, because in that position he is forced to use his potential to the maximum. He probably learns more than any other person how to be skillful in handling people. In her memoirs author Kathleen Norris recognized the importance of competition within a family. She was second among six.

"I want to place my own considered theory of the main causes of human behavior beside Freud's and those of Freud's whole school," she wrote. "The abiding genesis of the way we act is based on jealousy. Jealousy and sex frequently intermingle, but jealousy comes first, starts earlier and lasts longer.

"I have seen it in babes of three months and in centenarians of 101." [3]

Case studies further demonstrate the personality development common to the second of three or more children.

One woman, the second of four girls, was the most competent, but she also took advantage of other people's weaknesses. If a friend exposed a weak spot, this woman was likely to plunge a verbal knife into it. One friend confided to her: "I didn't realize how hard the job would be." This woman retorted acidly: "You remind me of the saying that fools rush in where angels fear to tread."

A man who was born between two sisters complained that he had difficulty relating to women. He felt that he must protect them from himself.

"I either allow them to dominate me or I try to dominate them," he said. "I've never been free of that struggle with domination."

Larry told me he could not see women as women but always as mothers or sisters. He felt either that they had to be protected from his maleness and from recognizing their own sexual needs, or that he must force them to submit to him.

I encouraged him to discuss his childhood relationships with mother and sisters in depth. He confided that he and his little sister had often engaged in sex play. Mother and older sister were protected by age and power, but little sister could be seduced. Guilt about these sexual activities persisted into adulthood.

As I worked with Larry I explained that this pattern was not unusual for men in his birth position, and he came to see that there was no need to carry the guilt of childhood over into relations with other women. His relationships then improved.

By contrast, another man, secondborn with three sisters, learned constructive techniques for dealing with women in childhood. He had kind, loving parents and sisters, and his adult relations with women were also kind and considerate. He has become the personnel director of a firm that employs hundreds of women.

THE LATER MIDDLES

Early in life the members of a family seize on small differences in traits, aptitudes, and interests to distinguish one child from another. These traits often become part of family banter and competition. Calling attention to such differences fixes them early in an individual's mind and distinguishes him in a group situation. This kind of differentiation is most true of large families, where individuals tend to become lost in a crowd's need for parental attention.

One girl was so humiliated when her sister was singled out as the pretty one or "the one with those beautiful big eyes" that she would run away when visitors came. She compensated by developing her mind, and became an outstanding lawyer. There may be a boy who is a math wizard and is always called on at family gatherings to demonstrate his cleverness, or a girl who wins a swim meet and thereafter is known as "the champ." Such children have established identities and know who they are. Others in a large family may not be so fortunate. One researcher has categorized the types of children usually found within a large family as follows:

1. The responsible one.
2. The popular and well liked.
3. The socially ambitious.
4. The studious one.
5. The self-centered loner.
6. The irresponsible.
7. The physically weak or ill.
8. The spoiled child.[4]

We must caution that such categorization is not fixed or universal. Many variations can result from age (and the years between any two children), as well as from sex, order of birth, and innate characteristics. This does not mean that every family with eight children will match the above model.

We have seen the woman who competed with a sister's beauty by becoming studious. Another remembers that she competed with an older sister by being brave during thunderstorms and remaining calm during family crises. She believes that her current position as supervising nurse in a hospital is a direct extension of her childhood role as the one who could meet problems with strength and courage.

Although there are many combinations of characteristics in later-middle children, some definite personality patterns are discernible. For example, a boy born in the last half of a family with a minority of brothers is likely to have high self-esteem, which tends to be greater if he is the only boy child. This same quality for laterborn girls does not seem to depend so much upon the sex of the siblings, but there is an advantage in the development of self-esteem if she is the first girl after several boys.

There is more variety in the life patterns of late-middle children, perhaps because the definition of their life role is more diffuse. As adults they tend not to think of themselves as part of a general group. Having fought for individual status within a large family, they value identities won in their own right. Rather than saying, "I am a businessman," a later middle is likely to be more specific, such as: "I own a car-parts business." He or she may be uncomfortable in crowds and belong to few social groups. These late middles rely less than others on outside evaluation of their performance. They often relate well in personal situations, may not require so much support from another person, and tend to be self-reliant and responsible. Because middleborns in a large family must cope with many peer situations without parental attention or intervention, they perform well under threat of physical stress or harm. They are less moralistic than other children, open in social relations, resist social pressures, and show less anger in commonplace situations.

Later-middle women tend to be less aggressive, less moralistic, and have less need for approval than firstborns. Like their male counterparts, they are also good at breaking down interpersonal barriers.

THE YOUNGEST

The youngest child is the baby, and will remain so in the eyes of family members throughout life. This position may elicit special privileges from parents who dote on the lastborn, or he may go relatively unnoticed in a large family where parents are overburdened. The youngest girl or boy may become the family pet, or be teased and put down by older brothers and sisters.

The youngest, if teased, may become irritable, shy, and prone to quick anger. On the whole, however, the lastborn receives so much attention (as well as hand-me-down clothes and toys) that, depending on the family situation, he grows up either spoiled, in the sense of always demanding more, or deprived, in that everything he gets was used by his predecessors.

The lastborn youngster is often more popular than older siblings, and can be lighthearted, cheerful, and playful. If suppressed by parents and other children, the youngest may suffer low self-esteem; but if reared in a benign environment, the child will have a high estimate of himself. This boy (or girl) may be unusually dependent upon others, because parents or brothers and sisters always helped solve his problems.

For example, Frank, who was youngest of three children, was described to me by his wife as follows:

"He is sweet, honest, and good," she said, "but he doesn't want to grow up. He acts like a little boy. He thinks if he acts cute, I will love him because he's a little boy. Many of his acts are attention-getting, as though he's saying, 'Love me because I'm a little kid.'"

Frank joined the Armed Services. It was not a final solution to his problem, but, as he said: "That will give me a place to sit and think without having to make decisions. Decisions are hard for me."

Low acceptance of repsonsibility is common among lastborns. A youngest girl was described by her husband as follows:

"She doesn't do anything around the house that she doesn't have to," he said. "She wants me to help with everything. She's a baby. She whines and complains, and she gives more affection to her dog than she does to me."

Another woman, age twenty-three, sought therapy because she was unable to remain close to anyone other than her mother, but her mother resented the fact that her youngest daughter returned home to live after being independent for several years. Gladys came to see me only to appease her mother, who also paid for the therapy sessions. The young woman talked about her lifelong habit of "having baby tantrums all the time."

As we progressed, she saw that she had developed this

tactic as a way of getting anything she wanted. When she was small her parents and brothers and sisters thought the tantrums were cute. Now they were no longer cute, to either her family or her friends. I directed my efforts toward helping her employ more adult methods of achieving goals.

Another example of this was Jonathan, the last of four children. Two older brothers were followed by a sister, and Jonathan was not born until ten years later. After he was five his mother started working and his sister became his substitute mother—cooking, caring for, and disciplining him. Jonathan's father was a businessman who was away from home a great deal, so that Jonathan's role model became his oldest brother.

As an adult Jonathan felt professionally inadequate in the business he owned jointly with his brother. He resisted change, as though his security depended on having his family remain frozen in the childhood pattern. He could not assert himself. Jonathan acceded to what other people wanted, as he had done with his older siblings when he was a child. He handled situations by covering up his true feelings to avoid offending anyone, but by so doing seemed to hurt everyone's feelings.

As we continued to work together, Jonathan came to recognize his persistent difficulties with people as a direct repetition of his childhood need to keep larger and stronger family members under control. He tried to make sure they would have no reason to be angry with him. As therapy progressed, he was better able to take his place among his brothers and sisters as an equal, as another adult, rather than as their "little baby brother." His case, like others, exemplifies an individual's fixation on a way of life in childhood that confounds and distorts adult relationships. Many vocational and marital impasses come from this source.

Jonathan's case actually illustrates two birth-order effects: (1) the result of being last in the family, and (2) the effect of a space of five years or more between siblings. As we have seen, the years between children can influence personality development, and should be considered along with birth order.

Such a combination of circumstances explained part of the problem for Charlotte, a charming, bright-eyed woman of sixty-eight who came to see me. She was trim and petite, but behind her quick smile I detected depression and tears near the surface. Charlotte was dissatisfied with herself. She had retired from teaching, but her husband, five years younger than she, was still working. She could find nothing to do all day, and felt stifled by depression.

Charlotte was the youngest of four girls, and when she was born her next oldest sister was already five. During childhood she had enjoyed the loving attention of her parents and sisters. Because of her size and the years between, they had treated her "like a little pet."

"One by one my sisters married and left home," Charlotte said, "but I wasn't interested in marriage. I never wanted to live anywhere except where I grew up. I couldn't imagine a happier life than being with my parents in our large, comfortable home. I loved teaching, and I was happy as a clam for many years."

Charlotte met her husband when he came to school to talk about his son from an earlier marriage. She was thirty-four and he was twenty-nine, "but I liked him right away." They "went together" for five years, but it was not until her father died that Charlotte consented to marry her friend.

"I was never the slightest bit interested in sex," she said, "but he won me over after we were married. He was so sweet and affectionate and seemed to need me so much that I went along with his wishes."

The couple had lived in Charlotte's home with her mother, who survived her father by only a few years. Charlotte had no children.

"By the time I was married my sisters were getting divorced or widowed," she said. "None of them ever had children, so they were free to do things with me and my husband. It was almost like the old days when I was little. We had a wonderful time together, my husband escorting the four of us everywhere. But then, one by one, my sisters have died. And I even lost my darling little Siamese cat three weeks ago."

Charlotte's problem is common to many people as they grow old. Because she was so much younger than her sisters, she had watched them drop away one by one, and she was alone in the sense that an only child is often alone. No one was left to treat her as the little pet. Fortunately, she had a loving husband who could partially take the place of parents and sisters and help her face the problems of aging.

In this and the preceding chapters I have shown the general personality development to be expected in the various birth-order positions. Next we will explore individual achievement as influenced by birth order.

CHAPTER 6

Achievement

Research and clinical experience indicate consistently that firstborn children are more likely than others to achieve advanced university degrees and to excel in such intellectual professions as science, psychology, medicine, and college teaching. This fact, which seems to give unfair advantage to the first child, is troubling to others. If it is so, why should it be this way?

Early investigators sought the answer in different intelligence levels among children, but there is virtually no evidence to support this notion. Most genetic studies indicate a high degree of similarity in intelligence among children from the same family. I believe that differences in achievement are due to the fact that children in various birth positions have different *opportunities* to develop intellectual potential, and that the environment of different birth positions may influence or train a child to prefer one line of endeavor over another.

Galton's pioneering study, which found a preponderance of first and only sons among eminent British scientists, also pointed up another fact: It is not just firstborns who generally achieve most highly but firstborn *men*. Social attitudes have prevented many women, including firstborns, from achieving positions of importance, although this tendency may be changing under pressure from the women's liberation movement. The size of a family and its economic status also may help determine how well any child succeeds. For example, if there isn't enough money to send all the children to college, the first child is likely to be favored, and often the first son, even if sisters were born ahead of him.

The disadvantage of laterborns' not obtaining a college education was pointed up in a study of middle- and top-management people.[1] It indicated that laterborns with college education seem better able than firstborns to rise to the top of the ladder in certain situations. In these high-level management positions it seemed that when laterborns *do* compete in the intellectual realm, they may be able to utilize their social skills to the disadvantage of firstborns in the same situation.

Beyond statistical findings, which tend to lump people into amorphous groups, we need to know whether a particular individual from any birth position is reacting to his own or to another's pressure for achievement. We must try to understand the whole pattern of development. Does this person have the capacity for development and, more important, for meeting his or her own standards? Did the relationship with parents and siblings help or hinder the child in developing potential? What are his goals? What is the relation between what he *wishes* to achieve and what has been, or can be, achieved?

MOTIVATION

We approach the matter by investigating *motivation* or need for achievement and the *actual level* of achievement in school grades, college attendance, and occupation. The need for achievement which a person *feels* depends on:

1. ordinal position of birth,
2. own gender,
3. gender of siblings,
4. pressure from significant others, such as parents.

Motivation, more than actual achievement, gives a vantage point for pertinent questions, because the two are not necessarily associated in the same person. A highly motivated person may be prevented by various conditions from achieving his goal. Conversely, an apparent high-achiever may not be highly motivated in the professional direction he has taken. This becomes an important distinction, one which gets at the root of much distress psychologists encounter in their clients.

In general, men are motivated to achieve more strongly than women are. The need is higher in firstborn males than in laterborns, and also higher for firstborn women than for those born later. The following table suggests the comparative levels of motivation generally found among only children and children of two-child families. Number 1 designates the highest degree of motivation, number 10 the lowest.

1. Older brother of a sister.
2. Male only child.
3. Younger brother of a brother.
4. Older brother of a brother.
5. Female only child.
6. Older sister of a sister.
7. Younger brother of a sister.
8. Younger sister of a brother.
9. Older sister of a brother.
10. Younger sister of a sister.[2]

The middle child in a family of three seems to have a lower need for intellectual achievement than oldest, youngest, or only children do, although motivation seems about equal among children in upper-class families. In lower-class families, which are usually larger, the youngest child often feels the strongest need to achieve.

Anxiety about school tests and fear of failure in business deter achievement. The greatest fear of failure is shown by the younger sister of a sister; next is the younger sister of a brother, and third is the older sister of a brother. The male only child is least afraid of failure. Next in order are the younger brother of a brother and then the older brother of a sister.[3]

It is also possible to be highly motivated but unable to fulfill ambitions as a result of lack of opportunity, insufficient funds for education, ill health, or because many children deplete the family's resources. Complexities such as these complicate psychological research and send people to seek therapy.

ACTUAL ACHIEVEMENT

Firstborn youngsters, including only children, generally are superior in schoolwork and dominate the rolls of colleges and universities. This correlates with parental pressure, but also reflects the fact that where family resources are limited the oldest child will probably receive the best education. Middle children are least likely to attend college or attain higher degrees.

The *appearance* of achievement may be misleading and can result in problems. A common example of apparently high achievement but low motivation is a person who has inherited an ongoing business. Problems may arise in several ways. The second-generation manager may attempt to meet high standards set by others because he feels responsible for the position into which he was thrust. He is forcing himself to comply with what he *should* do rather than having the freedom to recognize his own wishes. If his motivation is lower than that of the ancestor who built up the business, he may develop emotional conflict about working and become distressed because he cannot meet the needs of the business.

BIRTH POSITIONS

The high motivation and level of achievement common to firstborns come from several sources. Onlies or oldests, because of their close relationships with parents, commonly develop high verbal ability. Since intelligence tests rely heavily on vocabulary and verbal reasoning, verbal facility may produce high test scores, good grades in school, and achievement in academically loaded areas such as science or teaching.

Mothers usually apply greater pressure for performance on firstborns than they do on later children. They pay close attention to first-child performance, and express disappointment when the child fails. Although generally proficient, first children later in life often feel the need to go back to Mother, or another authority, for confirmation that what they are doing is right. This is especially true of only children.

One example of this was a young man who established

a business with the help of his mother and a friend. Later his mother died and his friend stepped out of the picture, and the only-child business manager was temporarily at a loss. He turned to me for help because he was reluctant, and sometimes unable, to make decisions for himself and the business. As his therapist (and temporarily a mother figure), I found this a relatively simple problem. As he discussed various approaches to a decision, all I needed to say was "It sounds like a good idea" and the pattern of inertia was broken. The only son was off and running again.

This male only child believed he could handle a problem if his mother told him he could, and it was helpful when she reaffirmed his sense of direction. Another case in point was aviation pioneer Glenn L. Martin, who throughout his life sought his mother's advice on how to operate his multi-million-dollar aviation business. The bond between mother and son was so strong that Glenn never married, and in fact lived only a short time after his mother's death.

This pattern also fits the firstborn astronauts, who exemplify self-confidence, motivation, and achievement but perform best when they can check back with "Mother Earth." During a flight into orbit or to the Moon the astronauts perform with precision, confidence, and heroism, but they are always in touch with higher authority through the radio umbilical cord to Mission Control in Houston. One theory suggests that daredevils, astronauts, and mountain climbers are continually challenging their dependence on "Mother Earth."

Mothers of only sons often attribute "miracle-making" powers to their children, but protect them from harmful or disturbing situations. Thus, the only male grows up confident he can cope with his environment, but he often needs support from a surrogate parent.

The pattern is more confused for the only girl child. For the man, parental pressure and society agree with his own inclination toward achieving the breadwinner role, but a woman may be torn between the conventional feminine role and her need to achieve outside the home as a liberated woman.

This dilemma was already apparent in a fourteen-year-old girl sent to me for counseling because she was depressed and unhappy and not working up to her level in school. The daughter of a wealthy businessman, Sheryl did not lack the ability to comprehend, but she had trouble finding practical solutions to common problems, and was uncertain about her judgment.

Her struggle reflected the tendency of parents of an only girl to solve problems for her, thus limiting her ability to solve problems for herself. Sheryl had not learned to experience and circumvent frustration, yet her father's achievements had motivated her toward high aspirations.

"Most of all I want to succeed in my goals," Sheryl said, "whatever they may be." In other words, she wanted success but she did not know what she wished to do. A high degree of achievement-need in the absence of personally expressive vocational goals is a combination dangerous to mental health.

Like many young women, Sheryl admired and envied the masculine role in society, and disapproved of the "weaknesses of women." She was depressed that she was not a boy, but at the same time she was experiencing the normal pubertal drive toward womanhood. This ambivalence toward the feminine role was intensified by the fact that her mother was having an affair. Sheryl came home from school one day and found her mother and the family physician embracing in the living room. This sharpened the girl's desire to achieve not as a woman but as someone who could do a better job than her mother of caring for her father. (Among other goals, she had fantasies of becoming a doctor.)

Both parents wanted Sheryl to becoming a charming and popular woman while also striving for intellectual achievement. With these conflicting pressures, it is not surprising that Sheryl felt anxious, tense, and depressed. It was not until late in our therapy sessions that she and her parents understood and accepted that they had rationalized her emotional conflicts by blaming the girl's low school performance on poor teachers and inadequate attention. I was able to help Sheryl accept herself as a developing woman *and* a potential achiever. Without help, she probably would have muddled through high school and settled for an adult niche in society below her potential.

The first child followed by brothers and sisters receives much the same parental pressure for performance that is imposed on an only son or daughter. The arrival of a second child seems to intensify his anxiety about performance, and thereafter the firstborn struggles to regain parent approval and love. Since parents give love and approval when a child performs, and withdraw affection when he fails, firstborns develop a strong need for the reassurance received when parents approve of what he does. Most clients in psychotherapy eventually say: "My parents approved of me only for performing in line with their expectations and never loved *me*." The motivation of many professional persons is undermined by this struggle.

Feelings of inadequacy or inability to meet standards often carry over into adult life for oldest children because of parental pressure for achievement and uncertainty about meeting parental standards. A mother who thinks she sees unusual talent in her first offspring takes steps to develop it. The "stage mother" is a prime example. Sometimes there is so much pressure for performance that as an adult the firstborn wants to be stage center but retains anxiety and fear because of childhood failure. The four-year-old girl who was forced into long hours of practice to become a dancer, pianist, or singer may carry into her adulthood resentment against parents for forcing behavior which she hated, along with a feeling of having failed someone important. Intimidated firstborns (they may be only children or followed by others) often retain such a great fear of failure that it may be difficult for them to engage in new activities.

The oldest child seems to identify with parental attitudes, including persistence and determination in reaching goals. Conflict often arises between parents and their first children specifically *because* the child has learned these values. He may pursue self-selected goals despite a parent's opposition. Thus, firstborns have been known to lead youth gangs. Motivation in such cases could be a need to rebel against the parents or society, which often is a surrogate for the feared or disliked parents. However, firstborns will use *methods* learned in their place in the family even though they do not fit the usual concept of conformity. Usually the firstborn eventually conforms to the parents' attitudes and values. Storms of conflict between teen-age firstborns and parents may later result in surprising conformity in the late twenties and beyond.

In general, the firstborn is in the best position for motivation and achievement, but may also encounter problems which complicate development. Such knowledge should serve as some consolation to second or middle children, who have been considered the most deprived among the birth positions. I emphasize again that each position contains its own special opportunities as well as detriments for personality development and achievement.

SECOND- AND MIDDLEBORNS

Joe, the younger brother of a sister, was thirty years old when he sought professional help. He presented some of his complaints openly, while others became clear only as we worked together.

He said that although he liked his work and was well trained for it, he found it difficult to produce. He procrastinated, was late for appointments, and failed to meet deadlines. He was uncertain about proper courses of action, though he had demonstrated ability and competence.

Later on, other negative tendencies surfaced. Joe was very concerned with the impression he made on others, was rarely able to be himself, was always on the defensive and often unable to assert himself. He allowed decisions to be made for him, worried about the capacity of his co-workers, and always saw his abilities as inferior to others. Consequently, he did not trust himself to cope with the present or the future, and allowed events to run their course.

I eventually helped him to see that his sister, three years his senior, had dominated him from her earliest years, and used him as a toy. She used to dress him in girl's clothing and forced him to attend tea parties for her dolls. Later she was better at baseball and bicycling than he was.

Joe also had to cope with another aggressive female—his mother. She was the family's top sergeant, directing her children how they were to fit into her beautifully ordered home. Joe's sister rebelled and clashed with her but Joe took the opposite tack of being subservient and nonassertive. He managed to get along well with his mother, and noted proudly that she seemed to prefer him.

Another factor in Joe's unsatisfactory achievement pattern was that his parents had never required him to produce. He had never been scolded for idleness or forced to study.

The troubling aspects of Joe's adult behavior soon became clear to him. Through young adulthood Joe had tried repeatedly to develop independent direction, but childhood domination by his mother and sister had always brought him back and thwarted his progress. (This is a common lesson learned from birth-order effects: Childhood family pressures create internal attitudes that stop progress, and even limit an ambitious and potentially successful young man like Joe.)

In therapy we probed deeper into Joe's motivations in personal relationships. As he gained insight into the reasons for his actions, he also became more assertive. Joe began to peel away the dominating influence of his mother and sister, see them objectively, and realize his own potential.

The sex of the second child in a family of three or more children—and that of the following child—is important in predicting achievement. Self-esteem is generally high if the second is the only one of his sex in the family.

It has been claimed that middle children are neglected. They may not receive the exclusive attention accorded the firstborn, or the doting affection often lavished on the last child in the family. Middle children are consistently underrepresented among those going to college and obtaining advanced degrees. Their relative lack of educational achievement may relate to economic limitations, because studies of higher-status families reveal a need for academic achievement—and achievement itself—among all the children.

How the middle child achieves in adulthood closely corresponds to how he was permitted to compete during early childhood.

Bernard Baruch, Wall Street genius and Presidential adviser, was second in a family of four boys.

"None of us ever really outgrows his or her childhood," he wrote. "How we meet the problems of adult life usually does not differ greatly from how we met the problems of growing up. Whatever I saw others accomplish, I was driven to try to do myself." [4]

A highly competent older brother or sister poses a special competitive problem for the middle child. They sometimes try to rise above the crowd to obtain parental attention, or do just the opposite and drift with the current among the children around them.

Ex-President Nixon's personality has probably been as thoroughly dissected as any man's in recent times, but he can also be studied from the viewpoint of birth position and achievement. He was secondborn among the four boys (although a fifth boy was born when Nixon was seventeen), and thus most of his associations were with his three older brothers. Two special conditions were important in Nixon's development: His older brother by four years was often ill, so that the mantle of seniority in a sense fell on his shoulders, and he was only a year old when his younger brother was born, suggesting that he did not enjoy much infancy. The fourth boy in the family died at age seven, when Richard was twelve. Thus, Richard Nixon was exposed to a great deal of tragedy during his childhood.

His mother described him as "always serious" and amazingly mature even at age five or six. His birth position, plus unusual childhood responsibilities, may account for the tenacity and stubbornness with which he tackled challenges in adulthood.

THE YOUNGEST CHILD

The youngest child, especially from a large family, may enjoy assets similar to the firstborn's in a small family, in terms of achievement. The last boy or girl also may avoid handicaps, like anxiety about achievement, which mark oldest children, because less is expected of the baby. If from a poor family, the youngest often shows a higher *need* for achievement than any other child except the firstborn boy. The youngest is more likely to complete advanced education if he is from a four- or five-child family rather than a smaller unit. The lastborn, although often favored and pampered by parents and brothers and sisters, may have low self-esteem if not encouraged by his family. If the family is overly protective, the youngest may grow up lacking courage and independence.

Three cases illustrate some of the problems encountered by lastborn children regardless of the type of family they come from.

They were men, all in their early twenties, who at the

time of therapy suffered extreme identity crises. Each was born last in a family of four children, and had one sister who was seven to ten years older and had been a strong mother figure. The father in each case had been away from home a great deal because of business or lack of interest in the family. Socio-economic and cultural conditions, however, were quite different for the three families.

Martin was a third-generation American with a lower-middle-class background. At age twenty-one he was attending college with help from his parents and the Veterans' Administration.

Jiminez, a first-generation Mexican-American, was also reared in the U.S. Most of the family income had come from welfare, and at age twenty Jiminez worked as a box boy in a supermarket.

Halel came from a wealthy business family in the Middle East. He had emigrated to the United States at age twenty-four, and lived on a small income from his family.

The specific career goals of these men were quite different. Martin sought an interesting profession, Jiminez needed a job to meet immediate practical needs, and Halel hoped to find a business in America where he could make a quick fortune. Each of the three, however, shared similar hopeless feelings about finding the kind of work he wanted. All of them were frustrated and angry that their needs were not being met, and would become easily irritated—even with those who might have been of assistance.

None of the three young men was married, and all complained of loneliness, even though they felt the girls they met were too demanding. Each was timid about getting what he wanted.

The three men also indicated varying degrees of ambivalence toward their older sisters. Martin had been deeply influenced by his sister, partially because his father had been at work long hours each day and his mother had been passive. Jiminez's mother had abandoned the family when he was a year old, and his oldest sister had become the mother for all practical purposes. His father had spent evenings away from home, giving the impression that he didn't like to be with his children. Halel's mother had been chronically ill; he had been placed under his sister's care, because his father had been preoccupied with business and men's activities.

In trying to find a mate, each man was looking for a girl willing to mother him, but at the same time each feared domination by a woman.

As I worked with each of these men in separate therapeutic situations, I occasionally mentioned the birth-order effects normally experienced by a youngest child. Once they considered this factor, each man viewed resentment toward his father in a different light. The patterns of behavior stemming from their role as youngest in the family were important to each of these clients. I supported their movement toward specific goals by helping them develop strengths to achieve them. Another aspect of treatment was to help them relinquish unrealistic expectations or demands upon others.

These were especially interesting case studies because birth-order effects were the same despite different social, economic, and cultural backgrounds. All three youngest children had developed similar behavior and personality limitations related to their place in the family. Because they had been considered weak and small as children, they continued to hold this image of themselves as adults. They had been neither encouraged nor helped to develop work and planning skills. They resented other adults for failing to substitute for strong older brothers and sisters, and most of all the dominant sister. These youngest children were frustrated because other adults did not care for them without being asked.

Martin eventually obtained a college degree and a technical position which met his needs. He resolved his social problem by marrying a girl somewhat younger than himself who identified strongly with the traditional female role and could "mother" him as well as their children.

Jiminez is attending junior college to learn a mechanical trade. His timidity and ambivalence about women caused him to vacillate between superficial relations with both men and women. Contacts with men were "easier to make," although they did not ease his loneliness. At age twenty-eight Jiminez was looking for a girl "who will love me and put up with my limitations."

Halel decided that he should take advantage of his family's economic position and became a U.S. representative for their business. He married a well-to-do girl whose family came from his homeland.

In the next section we shall examine more closely the relationships between ordinal position of birth, the selection of vocations, and ability to work in the business and professional world.

SECTION

III

---

*The World
of
Work*

CHAPTER 7

Vocations and Creativity

Selecting a vocation is aided and complicated by many factors, including childhood interests, family labeling and pressures, influential teachers, and educational opportunities. The relationships one has with parents and brothers and sisters also play an essential part in this important aspect of an individual's functioning comfortably in a life role.

A successful woman artist, for example, had three sons, who fell principally under her influence because she was the dominant parent. The marriage was a good one, and the father was interested in his boy's development, but his level of education was lower than his wife's. He bowed to her desire for their sons to excel in education and the creative arts.

The oldest son readily learned and accepted his mother's values. He drove himself to study, and became a successful, hard-working artist.

The second son tried to follow his mother's direction and compete with his older brother. At his mother's insistence, he took music lessons for several years, yet he was always more interested in athletics and building model cars. He became a professional automobile racer.

The youngest son made no effort to conform to his mother's artistic drives or to follow either of the other boys. Without emotional conflict or trauma, he chose a field which seemed to offer the advantages of good living and social contribution. He became a "very relaxed" and competent teacher.

The birth-order patterns are clear-cut in this family. Each of the three sons adjusted successfully to the life role indicated by his position. The oldest adopted some of his mother's feminine characteristics and responded to her guidance and pressure. The second tried to meet her standards and interests initially, but needed to be different from his older brother. He developed different interests and chose a different career. Because his two older brothers received the brunt of their mother's attention, the youngest boy escaped the direct pressure of her ambitions. However, the youngest son *did* satisfy his mother's desire that he obtain a better education than his father had.

No member of this family ever needed or sought therapy, because each resolved successfully the impositions of his place in the family. Others are not so fortunate in selecting vocations. Awareness of birth-order patterns may help them adjust more satisfactorily to their chosen professions.

One strong indication from birth-order research is that firstborns prefer working with ideas while laterborns are more interested in practical pursuits involving social interaction. Drs. Mark I. Oberlander, Kenneth J. Frauenfelder, and Helen Heath, of the Institute of Juvenile Research in Chicago, measured the interest patterns of 299 eighteen-year-old men and women. They found that firstborns leaned toward non-personal intellectual activities while laterborns were inclined to choose activities with social interplay.[1]

CHOOSING A VOCATION

It is impossible to pinpoint a vocation or profession best suited to each birth-order position. We would expect family resources, availability of jobs, and imitation of parents to prevent a direct correlation between occupations and sibling roles. Despite this, there are some signpost categories that seem sufficiently supported by research to offer suggestions.[2]

Any list of *eminent* scientists is likely to include a disproportionate number of firstborns. However, scientists in general may include not only firstborns but also youngest children from large families. Second, third, and fourth children study and practice the sciences less often.

According to Alfred Adler and others, creative mathematics is dominated by eldest sons. Adler noted:

> It is tempting to approach the nature of mathematical creativity by describing the nature of creative mathematicians, but that is the wrong way to go about it. For example, the approach cannot explain the fact, amusing at first and then puzzling, that nearly all mathematicians are eldest sons. The few exceptions tend to be mathematicians whose older brothers also are mathematicians.
>
> Mathematical gifts cannot be unique to eldest sons. It must be that the discipline itself is crucial, that it provides a domain in which mental power and creativity can be wielded in a manner congenial to the special qualities of men who, for a time at least, were the only sons in their families.[3]

Various researchers have found a tendency for firstborns to choose (in addition to mathematics) engineering, physics, architecture, and chemistry.[4] These occupations require a college education, and so we could expect to find many firstborns and onlies in them. Those occupations also require a high level of abstract thought, and do not reflect much interest in social contacts. The fact that other occupations have not been as thoroughly studied in relation to birth order may be because firstborns are more likely to be the college faculty members who study such matters and are more interested in occupations that require college education. Also, the subjects of study they have available are college students.

Laterborn men and women make up the majority of those practicing the creative arts. William D. Bliss, of the University of Montana, found, for example, that writers tend to come from the ranks of laterborns. Among writers polled in a statistical study, only 23 percent were oldest children. Nine percent were onlies. There was a tendency for prose writers to be among the younger half of the children in a family, and more novelists and short-story writers were laterborn than were poets.

"The advantage of the late-born over the firstborn in creative pursuits," Bliss said, "would seem to derive from his or her greater ability to work independently and tolerate isolation—surely qualities required of an artistically creative person." [5]

Unexpectedly large proportions of laterborns have been found to study music and language.[6] It is a surprise to find laterborns among language majors, since firstborns are so often more adept at verbal skills. A probable explanation is that laterborns are eager to communicate with others, especially their peers. They are also more likely to reveal personal information than firstborns are.

It seems that laterborns can tolerate isolation in work situations and also work better in a team than firstborns can. Laterborns were shown to continue working as night nurses more often than firstborns, apparently because firstborns in such an occupational situation could not find the support from others that they need.

Musicians most often play in team situations—orchestras or groups—and a high degree of social cooperation is required. In other situations requiring teamwork, as in assembly-line operations, laterborns appear comfortable and successful, fitting in with the group.

Other findings have shown firstborn art students to be less creative than laterborns. This may relate to the fact that the first child is more conservative and conforming to authority and therefore less free to be original and innovative. A second or later girl also seems more likely than a firstborn to be an actress. We know that later children have their life roles less clearly structured by parents and are freer to indulge in fantasy, to pretend and play varying roles.[7] Second daughters with older sisters often participate in high-school and college plays. They also are often better actresses than firstborn girls, but *not* better than only children. Jane Fonda, Barbara Walters, Jennie Churchill, and Joan Crawford were second sisters. Since only daughters also need to be the center of attention and to dramatize themselves, it is not surprising that a number of well-known actresses were only children—Marilyn Monroe and Mary Astor, for example.

Interest in becoming a college professor was expressed by a majority of junior and senior college students polled in one study.[8] Firstborn women were more interested in the academic field than laterborns were, while first- and laterborn men ranked with firstborn women. Oldest men and women seem to dominate the fields of medicine, law, and psychology, and the preference for such advanced study is strongest among students whose fathers were in these occupations or who had been frustrated in professional ambitions. This symbolizes the way in which many fathers encourage their children to fulfill the father's ambitions. The findings also relate to socioeconomic situations in which a family's first child is given the best opportunity for obtaining an education.

Among a group of Peace Corps volunteers, firstborns excelled in math-science programs, while second- and thirdborn men and women were superior in teaching English. Another study of teachers indicated that family size had no apparent relationship to making a good teacher, but only children predominated among teachers with the best high-school records.[9]

Again, we emphasize that these categories are not firm, fixed, or unchangeable, but only show *general trends*. Parental role assignments can be defied as well as accepted.

The military services also provide data regarding birth order and choice of vocation. It was found in 1971 that 56 percent of the Army officers studied were firstborns.[10] This proportion is consistent with that of college education, but the same study also found that 46 percent of the sergeants, usually not college-educated, also were oldest sons. (Clinical observation corroborates that firstborns may prefer regulated, organized activities, and that they may become leaders in them.) Sixty-seven percent of superior Navy jet pilots were firstborn men, compared with 55 percent of Navy pilots picked at random.[11] The fact that outstanding jet pilots in all services were most often first sons with close father-son relationships suggests that firstborns with such relationships become competent and confident.

One odd finding on the preponderance of firstborn men among military leaders is that oldest children (both men and women) are more likely to be fearful in stress situations than laterborns. The military certainly offers fear- and stress-producing situations. However, this apparent contradiction is cancelled by the firstborn's tendency to seek affiliation with others when under stress. The tight structure and repetitive training of the military seem to offer the affiliation and reassurance these firstborns need.

The high proportion of firstborns among military leaders also relates to the oldest child's tendency to conform to authority and carry out orders from above, even to the point of denying or overriding his fears.

We have mentioned that most of the early American astronauts were firstborns or only children, but how specifically does this fit in with what we know about oldest children? (Of course, 50 percent of the firstborns have been eliminated, since no women are allowed in the program.) The astronauts follow the firstborn pattern with their: (1) high need for achievement; (2) high responsibility scores; (3) low test anxiety; (4) strong self-discipline; (5) need for approval of others; (6) susceptibility to social pressure; (7) conformity to authority and regulation; and (8) task orientation.

Laterborn men, by contrast, conform less to authority and are more oriented toward social relationships than to fulfilling a task. Firstborns seem more likely than laterborns to feel confident that they can control what happens to them.

Another area where the social abilities of laterborns may be important is in athletics. Although the laterborn may be directed toward an interest in sports because he could not compete with his academically achieving older sibling, his success in team sports may be enhanced by his ability to participate in cooperative group situations. Firstborns are less likely to engage in body-contact sports, where there is a prospect of physical injury.

The following are some conjectures comparing first- and laterborns. In any of these situations, specific working conditions would be important.

Salesman: Probably firstborns would be more comfortable, as they have verbal skills and they like to guide people into doing "the right thing." Top salesmen usually believe that what they have to sell is important to other people.

Waiters and waitresses: Probably laterborns would be better as they are usually interested in serving others.

Secretaries and stenographers: They are more likely to be laterborns, who often enjoy serving as a substitute parent or older sibling.

Generally speaking, in relation to vocational aptitudes, firstborn children benefit intellectually from their birth positions, while laterborns benefit socially. This difference reveals a good deal about how a man or woman may emerge from the family and take his or her place in the working world. But how well do they succeed in working with other people, in taking direction and directing others?

WORK RELATIONSHIPS

"I don't want any weakness in me," Harris, an oldest son, said, "and I don't like any in those with whom I work. I have a job to do and many responsibilities, and I don't want any decisions made by anyone that will make the job less than the best that can be done."

It was a familiar reaction—the super-conscience and sense of personal responsibility learned by the firstborn from close association with parental values were speaking. But Harris was disturbed about his work relationships. His boss told him one day:

"You come on very badly with your people. You see something to be done and you're not very tactful. They complain to me about your attitude."

"I should be more relaxed with people," Harris admitted as we began consultation. "I know it's important to keep this in mind. At work the other day I told these people that what they were doing was wrong. I really didn't consider their feelings."

After our first meeting Harris began to see how he had developed under close and rather harsh parental direction and how he had carried those attitudes into adult life. He described the next encounter with his employees:

"At our next meeting I kept my mouth shut and did more thinking. I know I'm right, but I must learn some way of getting the message across without antagonizing them."

Still later he said:

"I've been staying out of people's hair. I've been talking to more people at work and getting their cooperation by the way I say things." As a result of his colleagues' more positive response, Harris began to develop more confidence in them and in himself.

"I feel different at work now," he said. "I think better things about myself. I'm not so concerned that they won't like me, and I'm not afraid to put myself and my ideas forward. I think I'm doing it in such a way that they'll listen with a positive attitude. I've found it's easier to work with people if you're more loose with them, let things flow, and don't expect so much."

His last remark was revealing. Typical of a firstborn, Harris had been anxious about his performance, and was never quite able to satisfy the high standards he had set for himself. Once he understood this, he also saw that he had been driving his subordinates to achieve in order to satisfy his own needs. He had been driving others as he had been driving himself.

A similar pattern governed Virgil I. (Gus) Grissom, one of America's original seven astronauts. The eldest of three boys, Gus drove himself unmercifully to excellence in a military flying career that was instrumental in his selection as an astronaut.[12] Grissom flew the second Mercury suborbital mission and the first orbital Gemini mission. Throughout his years as an astronaut he participated in the engineering and construction of his spacecraft, often irritating engineers and technicians with his demands for excellence. His driving ambition was to be the first man on the moon, and he almost made it. Grissom was killed with two other astronauts in 1967 when a fire swept through their Apollo spacecraft during a flight rehearsal on the launch pad at Cape Kennedy.

Oldest children of both sexes tend to be seriously task-oriented, and will often ignore human relationships in favor of the work at hand.

Because of their conformity and respectful attitude toward authority, firstborn men and women become more deferential employees than laterborns. They perform at a lower level when anxious, and therefore may require a high quality of supervision. When a firstborn is made comfortable, he will perform far better than when under pressure.

Since firstborns are motivated toward achievement, they usually work hard when there is opportunity for advancement. A common problem firstborn employees share is that of relating to their supervisors as parent figures. For example, a firstborn woman (with a younger sister who was her rival in childhood) was placed in a situation of competing with another female employee for the supervisor's attention and approval. The situation became sharp and bitter before she was able to see the childhood roots of her actions.

It is not unusual for a person to see supervisors as parent figures and fellow workers as latter-day brothers and sisters. This is why it is important to teach cooperation and adjustment to the needs of others during childhood. An "uptight" firstborn may be difficult to supervise, but in turn will make a conscientious, hard-driving supervisor.

The situation is different when the firstborn is an only child. The male only child tends to be considerate of the needs of those with whom he works, usually because his own needs were met by a concerned mother. He is self-confident and noncompetitive. The female only child also tends to be this way, but she may have difficulty competing with women if she had a hostile relationship with her mother. Women who were only children frequently seek positions where they work alone or with male associates. They may take such positions as a legal secretary who is the only female in the office.

Only children are most likely to be confident in relating to supervisors and fellow employees, and, as one said: "I haven't any close friends, but I haven't any enemies either. I can get along with almost anybody."

Although more considerate with employees than an oldest child, the only adult may be more susceptible to quick anger.

"I tend to get more angry with my friends and bosses than I should," one man said to me. "I think it's because I feel they will like me no matter what I do. I felt that way about my parents. When you're an only child, you reason that way."

One question among birth-order investigators is whether or not the high motivation of firstborns impels them automatically to top leadership positions. I believe that the qualities of firstborns will guide them to leadership in *certain kinds* of work situations, but laterborn qualities lead just as directly to the top in other vocations. This question may not be whether a first- or laterborn might get the position, but whether the position *requires* a firstborn or laterborn.

Corporate executives might examine this question before promoting a person to a high position. Firstborns tend to be task-oriented (sometimes at the cost of human relations), while laterborns may be more human-related (sometimes at the cost of getting the task done). The higher a person goes up the corporate ladder, the more important it is that he pays close attention to interpersonal relationships with his employees, and laterborns are best at this. At the same time, there is a risk that the second- or laterborn child may become so concerned about human relations that he doesn't get the job done.

One secondborn man (with an older sister) felt his success was limited because he needed "to be kind to everybody." This need prevented him from achieving his career goal. Some laterborn men suppress normal anger and assertiveness, because they have witnessed a rebellious struggle between older siblings and their parents. Excessive restraint of emotions can be just as troublesome as insufficient control.

"I was supposed to be teaching people my skill," this young man said. "I couldn't bring myself to criticize anybody. That would be unkind. Nor could I express myself fully, because they might think I was being too aggressive.

"I tried to keep cool, controlled. I didn't let myself get excited. As a result, nobody got excited about what I had to say, and I wasn't asked to come back."

Therapy loosened up this man so that he felt comfortable expressing his feelings.

Youngest children are usually relaxed in relations with other people, and if they are from a small family, may be less interested in vocational achievement than in maintaining those relationships. If from a large family, they may be motivated to achieve because they were helped and stimulated by parents and brothers and sisters. Some youngest children, especially women, may lack self-confidence, as they were overly protected and felt inferior when competing with the older children. One youngest son came to me for help in this regard.

"I'm unable to do anything because I'm so afraid I won't succeed," he said. "Everyone else seems so much more capable than I. I always see strangers as better able to cope than I can. It's as though I'm always the baby."

A youngest daughter said: "I can't make plans. I never think anything will work out. I'm frightened of everything, including new people to work with."

Another young man, youngest of five children, sought help because he was frightened by his violent anger. Jim was unable to hold a job because he made offensive remarks to employers and customers and fought with fellow employees. This happened in response to what he called the offensiveness of others and overbearing authority by his superiors.

Jim described his father as a self-righteous, sober man who never used bad language, but who had such an uncontrollable temper that "he scared the living hell out of me." The father had used a belt on his three boys and pulled the girls' hair when he punished them. When Jim was a preadolescent his father had once broken his nose. Trying to describe how he felt about his father, he said: "We were so far apart it wasn't fair."

As we worked together, I helped Jim examine how he had come to expect nothing except criticism and punishment from his father and older brother. He was furious inside, but afraid to express his anger or struggle with his brothers and father because he was so much smaller. Now, as an adult, he reacted with the same fury to criticism and bossiness; only, as an adult, he *did* strike out physically at work.

Jim appraised himself more realistically as an adult no longer subject to family domination, and began to listen without taking instant offense when a supervisor or fellow employee criticized him. His work improved, and when I last saw Jim he seemed on the way to overcoming the handicap of his place in the family.

No matter what the birth position, work situations often seem to echo the parent-child relationship; competition with brothers and sisters is now represented by competition with fellow workers. Problems with supervisors and peers seem to follow characteristics of the birth-order pattern in which the person was reared. A firstborn woman, for example, was extremely angry with her male supervisor.

"He treats me like a child," she stormed. "He calls all of us in his unit 'my children.'"

What this woman did not like was that she was made *one* of the children, whereas in childhood she had held the special position of being *in charge* of the other children. Another woman, named Mabel, the older of two girls, complained:

"My superior is rude and arrogant. She knows how to put a person down. I feel she's doing it deliberately to make me mad."

It developed during therapy that Mabel had taught

herself as a child not to express anger or other emotions in reacting to a younger sister in order to retain her mother's approval. Both her mother and her supervisor related to Mabel in a critical and derogatory manner. As she examined the situation with me, and also with a sympathetic colleague and friend, Mabel began to question her own contribution to the relationship with her supervisor.

"You just let her treat you badly," the friend said. "You sit and take it."

Mabel began to assert herself, quietly making her points. Soon she reported improved conditions.

"I guess I was just trying to get along with her the way I got along with my mother and sister," she said. "In neither case did I earn any respect."

Mabel also complained about the close bond between the supervisor and one of her fellow workers. She felt threatened by any closeness between the supervisor and her colleague, just as she had resented any intimacy between her mother and younger sister. Understanding the origins of her feelings was the primary step in resolving Mabel's working relationships.

Although we could examine in greater detail the correlations of birth order with aptitudes and performance in the business and professional world, these brief studies should help many men and women find greater professional satisfaction and comfort. Next we will explore more specifically the birth order of women who achieve.

CHAPTER 8

Women Who Achieve

"I never had a chance," the woman said. She sat crying in an armchair, her voice shrill with rage.

"Everything was for my brother. My parents preferred him. They were so proud of their boy. Sure, they saw me as the cute little girl, but he was the one they encouraged to learn things like swimming or skiing.

"They always talked about his going to college, what school he would go to, things like that. They let him be free. He usually could go anywhere, be with anyone he wanted to be with. I was simply my brother's little sister all my life."

How often I have heard that cry from the hearts of unhappy women who felt a poignant need to achieve in the creative or business world, but who were blocked not only by society but by parents and brothers and sisters.

It is not a battle cry against men, as many suppose, but a plea for emotional comfort and self-realization. A woman, like a man, seeks only to apply her talents and abilities in the areas where she can function best and which give her a sense of significance and satisfaction. The problem is that women, more often than men, are pressed into molds of servitude and life roles of subordination to others. This has been going on for centuries—

and the reasons for it lie in the history of the human race
—but the proponents of women's liberation are attacking
this pattern of sex roles, as it operates unnecessarily in
today's world. They deplore the pressure on women to
cultivate qualities, behavior, and attitudes related to duties
within the home, and the concurrent social support for exclusive male achievement outside the home.

If a woman has a high need for achievement and wants
to be a creative artist, society should not inhibit her
efforts. If she has the aptitude and intelligence of a business executive, she should be free to become one. If she
is happy as a wife and mother, fulfilling her life by sharing
it with her husband, let her *be*. Her achievement is no
less as a wife than as president of a firm if it is her own
choice.

The more common condition, which depresses and dis-
satisfies many women, is that the life roles imposed on
them as children becomes so accepted and ingrained that
they do not discover their true personal inclinations until
later in life. At that time it may be difficult or impossible
to obtain either training or the opportunity to express
themselves.

I met Jane when she was twenty. She was secondborn
in her family, with a brother four years her senior.

Jane came for counseling because she was depressed
and unable to find work that interested her. She hated
school and had no career goals. She couldn't find a job
that paid as much as she wanted, since she had no training, and was angry at her parents but accepted their
financial support. More than anything else, Jane wanted
to get married, but all the men she knew seemed childish.

Jane's father was domineering, and she feared him. But
he adored his wife, and was eager to satisfy her wishes.
Jane's mother enjoyed her role as wife and mother, and
placed few stresses on her aggressive husband.

This was the background with which we began. Soon
Jane complained about her older brother, who was a grad-
uate student. Throughout her early childhood and adolescence, he had often insulted her.

"He made me feel completely dumb and unattractive,"
Jane said. "He said I was frivolous and criticized my
appearance, like my hair and clothes. He never would

talk to me as an equal, but was always big on giving advice."

As Jane described the relationship with her brother, she provided the clues I needed to guide her treatment, clues which fit the birth-order pattern of second and last children, especially if that second child is a girl. She complained also that her mother and father had been more interested in her brother than in her. Jane's father (the model for her brother) also had talked down to her. Jane's mother had taken her shopping and watched her diet and personal development, but she also had seemed prouder of and more concerned about her son than about Jane. From brother-criticism and fear of her father, Jane had grown timid with boys. She doubted her attractiveness and agonized about her appearance.

As we proceeded, I was able to show that her brother had followed the usual pattern of an older brother with a younger sister—that it had been his way of competing and protecting his firstborn superiority. Gradually Jane felt her hostility diminishing, and began to relate to him as an equal adult, rather than as a younger sister. This was aided by some discussions between them. I also encouraged her to examine objectively the attitudes of other young men toward her. She began to see, and accept, that they found her attractive. Because both Jane's brother and father had seemed stronger than she and her mother, Jane had idealized the two males and desired an "ideal" male as a husband.

Later she became more realistic in her expectations of a mate as she began to see her brother as another human being with human weaknesses as well as power and strength. She stopped trying to emulate the family men— a task which had contributed to her depression—and began to appreciate her mother's qualities. More importantly, she began to appreciate those qualities in herself.

Two years later Jane had a job which matched her abilities, and was saving money to pay for her pending wedding. She and her mother had developed a mutually satisfying relationship, while her father and brother watched with astonishment. Jane grew to accept herself as an attractive young woman, and was ready to enjoy the feminine life role she had both disdained and desired.

Family interactions springing from birth order play a

strong part in assigning a woman her place in society.
Conflicts may arise, for example, when a firstborn woman
seeks intellectual achievement to cement her family status
and then tries to reconcile business success with rearing a
family.

One woman, the oldest of three children, complained
of tension. Darlene told me that she felt under constant
pressure "to do what I have to do." She was irritable with
her husband and children.

"What is worse," Darlene said, "is that I'm snappish
with people at work."

She held a managerial position with an erratic schedule
plus evening and weekend work. A housekeeper looked
after her two children, but she was never confident that
the housekeeper would return from her weekends off.
Darlene's husband did not object to baby sitting on weekends, but his own business schedule precluded helping
during the week.

Darlene's problem, of course, was that she had too many
jobs. She wanted to do them all—wife, mother, homemaker and businesswoman—but she was spread too thin
to give full attention to any one task.

In therapy she came to understand that she was driving
herself to achieve outside the home because of her
mother's dissatisfaction with the conventional feminine
role. Her mother, a second daughter, had hoped to achieve
fulfillment of her own ambitions through her child, but
Darlene did not share her mother's disdain for the housewife role. She felt she had a *right* to be wife and mother
as well as to engage in other activities, provided she could
manage them comfortably and satisfactorily.

This was the direction we took all through therapy, and
Darlene came to terms with her conflict. Although it required temporary compromise, she decided to concentrate
on the most urgent aspects of her life at that moment:
being wife and mother. She reduced her outside work
schedule, building it up again later as the children spent
more time in school.

Women who were only children are often dissatisfied
with the homemaker role, though some ambivalence is involved. This is especially evident with the growing strength
of the women's movement, which has encouraged more
women to think and talk about their feelings. Female only
children have a moderately high need for achievement,

but they think of reaching it *through the help of others,* particularly husbands. They often identify with the feminine role which sends them into early marriage and motherhood, but these activities may not satisfy them for long.

This was true of thirty-two-year-old Margaret, who complained that she was bored. She felt hopeless, useless, and that "nothing is going to happen that will be interesting."

As an only child, Margaret had been indulged by her parents. They had delighted in her charm, her beauty, her gentleness. She had wished for little except to please them. Her parents had made no demands upon her other than that she be—for them—the delightful daughter.

Margaret had married a wealthy young man when she was twenty-one. She had continued performing as the delightful daughter by producing two children to please two sets of grandparents. She had wealth, a devoted husband, a fashionable home, and two lovely children. But Margaret, at age thirty-two, was bored.

Her first insight, as we began talking, was that she had made an almost effortless transition from under the wings of devoted parents to the protection of an equally devoted husband. During childhood she had rarely experienced anxiety or insecurity, because her parents had shielded her so carefully. Now that she was married, Margaret expected her husband to provide the same barrier against discomfort, including the anxiety of boredom. If she needed goals, she expected him to define them and push her toward them.

As we worked together, she came to see that she must take responsibility for her own happiness, that she must find out for herself what she *could* and *might like* to do. She saw that she would find life interesting only if she worked at something she considered important. Gradually she decided that she wanted to be a fashion designer, and entered training. There was no economic problem in caring for her children while she went to school. Margaret planned to maintain her studio in her home, thus achieving the best of two careers: mother and profession. Needless to say, Margaret's boredom vanished.

Part of the pattern for firstborns, especially those with brothers and sisters, is a lingering concern that they are not achieving enough. Emotional disturbance related to this concern often reveals itself in dreams about test situations, even years after a person has completed school. Such dreams may have to do with being unprepared, or facing unexpected questions, or failing to take the test. An example of this is the older sister of a sister who related the following dream:

"I had to take an important test. I was already sure that if I didn't hurry I wouldn't get to the test room in time, but I stopped at a cafeteria on the way and stood in line for food, even though I was anxious about the test."

This woman's dream shows the basic drive—for food, for comfort, for Mother—to which she gave precedence and which underlay her childhood and adolescent preoccupation with doing well in school. The dream also showed her changing needs during therapy: She had reached the point where she could permit herself to satisfy a basic need even though still anxious about not being there "to meet the test." Later in therapy her dreams shifted to both meeting the need for comfort and arranging matters so that she could take the test.

FIGHTING BACK

In the continuing struggle to secure equal rights for women, which birth position is most likely to produce a woman angry enough to fight back against the established order? Which is the most likely candidate for the feminist movement? Since women's liberation is interested in changing sex roles, perhaps our target is the girl who, in her birth position, is most dissatisfied with her sex role.

Firstborn women, both only children and those followed some years later by others, tend to achieve at levels relatively consistent with their motivation and goals. The older of two girls is more apt to achieve along academic lines than her younger sister is, but the differences do not suggest that either will be deeply dissatisfied with her sex role. The older sister of a brother is more likely than he to attend college, and the same is true of the older brother of a sister.

Zeroing in upon second girls behind brothers, Dr. William Altus, professor of psychology at the University of California in Santa Barbara, said:

"I have found that on self-rating tests a girl from a two-child family tends to check more disparaging adjectives about herself if she has an older brother than if she has an older sister." [1] (In other words, the younger sister of a brother has lower self-esteem than the younger sister of a sister.)

"The same girl with an older brother," Altus added, "tends to check more unfavorable adjectives about her brother and her father than does the secondborn of two sisters."

These data indicate that the girl with an older brother develops a negative attitude toward two important males in her life. Other studies suggest that this attitude carries over to relationships with men in general. Secondborn women with older brothers often are dissatisfied with their sex role.

When we recall that laterborn women with an opposite-sex sibling tend to be nonconformist, and connect that with sex-role dissatisfaction, it seems that the younger sister of a brother is the most likely to rebel against the established norms and strike out in experimental directions.

One father consulted me about his two children.

"The older boy is at the university working on his Ph.D.," the father said. "His sister will soon enter college, but I don't understand what has happened to her. Her brother is what I suppose you'd call straight or square, but she has adopted a hippie philosophy."

I assured the father that the pattern is typical. The older brother identified with the parents' values and followed intellectual pursuits. The sister, probably with equal academic potential, chose rebellion as a way of getting even with the males who had dominated her life. Many such younger sisters become political or social radicals.

Dissatisfaction with sex role can be almost as acute for the second sister in a family of girls. We have referred to Kate Millett, the middle of three girls who "were constantly reminded that we weren't sons." One of the outstanding theorists of the women's liberation movement, Millett wrote *Sexual Politics* as her Ph.D. thesis. She was fired as an instructor at Columbia University "because I was too much of a middle-class threat. I wore sunglasses to faculty meetings and took the student side during strikes."

With all her achievements—a Phi Beta Kappa key, a B.A. *magna cum laude* from the University of Minnesota, and an honors degree from Oxford—Millett recalls what it was like looking for a job in New York.

"Everywhere it was the same question," she said. " 'Can you type?' "

That three-word question has stopped millions of women as they attempted to enter the world of business and creative arts. Higher aptitudes or abilities are frequently overlooked or ignored on the assumption that a woman will be a typist or a secretary.

"Women feel so insecure because they have so little self," Millett said. "You go around feeling neurotic and then, Christ, you find out you're not alone." [2]

Much evidence, clinical as well as statistical, indicates that women alcoholics tend to be laterborn girls. This certainly does not imply that all laterborn girls are potential alcoholics, but suggests that birth-order conflict of sex identification may drive a woman to rebel against the feminine stereotype and strive to achieve in the so-called man's world. Excessive drinking may be one escape when such an attempt is thwarted.

Next in line as a candidate for nonconformity and women's liberation is the older sister of a brother. In this case the dissatisfaction with the life role does not come from feelings of sexual inadequacy, but from difficulties in competing with men in occupations for which the women may be as well as or better prepared than their brothers.

WOMAN'S WORK

The old pattern (old but now changing) is constrictive in that the minority of women who escape the narrow world of dish and diaper washing may then find themselves restricted in what may be to them a second narrow world of file drawers and steno pads.

One survey of women's work patterns conducted in England studied 371 married women selected from British university graduates of 1960. Eight years after graduation the women were asked whether they were working (or intended to work) full time, part time, or not at all outside the home. Firstborns were highest in following professional careers, but a husband's approval or disapproval was a major factor in their deciding whether to work full or part time. Laterborn women most commonly were non-working, although some considered part-time work with their husbands' approval.[3] These facts illustrate how marriage, the primary occupation stressed by society for women of all birth positions, deters feminine work motivation and achievement. Most married women still will not pursue an outside vocation without their husbands' approval, but firstborns are most assertive in rising above such male-imposed inhibitions.

What about feminine achievement where such constrictions do not exist? Consider, for example, those women who turn to religious vocations out of a sense of responsibility, moral conscience, and spiritual values. Scientists in one study surveyed 583 Carmelite nuns from 56 monasteries in the United States. Of 380 responses, they found an unexpectedly large proportion were third children, consistent with the clinical observation that thirdborn girls tend to be gentle and idealistic.[4]

The creative arts are most often practiced by women born later in the family, as shown by a study at Mills College in Oakland, California. The study was limited to women students who showed creative potential in the arts, sciences, or humanities. Because of sibling rivalry, these women felt deprived of affection and attention, which aroused rage and self-concern and encouraged a process of separation from parents, attended by feelings of weakness and guilt.

It was suggested that this complex of feelings may lead to the development of creative skills which play the dual role of making oneself emotionally self-sufficient but also capable of "winning back" the parent. Most of these creative women had an older brother who had served as a model, and a younger sister whose competition had pushed them toward independence and the development of skills.[5] The creative potential itself suggests personal attention to one's own unique feelings and perceptions.

SOCIETY'S PRESSURE

Society generally coerces women into marriage, urging them to find a husband for security to replace the shelter formerly provided by parents. Other pressures, however, also force women into positions that inhibit their vocational development. I recall two clients who were literally victims of being older sisters of sisters.

One of these women had had a domineering mother and a weak father. When her younger sister contracted polio, she had been given the responsibility for her sister's care. Moreover, she had been made to feel guilty because she had escaped the disease. This woman had been so overburdened with responsibility as a child that by the time she reached adulthood she had no interests or enthusiasm. She withdrew and went through such intense periodic depressions that shock treatments were necessary.

The second example of this older-sister syndrome was a woman five years older than her sister. When the elder child was fifteen, their mother died and the teen-ager was forced to take responsibility for her ten-year-old sister. She grew up and married, but even then she looked after her little sister. At age eighty she was still taking care of little sister and doing it willingly, although she sometimes thought wistfully of the career she might have had if her sister had not been there.

The pressure of economic necessity also drives women into certain vocations. Some have the freedom of choice, while others must take what is available. This limitation certainly is true of prostitution, said to be the oldest of professions. It is only one of the ways a woman may sell her natural endowments to get along in the world. A basic contradiction in women's liberation is the fact that many women use physical assets and feminine charms to compete with men in commerce and business. By doing so, they negate their complaint that they should not be considered sex objects. This inconsistency evokes the cynical male comment that women are superior because they are born with something to sell, but in truth everyone—male or female—sells whatever talent, aptitude, appearance, or ability he develops.

Professors James K. Skipper, Jr., and Charles H. McCaghy of Case Western Reserve University conducted a sociological study of seventy-five striptease performers in clubs and theaters in major cities from Honolulu to New York. They found that almost all of the women were firstborn children. Firstborn women usually have a more accurate and practical image of their bodies than laterborns do, and look for assets to use in achievements, so why not apply this to their appearance and their bodies?

Significant, however, is the fact that the researchers found that the strippers, in addition to being firstborn, had received little affection from their parents. The fathers were generally absent from home by the time the girls reached adolescence. Most of the women presumably were lured into their vocation by the promise of high incomes and were disrobing for profit before they were old enough to vote. Some moonlighted as prostitutes.[6] What a neat way of being paid for receiving needed attention and admiration, and perhaps mocking the admirers.

Not all strippers or exhibitionistic performers are driven to an "unwanted" profession by economic necessity. Some, especially laterborn women, enjoy the attention they receive from the audience. One such example is Liz Renay, the famous ecdysiast, who originally wanted to be a movie star. She was a beautiful young woman, the second of seven children, who went to the city from a small town to chase big dreams.

"I was going to be the biggest star at Warner Brothers," she said, "if all this hadn't happened . . ."

Her husband calls her an exhibitionist, and Ms. Renay admits that she likes to go where she can be admired as a beautiful woman. At the age of fifty Ms. Renay was still stripping, at a salary of $1,000 a week.[7]

OTHER OCCUPATIONS

We also find birth-order effects operating among more conventional feminine occupations.

One survey of beauty-shop operators revealed that most were secondborn children, relating to the laterborn woman's tendency to be easygoing and seek harmonious relationships. Other evidence indicates that oldest daughters from large families are more likely to become pediatric nurses than girls from other birth positions.[8] Do oldest daughters tend to identify with their mothers and choose occupations where caring, responsibility, and gentleness are required? The pattern does not hold true with women from families of two or three children. We believe that oldest daughters from large families learn how to care for others out of necessity, and thus gravitate to such work when looking for a job. Another comparison of nursing

students with women taking other college majors revealed
that a large number of girls with younger brothers and
sisters selected the nursing major. Such women may gain
satisfaction from feeling superior to the person who is
hospitalized [9] and thus relive their childhood position of
dominance.

Generally speaking, women born later in a family remain feminine and close to their mothers. They achieve
good marriages, run their households successfully, are
good parents, and enjoy caring for their husbands. Older
sisters who have stressed academic and other achievement
outside the home tend not to follow this pattern. They are
chagrined by their younger sisters' success in domestic
life, which they secretly envy and value as much as outside achievement. When therapy is needed, it usually requires strengthening the older's confidence in her femininity and belief that she is appreciated by the men in her
life. This is also true of older sisters of brothers.

One twenty-three-year-old woman came to me suffering
from moods of withdrawal and depression that interfered
with her relations with men, who were bewildered by her
erratic behavior. Nora was concerned with "getting the
job done," but couldn't feel close to most people. She
clung to faltering relationships with men even though she
did not want them.

During therapy Nora explored her feelings that her parents had preferred her younger brother. She anticipated
rejection, the feeling she had had when her brother was
born. As we worked together, Nora became engaged and
spent a long time examining the relationship with her
fiancé in terms of the competition she felt with her brother.

She eventually married, made a success of it, and had
several children. She succeeded partly because she learned
to expect less of herself and of others, and to be more
tolerant and relaxed. Her self-confidence increased to the
point where she could feel she was really loved.

Another woman, the older sister of a brother, described
herself as "a woman in a man's world." She worked in an
occupation usually reserved for men, and sought counseling because she was considering a divorce.

During Marcia's childhood her mother had been hostile
toward both children, especially Marcia. When her brother
was born, Marcia turned to her father for comfort and
companionship. They had gone on camping and business

trips together, and she had identified with him. In this case the identification was extreme, and her masculine orientation was so strong that she could not accept a feminine role. While not homosexual, Marcia was strongly dominant in all her relationships with both males and females. When she was able to understand her dominance more clearly, her marriage improved.

Let's summarize the effects on women's achievement which may be anticipated from birth order. The only child is feminine but achievement-oriented. She admires achievement in those close to her and wants to participate as wife, mother, or daughter. She is usually competitive, but only with other women.

The firstborn woman with brothers and/or sisters emphasizes getting a job done, but the job is not necessarily outside the "standard" feminine role. She is task-oriented and, like her male counterpart, may downgrade personal relationships in favor of the task. She is competitive with men.

The middleborn woman is likely to be disinterested in competition and more interested in human relationships such as rearing a family than in outside achievement alone. She may also be artistic.

If a woman is lastborn, her attitude toward achievement may depend on the size of the family. If it is small, she is likely to be relaxed and not motivated toward professional or occupational achievement. If she is from a large family, she may be interested in other than domestic achievement (but not driven) because her ambitions have been stimulated by older brothers and sisters.

CHAPTER 9

Power and Politics

A woman approached me for advice concerning a severe problem with her fifteen-year-old son.

"He curses me," Mrs. Harlowe said. "Whenever he's angry he pushes me down or hits me, and he does the same things to our two younger girls." She was afraid to report her son's behavior to her husband.

"He has such a bad temper he might kill the boy," she said. "He has always been harder on my son than I think he should be."

Obviously, the boy was exerting power the same way he had seen his father control a wife who was afraid to talk with her spouse. Such a situation does not develop in a month or a year. Mrs. Harlowe had contributed to it by accepting her husband's anger and violence, with undertones of masochism. She also accepted her first child passively, watching with pride when as a youngster he began to adopt his father's ways of mastering situations.

"As soon as he began to walk, whenever he was upset, he would hit me or kick at my legs," Mrs. Harlowe said. "It looked cute in such a little thing."

Her pleasure in the forceful assertiveness of "such a little thing" turned to anxiety and fears as the boy's uncontrolled use of power turned him into a young tyrant.

The reason Mrs. Harlowe turned to me for help was her fear of greater violence between father and son.

After gaining some insight into her own role in this situation, Mrs. Harlowe insisted that her husband control *his* temper. He came to conjoint therapy with her, learned how he had been modeling for his son and how the boy was terrorizing the women of the family. The son also required therapy, but this did not take long, because both parents were able to help him themselves. Gradually a relative peace replaced the exercise of unbridled power in this family.

It is not unusual for a teen-age boy to resort to violence now and then in rebellion against parental discipline, but as a pattern it is often the oldest son who identifies with the father's harshness. One oldest son told me of cruel, methodical whipping by his father in childhood. Although he had no children, this client revealed his father-identification by dominating women sadistically as an adult. Sometimes he even beat them.

Such direct translation of raw power over other people reveals itself in modern society as violence and destructiveness, and the strain is as old and deep as the story of Cain and Abel. These examples begin to show how the position of birth and the interrelationship among family members determine the way in which striving for dominance manifests itself in behavior and personality. Children observe their parents' interaction, relate to the push and pull of discipline, and maneuver for a dominant position among the other siblings.

To recapitulate, the firstborn has the opportunity to closely watch the rituals parents enact with one another. He observes how they make family decisions and discipline and direct them. If one parent persists in dominating, the firstborn is likely to model behavior on the seemingly more powerful parent. Since the firstborn internalizes the parents' attitudes toward him and later makes their attitude his own, we may expect him to be stern and harsh if that is the way he was treated in childhood. His place as the oldest and strongest contributes to his belief that he has the right to be authoritarian, and control and lead others. On the other hand, if the parents are equalitarian in their household decisions, the firstborn learns to be reasonable in the demands he makes on others and in his ways of exercising power.

The laterborn child must find some way to achieve dominance, even though there is an older child as well as parents who must be persuaded to give him what is needed or wanted. Since parents are the usual source of good things—whether attention, affection, or possessions—the laterborn child competes directly with the firstborn to achieve dominance. Since the older brother or sister is often engaged in a direct struggle with the parents, the younger brother or sister often adopts the opposite method of being sweet and good. If older brother or sister has been compliant in meeting parental requirements, the younger child is likely to be demanding and aggressive. Any laterborn tends to manipulate his way around an opponent or problem, because this was how he was required to maintain and enhance himself in the power struggle with his brothers and sisters.

Out of these childhood conditions develop the ways a person exercises or succumbs to power in adulthood. What has been learned in childhood colors adult relationships, determining whether a person tries to dominate husband, wife, or children and how the person relates to friends, employers, and employees. It is my belief that attitudes and techniques learned in the nursery manifest themselves in the quest for wealth (wielding power with money), the direction of big business (wielding power over people), and in politics at all levels (wielding power over people and nations).

POLITICAL LEADERSHIP

Because kings and queens have traditionally been firstborn children and ascend to the throne regardless of aptitude, desire, or ability, we generally assume that firstborns will hold the highest political offices. This often happens, but not always, as different kinds of leadership may be needed at different times in situations where the routes to power are more or less open-ended.

Even in a democracy we cannot accurately relate birth-order position to political leadership, because most power in politics has been traditionally held by men. Therefore we must refer largely to first or laterborn men, and can only speculate about women's roles in politics according to their birth order.

My hypothesis is that firstborn sons (and now daughters) might be expected to run for political office in large proportions. The second of two children may not strive for political power unless that secondborn is a girl who follows a boy. The second child of *more than two* is very likely to run for office, whether man or woman. Richard Nixon is a prime example of this.

Later-middle children may succeed in politics because they strive for identity and are often skillful in indirect ways of achieving their aims. Youngest men and women seem least likely to run for office, unless they come from large families. Youngests from smaller families tend to leave the responsibilities of leadership to others.

A study conducted at San Francisco State College in 1970 indicates whether or not the hypothesis is supported by fact. Researchers analyzed the birth positions of 258 American Presidential and Vice-Presidential candidates. They found that Presidents have come predominantly from the ranks of first- and thirdborn sons. Secondborns were lower on the scale, and men born fourth or later were virtually absent.[1] Thus, we see that firstborn and later-middle children, as represented by a thirdborn son, were well represented among these top politicians, while secondborns and youngest sons were not.

An excellent example of the tendency for a firstborn son to follow in his father's footsteps is that of John Quincy Adams, who became sixth President of the U.S. the year before his father, John Adams, our second President, died.

The Kennedy family provides an excellent opportunity for a specific comparison of birth-order effects on Presidential aspirants from the same generation of the same family. This is an exceptional case for several reasons.

First, the father, Joseph Kennedy, was cut short in his powerful career, but motivated all his sons to aspire to high office. Death, by assassination and otherwise, determined which of the boys made it. The eldest son, Joseph, was killed accidentally. Assassinated President John F. Kennedy was second of the nine children, and Robert, seventh in line and a later middle, was killed before Presidential ambitions could be realized. Senator Edward Kennedy, last in the family, stated repeatedly that he would not run in 1976. Although family scandals and tragedies are familiar, it would be interesting to know to what degree Teddy's sibling and parental interaction have contributed to his decision not to run for the Presidency.

As a psychologist and student of birth-order, I had long been interested in the Kennedy family and the mystique among the brothers and sisters. I was convinced that Ted Kennedy, even though forced into the family pattern of political power and prestige, would not be *personally* motivated to become President. As the youngest, he might weigh the responsibilities of such an office against the opportunity for personal freedom.

Some light is shed on this subject by Rita Dallas, who served as a private nurse to Joseph Kennedy, Sr., after he suffered a stroke while playing golf. In her book *The Kennedy Case,* Dallas relates that Teddy, the lastborn, was a happy child who sang around the house. His favorite expression was: "Let's make it a fun time."

"Teddy was the youngest," Ms. Dallas wrote, "and although he had won election to the Senate, he was the baby of the family. . . . The family responded to his exuberance and seemed to treat him like a loveable puppy who was not quite house broken." Other traits noticed by the nurse were Teddy's "flamboyance, his hale and hearty political mind, his quick wit, his tendency to cut corners, his smile. . . ."

After his brothers were assassinated, Teddy was left in solitude and loneliness. "He seemed to be lonelier and more lost than anyone at the compound," Ms. Dallas said.[2]

Although Kennedy may yet run for the Presidency, it is my belief that this would be a surrender to family and political pressures against his natural inclination as influenced by the position of his birth.

The San Francisco study of Vice-Presidential and Presidential candidates also revealed a close relationship between the temper of the times and birth order of the President. It is interesting to note that in times of crisis, such as war or impending conflict, national leaders were firstborn and only sons. In less troubled times they were more often younger sons. During World War II, first sons Franklin D. Roosevelt, Winston Churchill, Adolf Hitler, Joseph Stalin, and Benito Mussolini were in power. Since 1960, when the crises that occurred had more to do with finding practical solutions than with solving national or international ideological differences, the leaders in the Western world have been almost exclusively laterborn sons, such as Kennedy, Nixon, Macmillan, de Gaulle,

Adenauer, and Khrushchev. (Brezhnev, Russia's current top man, is a youngest son.)

The theory of Dr. Irving D. Harris,[3] which is supported by these findings, is that firstborn and only sons tend to carry on and protect tradition (connected with the past), while laterborns tend to move toward new things and plan along pragmatic lines (disconnected from the past). During war, when a country needs to be united so that its resources are utilized efficiently to support traditional values, the emotional and intellectual direction of the people is toward firstborns who can draw them together. In more peaceful times, as former President Nixon said in his first inaugural address, we must look and move forward. Therefore, the people may see laterborn sons as potentially more effective.

Only children, sometimes eminent in politics, are often friendly and well liked. Like Franklin D. Roosevelt, they may have that charm and personal magnetism known as charisma. Only children also gain a strong sense of independence and self-reliance from the circumstances within their families. Buddha and Stalin were only children. Also in this category are Indira Gandhi, the first woman prime minister of India; Mary, Queen of Scots; Eleanor Roosevelt; and the Duchess of Windsor.

Among firstborns (followed by other children) who have been great leaders was Harry Truman, first in a family of three. He took over the Presidency near the end of World War II after Roosevelt's death. Reflecting his belief in traditional values and direct confrontation of problems, Truman had a sign on his desk which read: "The buck stops here." His favorite quotation was: "If you can't stand the heat, you better stay out of the kitchen." Long after he had left the Presidency, in 1966, Truman said:

"It all seems to have been in vain. Memories are short and appetites for power and glory are insatiable. Old tyrants depart. New ones take their place. Old allies become the foe. The recent enemy becomes the friend. It is all very baffling and trying, but we cannot lose hope, we cannot despair. For it is all too obvious that if we do not abolish war on this earth then surely, one day, war will abolish us from the earth." [4]

The late President Lyndon Johnson, who caught the blame for escalating America's involvement in the Vietnam War, was a firstborn. George Washington was the first of five children, and Alexander Hamilton the first of two. Henry Ford and Winston Churchill were firstborns. A first son (after three daughters) who exercised spiritual authority over a large part of the world's people was the late Pope John XXIII, who came from a family of twelve children. Giuseppe Roncalli did not seek power, but it came by the way he exercised benign authority over his flock.

"I knew he was cut out for important things," said his younger brother. "Giuseppe *wanted* to go to school. I only went when it rained."

Although he was an old man when named the Vicar of Christ, and died soon after, Pope John set in motion the Council which "let some fresh air in here" and led to the most profound changes in the Catholic Church in five hundred years.[5]

If Pope John's humanitarian approach was partially rooted in birth-order effects, it probably resulted from the fact that he followed three girls. I have pointed out elsewhere that girls in a family preceding a boy tend to make that boy less authoritarian and less committed to dominance and aggression. Even though a firstborn son, Pope John was a later middle with the ability to compromise and see many points of view, as well as having less respect for tradition than a firstborn.

When the Machiavellian tendency of the second or later child is combined with a strong verbal ability, the result may be an outstanding politician. This pattern fits Nixon, who was second among five boys. It also fits Hubert Humphrey, the second of four children, but there was a difference in the makeup of their families.

Nixon's political skill in manipulating people began developing at an early age. His brother Harold's death, at age twenty-two, and Arthur's death at seven, threw a pall of sadness over Richard's early life. His seriousness was intensified by the family's economic hardships in the 1930s. Brothers Donald and Edward, who remained in the background during Richard's rise to political power, remember they had to "hustle" to keep Richard at school at Whittier College.

The ex-President's obsession with the crises in his life, and the feelings of persecution which seemed to mark his decline, were signaled as early as age ten, when he wrote a letter to his mother, who was then away on a trip. He fantasized himself as a poor beaten dog:

> My Dear Mother,
> The two boys [brothers] that you left me with are very bad to me. Their dog, Jim, is very old and he will never talk or play with me. On Saturday the boys went hunting. Jim and myself went with them. While going through the woods, one of the boys tripped and fell on me. I lost my temper and bit him. He kicked me in the side and we started on.
> While we were walking, I saw a black round thing in a tree. I hit it with my paw. A swarm of black things came out of it. I felt pain all over. I started to run. As both of my eyes were swelled shut, I fell into a pond. When I got home I was very sore. I wish you would come home right now.
> Your good dog, Richard [6]

From such a letter a psychologist could draw on many symbols concerning Nixon's personality, but for our purposes it draws attention to the fact that the roots of his thinking were imbedded in the emotional soil created by his siblings.

Former Vice-President Humphrey had an older brother, with whom he was "combative," and two younger sisters. He felt responsible for them and for his mother. This strain of gentleness, due to birth order, may have indirectly hindered him in reaching the top of the political ladder. However, he may yet run again for the Presidency.* A brilliant student and teacher, Humphrey found

---

* It is not appropriate to consider President Ford in the birth-order pattern of Presidents, because he was appointed rather than elected. However, I shall again presumptuously suggest that as the next general election approaches, it might be well for political parties to consider the birth order of the candidates they nominate. The country seems both to be swinging toward tradition and to be amassing a staggering number of problems to be solved. In this situation a successful candidate might be an only child who can be charismatic, give the impression of being a father figure, and yet who has had much practical experience. Oddly, President Ford would seem to fit many of these qualifications: He was the only child of his two parents but had to assume the position of eldest with stepbrothers and -sisters, and he did not know of this relationship until he was 17.)

as a secondborn that it is necessary in life to sometimes
fly with the wind instead of in the teeth of it.

"The politician must curry favor of the people," Humphrey said. "The successful politician . . . watches the
clock and knows what time it is. . . . The politician must
be reasonably adept at satisfying or conciliating the rival
interests and aspirations of others. A pragmatist." [7]

Leaders who came from the *second* birth position have
included Theodore Roosevelt (second of two), Benjamin
Disraeli (second of five), John Q. Adams (second of
four), and Herbert Hoover (second of three). Bernard
Baruch, powerful wall street financier and adviser to Presidents, was the second of four boys. He wrote:

> As a child, I was shy and sensitive, something of a
> mama's boy. I always sat at mother's right at the
> dinner table and I remember how fiercely I fought
> for this privilege.
>
> Only after much effort did I learn how to control
> my feelings and what I could do best, leaving what I
> could not do well to others. If there was any "key"
> to this process of growing up, it lay in the systematic
> efforts I made to subject myself to critical self-
> appraisal. As I came to know myself I acquired a
> better understanding of other people. . . .
>
> To reach the top in any endeavor, you must learn
> to take the bitter with the sweet—the ridicule and
> taunts of other boys, the sneers, threats and sleepless
> opposition of other men, and the anguish of your own
> disappointments. [8]

Later-middle children who have risen to powerful positions include Robert F. Kennedy, seventh in the Kennedy
clan. Woodrow Wilson was third in a family of four, and
Dwight Eisenhower was third of six boys. Benjamin Franklin was eighth among ten, the last two of whom were sisters. As he said: "I was the youngest son of a youngest
son for five generations back."

Brezhnev of Russia is a notable exception to the trend
of youngest children not to gravitate to positions of power,
But it is common to find a youngest serving alongside a
power figure. Marie Antoinette was a youngest daughter.
Pat Nixon is the youngest in her family (with two older
sisters), and Lady Bird Johnson is the youngest of three.

WINNING AND LOSING

A high need for achievement (often found in first-borns) is a prerequisite for *seeking* power, but other traits must be present if a politician is to win.

A psychologist at the University of Tennessee, Dr. Cabot L. Jaffe, found that sheer *quantity* of speech often outweighs quality when it comes to influencing people. Jaffe brought together groups of student women for discussion and debate. Those who monopolized the sessions, even though often wrong, emerged as leaders. Quiet girls, who often were accurate in their opinions, had comparatively little influence.[9] This experiment could be unsettling if it indicates that people with good ideas remain on the sidelines while the thoughtless are elected and permitted to run the world.

We suggest that only and middle children with good ideas should speak up more than they might be inclined to do. In a study at California State University at Hayward [10] only and middle children were found to be much less talkative than first- and lastborn students. First- and lastborns were equally talkative, but firstborns talked more about themselves than did lastborns. Since people often accept our own expressed view of ourselves, these facts about talkativeness might explain part of the preeminence of firstborns in politics.

The willingness and ability to express oneself relate directly to winning and losing in politics, as demonstrated by one of the few studies conducted in this area. Gordon B. Forbes of Milliken University in Decatur, Illinois, recognized the evidence which relates birth order to intellectual ability and academic training, but he wondered about the sparseness of information in areas not associated with intellectual achievement. Because it is difficult to obtain objective data in most nonacademic areas, Forbes focused upon politics, where success and failure are measured at the ballot box.

"Because of the clear over-representation of firstborns among the college-educated and because firstborns tend to be more academically successful and have higher achievement need," Forbes said, "it seemed reasonable to expect that firstborns would be more likely to enter politics and also more likely to win elections.

"On the other hand," he added, "laterborn children tend to excel over other ordinal positions in personal popularity and the skill with which they manipulate others. Both traits appear to be very useful in political life. Consequently, it was hypothesized that first and lastborn children would be more likely to enter politics and more likely to win elections than middle-born children."

Forbes sent out questionnaires requesting the birth order of all 228 candidates for contested seats in the Illinois State Senate and General Assembly of 1970. A review of the 128 questionnaires returned showed that no one birth position ranked unexpectedly highest among the candidates. However, more first- and lastborn candidates *won* their elections than did middleborn candidates. Forbes also found that winners more often returned the questionnaire *before* the election than others who subsequently lost. This early response suggested the possibility that a test— such as the return of a questionnaire—might be useful in predicting election outcomes and that the use of verbal communications by first- and lastborn might again relate to their political success. [11]

SOCIAL JUSTICE

Which people are most likely to become leaders when the winds of social change are rising? Only partial answers can be deduced from birth order, and these are derived from specific examples:

Susan B. Anthony, famous for her work in women's rights, was a second daughter in a fairly large family. The same is true of Joan Baez, one of the more prominent voices during the late 1960s and early 1970s in the outcry against America's involvement in the Vietnam War. In England, twenty-eight-year-old Susan McCormick was named the first female warden of a British prison. She is the oldest of four daughters.

A number of black people have recently risen through the American political process to the office of Mayor in several major cities as well as prominent state offices. Although no accurate survey has been made, the pattern of these black men and women seems to follow that of the firstborn, combining need for achievement with the best resources a family may have to offer. One such example is Wilson C. Riles (an only child), who won election over a popular incumbent to become Superintendent of Public Instruction for the State of California. Ralph T. Bunche, known for his distinguished State Department career, was the first of two children.

One of the loudest voices against social injustice (and *for* Communism) in the past decade was Angela Davis. She is the oldest of four children.

"If there was anything she really wanted to do, she would do it," Angela's mother said. "She had this self-determination . . ."

At age twenty-six, Ms. Davis became a fugitive from justice after her alleged involvement in a courthouse kidnapping and shootout in San Rafael, California, to free blacks and Chicanos she believed had been incarcerated unjustly. As early as age twelve she was helping to organize interracial study groups in Alabama. She won scholarships to go through college, to study in Europe, and finally to obtain a position as professor of philosophy. She became a Communist and supported radical issues.[12]

The important point is that some of the power tactics, force, or manipulation which an adult uses to maintain and enhance himself in society are learned in childhood relationships with parents and brothers and sisters. This is as true of people in high places as it is of those in average circumstances. Governors, Presidents, kings, and corporation executives all grew up in a family situation.

I hope to contribute not only to your own self-understanding, but also give insights into what family influences tend to develop men and women who can manage world affairs in a manner that will benefit all of humankind. Whether we have peace or war, a world of wasted or wisely used resources, whether there will be possibilities for personal development of all people may depend upon our interaction with parents and siblings in our childhood homes. It is our premise that this is where the individual learns to be violent or gentle, cooperative or dictatorial, tolerant of the weaknesses of others and respectful of the strengths of others. The values and attitudes we learn at home will be reflected in our choices of leaders and, ultimately, in the kind of leadership we receive.

SECTION

IV

*Sexual Development
and Social
Relationships*

CHAPTER 10

The Social Network

The family is a child's first social group, the rehearsal hall for a larger drama to come in adulthood. Playmates meet on the sidewalk, boys and girls explore the new environments of classroom and schoolyard, and teen-agers banter and wrestle with the coming of sexual awareness. Adult society then comes together as a network of men and women meeting, touching, parting, mingling casually or deeply as circumstances permit.

The web of human contact may be serene and symmetrical or tangled and distorted, but a person is always influenced by the life role molded by parents and brothers and sisters. We spend our lives seeking human relationships for comfort and warmth, for a sense of belonging in work and play, for friendship and love. As those relationships develop, or fail to develop, we seek greater understanding of the forces which shape our methods of maintaining and enhancing ourselves.

In the family setting a child learns much of what it is to be human. Information and skills furnished by parents and older siblings eliminate the need for each person to learn everything in life through individual experimentation. On the other hand—especially in the current generation influenced by various subcultures—parents often are not believed (sometimes rightly). Their experience is ignored, and young people tend to accept the ideas of peers rather than those of knowledgeable adults. This is one reason why birth order may play a more important role than ever before in determining how a child learns to fit into the social network—siblings may tend to influence the individual to a greater extent than parents do.

Regardless of generation gaps and change, which is always with us, there remain some relatively reliable criteria by which you may measure your aptitudes, inclinations, and capabilities in forming and maintaining social relationships. There are many such yardsticks but the major ones are:

Self-esteem—How approving are you of yourself?

Need for approval—Are you the best judge of the adequacy of what you do, or do you need others to approve?

Self-sufficiency—Are you dependent upon other people for support, comfort, reassurance?

Sociability—Do you *like* being with other people?

Conformity—Do you feel uncomfortable when your ideas and behavior differ from others'?

Morality—How strictly do you adhere to the moral and ethical standards of society?

Let's look at these in more detail to see how they relate to birth order.

SELF-ESTEEM

The maturation process involves a decrease in the need for approval as a person develops inner confidence in his or her own judgment. Maturing means greater self-approval or self-esteem. Helping a person move from dependence upon the approval of others to reliance upon his or her own inner values is often a major step in psychological therapy.

Firstborns (both male and female) followed by other children have more need for approval than laterborns and only children. Therefore, firstborns, in general, have lower self-esteem than later children do. Only children tend to have higher self-esteem than those from any other position in the birth order.

The development of self-esteem seems more difficult for women than for men. Ingrained social patterns establish the attitude of parents toward the gender of their child. Even today, in most parts of the world, a son is preferred to a daughter. No one can escape this evaluation, because it is reflected by parents, siblings, and others who surround a child; it also relates to the need for approval from parents, teachers, and others. Whether you are first- or later-born, your gender cannot help affecting your self-esteem.

Highest of all in self-esteem is the only male in the family, whether an only child or with one or more sisters. Next in line is the laterborn male who is not pressed to achieve, and thus feels less guilty if he fails. Since first-borns depend more upon external opinions than laterborns do, the conflict between self-esteem and need for approval is intensified if the firstborn is also a woman. Female laterborns seem to have higher self-esteem than oldest girls, but the sex difference continues to matter, because a young sister with an older brother usually has a lower opinion of herself than a girl with an older sister.

Frequently women tell me: "I don't like to be with other women. I much prefer being with men." Such remarks usually contain a certain smugness, since the woman feels she is conforming to parental and society's evaluation (and her own) of women in general. She feels she is somehow setting herself apart from the low image traditionally held by the feminine half of society and saying: "Approve of me because I depreciate women also."

One young woman and I had been working together for some weeks and, since we had several problems to consider, the question of her relationship with other women had never come up. Then one day she said happily:

"I don't understand what's happening to me. I'm finding that I enjoy being with other women. In fact, four or five of us at work enjoy getting together and we have a kind of little clique."

"What this means," I answered, "is that you're getting to like yourself better—yourself as a woman."

I explained that a woman who does not like other women is negating her own value. She doesn't like that part of herself that is female. If she is to have the confidence that will make her comfortable coping with the world, she needs to appreciate those characteristics of herself which she cannot avoid, and being *feminine* is one of them. It is a delight to see how pleased women often are when they come to terms with this aspect of their behavior.

Another woman told an acquaintance: "I know you find it hard to relate to me. It's evident that you don't like other women, but after a time in therapy you will learn that, as you like yourself better, you'll like other women as well."

The tendency of the firstborn to identify with the father after a younger sibling is born accentuates the problem. A girl can never quite make it. She may adopt her father's values, attitudes, and behavior in many ways, but she cannot change her gender. Until she and society come to value femininity, this struggle will exist for the ambitious woman. This was true of a teacher who was concerned about problems at school and personal relationships with men. Other women teachers were uncooperative, and complained that she was not sociable. Her only good professional relationships were with male teachers. She could get along with her principal but not with her immediate supervisor, a woman.

Christine had a series of boyfriends. Men were quickly attracted to her but the romance was always short-lived. After each hostile and unhappy ending, which recurred every few weeks, the man of the moment vehemently criticized her. She assumed the attitude that, as a woman, she was not appreciated for the great person she was. The pattern was repeated again and again.

In the course of therapy, Christine uncovered her deep hostility toward her younger brother, which had developed out of competition for their father's attention. She understood that now she was using her seductiveness as a weapon to conquer men. When they succumbed to her sexual attraction, she taunted and rejected them. While using it as a weapon, Christine actually was denying and rejecting the femininity which had caused her to feel inferior to her brother.

When she finally accepted her femininity, Christine's relations with other women teachers improved. She never came to regard other women as equals, but she was able to relate to them without disdain. As Christine became more self-accepting and confident, her belligerent sexuality also diminished. She began to accept men as companions rather than as opponents on a battleground.

NEED FOR APPROVAL

It follows that firstborns usually have a stronger need for approval than laterborns and the tendency is stronger for women than for men. Oldests have been found to be inhibited in competitive learning in the presence of others, whereas laterborns learned better under this condition.[1] The investigators believed the firstborns were affected by reluctance to irritate others. Another explanation is that the firstborns were overly concerned with the opinion of the observers.

Firstborns (including onlies) have been found to seek the approval of persons important to them from very earliest years. Laterborns do not place such high value on the approval of parents, spouses, and employers. It has been found that young laterborns tend to lose interest in pursuing academic projects if they are given much approval, while firstborns are encouraged to improve when they hear approval from others.

SELF-SUFFICIENCY

The personality characteristics we are describing overlap one another. A person is self-sufficient who has high self-esteem and depends upon his own approval of what is accomplished. Another aspect of self-sufficiency is the extent to which a person is dependent on others for help, support, comfort, and reassurance.

Firstborns often appear independent because they proceed persistently to accomplish their goals. Nevertheless, there is a deep-seated dependency within firstborns that is often hidden from all but the therapist.

The transition from only child to first of a series of children can be a traumatic one. The pressure of the parents' wishing for another child and the concomitant diversion of parental attention from child No. 1 requires adjustment. The firstborn must now learn not only to share attention, but to expect less concern for his dependency needs. The parents' awareness and willingness to deal with this transition will determine how much deprivation the child experiences.

In laboratory situations dependency shows up in various ways. One researcher [2] discovered that the mere presence of other people in a situation of high anxiety relieved firstborn anxiety, even though the subjects were not permitted to talk with one another. In another study [3] of college students, oldest and only children had a greater desire than laterborns to seek the support of others under conditions of high anxiety.

At 6 A.M. on February 9, 1971, a major earthquake jarred a large section of Southern California. Lasting for about a minute, the quake resulted in more than fifty deaths and millions of dollars' worth of property damage. The day after the quake, Michael F. Hoyt of Yale University and Bertram H. Raven of the University of California in Los Angeles questioned 428 undergraduate students concerning their reactions to the quake and their levels of fear and anxiety.

Anxiety and the need for support, as shown by how quickly the students called their parents or other people, did not seem to vary according to birth order. However, among 112 subjects who were *alone* at the time of the earthquake, firstborn women were more afraid and affiliative than firstborn men and laterborn women. Among men, firstborns gave more assistance than laterborns. This corroborates our observation that firstborns often assume leadership in times of disaster to ease or deny their own anxiety, and find affiliation and support by helping others. [4]

Similar reactions were found among adults in South Africa in September 1968, when a flash flood struck Port Elizabeth, a coastal city of 296,000. [5] A number of other investigations support the observation that oldest women in particular are less anxious if they are with other people during a stressful situation.

SOCIABILITY

Sociability is the natural disposition to join other people for companionship and social relations rather than to satisfy a need for emotional support and approval.

Later children in general have been judged more socially adept than their elder siblings in tests based upon their ability to talk freely about personal matters. Since there is more interaction among peers as a result of being born later in the family, the give-and-take between brothers and sisters carries over to easier social relationships with adults. On the average, firstborns are less popular than laterborns and may anticipate less acceptance in casual social relations.

The question often arises as to who is more likely to be a "joiner." It has been convenient on college campuses to study students who join fraternities and sororities. The results suggest that, among men, birth order isn't related to joining fraternities, but there is a tendency for more only and firstborn women to join sororities. Since these college social groups often seek out good students to raise grade averages of the whole, it might be expected that firstborns would be sought as members. Firsts and onlies also are more likely to be asked to join country clubs or other exclusive groups where socioeconomic status is important.*

Laterborns are invited into groups where popularity is the criterion. Their enjoyment of others because of personal characteristics, rather than social or economic status, is probably the reason. They have been found more likely than firstborns to be leaders in small groups where the quality of personal interaction is important.

To summarize:

Only children usually rank high in social acceptance, probably relating to their generally high economic status. However, they are slow to volunteer in group activities, perhaps because they are accustomed to being alone and do not like being regimented.

Firstborns, with other siblings, like associating with popular people but may be less popular themselves. Oldest women tend to have more dates than laterborns, because they drive to achieve, and make use of their physical attributes at an earlier age. Because they try harder, firstborns may belong to more formal groups, such as fraternities and sororities, than would be expected considering their general level of social acceptability.

The second of two children, if a girl, is not likely to be a joiner, and if a boy may be interested in sports but not

---

* Onlies tend to come from higher social status than persons from other birth orders, and thus would swell the numbers of invited firstborns.

in joining clubs for reasons of status. Later middles and secondborns in families larger than two children are less inclined than firstborns to join organizations.

Youngest children are usually popular and more apt to join organized groups than other laterborns.

CONFORMITY

The conforming person submits to the model opinion of a group. He is uncomfortable if his ideas and behavior differ from those of the majority.

In laboratory situations tests of conformity usually present a situation requiring an opinion or judgment, and then measure how readily each person conforms to the opinion of someone else believed to have the correct answer. The results of many studies indicate that firstborns are more susceptible than laterborns to social pressure.[6] Firsts are more likely to agree with established mores and institutions, as taught by their parents, and later to conform to pressure from other adults.

From a pragmatic point of view, one might wonder if firstborns are more influenced than laterborns by televised reports of early election returns shown in areas voting much later, such as California or Hawaii.

MORALITY

We are not concerned here with criminal behavior and other such divergences from established mores of society, but with everyday situations of ethics and responsibility.

At the University of Nebraska researchers studied resistance to temptation among teen-age boys. The findings indicate that firstborn children develop stronger self-control as a result of greater exposure to their parents' views about moral and ethical standards.[7]

This same pattern also held true in a survey of what type of person is best able to keep a secret. It seems that the eldest child is least likely to tell, while a laterborn may find it rewarding to run to older brother or sister with a tidbit of gossip. A secret is one of the gifts a younger, weaker child can carry in triumph to his lords, the elders. The possibility that the habit may carry over into adulthood is indicated by the fact that laterborns are more likely to write family histories and autobiographies, thus perhaps divulging secrets and information their elders would like to keep hidden.

Evidence shows that all through the years of elementary school, high school, and college, laterborns are more likely than firstborns to transgress the rules. They are less likely to meet teachers' expectations, and more likely to be placed "on the carpet" in college. They are less inclined to follow the rules of authority figures, and more likely to accept those of their peers.

It is one thing to separate and examine the major threads which form the tapestry of a social or non-social person, but quite another to show how the threads mesh together to form an individual personality.

THE ONLY CHILD

Everyone feels lonely at one time or another. However, the child with brothers and sisters—particularly older brothers and sisters—rarely complains of loneliness as does the only child. In many instances the only child will turn to a self-destructive, clinging relationship with another person just to avoid being lonely, and may move from one unpleasant relationship to another in the quest to be close to someone. Sometimes the only child has difficulty understanding other people.

"I was always more involved in daydreams than with people," one only child said. "I expected people to be like my fantasies, and now I'm puzzled when they aren't."

Confusion, loneliness, and fantasy can become tangled with outright fear of other people if the only child is subjected to excessive control (often the mark of parents who treasure their single youngster), with personal contacts limited to the adult world of father and mother. I had the unusual occasion to witness this complex process as it was occurring in a five-year-old boy brought to me for therapy.

Gene was a sensitive, intelligent youngster. His parents both worked, but carefully scheduled his life, forcing him

to eat, sleep, and rest at specific times. Some of his
mother's overprotectiveness stemmed from the fact that
Gene had suffered an unpleasant throat infection when he
was an infant. Now, four years later, he still cleared his
throat uneasily whenever he felt anxious or uncomfortable
with other people.

When I began working with him, Gene was uncooperative with teachers and other children in kindergarten. He
feared freeways (reflecting his mother's fear), and was
repulsed by physical contact. At the same time, his fantasy
play was often violent, involving cowboys and killing, and
he even occasionally struck his mother. He was continually
on guard against violence, and insisted upon carrying a toy
weapon with him to school. For a child his age, he had
exceptional control against expressing emotions with people other than his mother.

As I counseled Gene's parents it became apparent that
Gene was confused and frightened by his mother's outbursts of anger and by his father's insistence on teaching
him boxing and wrestling. The boy's confusion came partly
from the usual Oedipal conflict, but more from mani-
festations, which he could not understand, that his parents
were dissatisfied with each other.

Basically, Gene's interpersonal relationships had not kept
pace with his intellectual development. He was lonely and
yet frightened of contacts with other children his own age.
He identified with older children. In drawings Gene de-
picted his father as a figure with huge hands: strong,
powerful, threatening, and frightening. He needed his
mother's support at all times, frequently remarking that
"Mother hasn't taught me" how to do something. He was
critical of his own performance, and was unable to perform at all whenever he felt the results would not reach
the expected level.

Gene's concept of human beings in general was confused
and undifferentiated. He seemed to feel secure in his
parents' love and attention, but frightened of anyone outside that small family realm. In fantasy play he called his
toys "little people." He talked about being a "fireman
dog" rather than a "police dog," and played with a toy
dog at putting out fires (which to him probably represented his parents' angry interchanges).

Through play therapy with Gene and counseling his parents, I was able to see considerable improvement in the boy within a short period of time. Gene's father stopped the boxing and wrestling, which had stimulated the boy's fear at a sensitive stage. I encouraged his mother to relax her solicitude about his welfare, because she was transmitting abnormal fears and anxieties to her child. Gene's parents cared about each other, but had found the frustration of early parenthood and achieving economic security a challenge to their relationship. They made real efforts to establish a more peaceful atmosphere in their home.

Gene began to enjoy school. His anxious throat-clearing went away. He learned to play baseball, which satisfied his father's athletic ambitions for him, and his stubbornness and savagery subsided as he felt less threatened within his home.

Some children learn to get along with people better than others do. Often the only child accomplishes this to a fine degree, possibly because he develops more sophisticated and adult attitudes through parents and their friends. It is not uncommon for the only child to be the most sought after in social groups because he is the least aggressive. Only children do not feel threatened by the presence of other siblings, and their dependence upon parental influence is significant in social relationships. They carry the older generation's ways into the new generation, but may be overwhelmed when peer ideas vary widely from parental attitudes. Especially strong peer pressure may lead to rebellion against parental values during adolescence when other disturbing factors are also affecting a child's development.

One important difference between the only child and one with brothers and sisters is that the latter learns to take for granted the interplay of emotions and affectionate or hostile behavior of peers. Usually the child with siblings learns not to be disturbed too much or for too long, and finds that angry competition for a toy can soon be followed by calm and happy sharing. Many only children become distressed as adults when they are faced with accepting both hostile and affectionate behavior from friends, acquaintances, relatives, and spouses. Many only children are bewildered by this normal interplay of emotions, which other children learn to accept as they are growing up.

THE FIRSTBORN

If you're an oldest boy or girl, you may have a more difficult time than others in forming easy friendships. The effect of emphasizing achievement, competition, and authority may lead to a less attractive personality than an only child, who learns to charm, and later children, who are more interested in human relations than in achievement.

In school, for example, the firstborn achievement drive may alienate you from other children who achieve at a lower level, and avoid you because you may appear aloof and superior. This can cause personality conflicts, particularly in adolescent years, when a young man or woman feels the acute need for companionship. One young man told me of the agonies he suffered in high school.

From earliest years Greg's mother told him repeatedly that he must be a "good boy," and that as her firstborn she expected him to achieve excellence in all things. Fortunately, his early schoolwork was easy for him, and he was able to bring home A's and B's to his mother.

"No matter how well I did, though," he said, "it always seemed that she expected something more of me."

As a result, he felt continuous anxiety, trying to find an exceptional accomplishment which would gain her unqualified approval and love.

Greg grew up on a farm with few opportunities for social interchange; thus, his anxiety was sharpened when he entered high school, even though he had graduated as valedictorian of his class. In the small-town high school Greg soon found it was not difficult to compete academically. Because of his response to teaching, he won the admiration of the faculty, but he did not understand why his accomplishments did not win equal admiration and friendship from other students.

Greg felt out of the action. When young people congregated in the halls he envied them their easy banter, and when he passed a laughing group he thought they were laughing at him. Greg liked several girls, but they ignored him in favor of the athletic types. In the morning before class he heard scraps of conversation among other boys who had been to a party or out on a date the night before. Greg was too shy to ask a girl for a date, and he was generally excluded from parties and other activities.

Part of Greg's problem was that his father required him to hurry home after school every afternoon to help with the farm chores, but instead it seemed that he was deficient in social attractiveness and that there must be "something wrong" with him. To compensate, he studied even harder and scored the highest grades to maintain the adult approval he had already achieved.

During his last two years of high school Greg gained some peer approval by playing on the baseball team, but he had few close friends and dated girls only a couple of times. It was not until he entered college that Greg found academic excellence could blend with social activities for mutual satisfaction.

This is not an unusual pattern for the first youngster followed by other children. In their eagerness to please parents and other adults, firstborn men and women grow up with feelings that they must accomplish all things for all people. Since it is seldom possible for anyone to achieve highly in all realms, this eagerness and anxiety also often translates into fear of failure in personal relationships.

Frank H. Farley of the University of Wisconsin and Wallace L. Mealiea of Indiana State University gave a fear test to 148 college students. They found that firstborns showed greater fear than younger brothers and sisters in social and personal situations such as being alone or parting from friends. Later children are generally more self-confident and more relaxed in such situations.[8]

We have emphasized repeatedly that birth order is only one of the major contributors to personality development and that one factor may cancel or intensify another. A pattern indicating that firstborn anxiety may decrease with age in women was found in a study of defensiveness among unwed mothers. Firstborn women were less anxious and less defensive than laterborns, but age may have been a crucial factor in this study, since the firstborns, on the average, were older than the laterborns.[9]

THE MIDDLE SECOND

The social graces of a second child who is the middle of three are forged in an atmosphere of competition with the older sibling, and complicated by a new competitive situation when a younger child is born. As a result, the second boy or girl may meet social contacts with devious methods of gaining an objective or with unusual aggression. The search for identity is difficult for the child born into this position, because he must continuously struggle for parental approval, affection, and a *place* in the family. An extreme example of this was a fourteen-year-old boy sent to me for help because he was having trouble both in school and at home.

Elmo had an older sister and a younger brother. His parents were unskilled workers, and both were forced to work outside the home to support their three children. Consequently, Elmo was required to help his older sister take care of their little brother, clean house, and prepare meals for the family.

The boy felt a total lack of companionship with his parents, especially the affection he needed from his father. One of his few good memories was of going to a show with his dad.

"My folks always come home tired and cranky," Elmo said. "They act funny most of the time. What they do makes me feel that whatever they ask me to do, I'll do the opposite."

In school he disrupted the classroom and teased other children, sometimes hitting or pinching them. He stole small objects from fellow students, and once brought a gun to school and fired it on the playground.

Because of Elmo's obvious slide toward serious delinquency, he was referred to a service agency for psychological counseling. He was sent to me for help, but I felt a male therapist would be more effective. This was a turning point for the boy. From the male therapist he gained the opportunity to identify with a male who could sympathize with him and understand his needs, the things he needed from his father.

Elmo began adjusting better to teachers and students at school, and seemed to gain some sense of identity as an individual, which he had never achieved under the pressures of his place in the family.

LATER MIDDLES

Later-middle children usually adjust more easily than first-, second-, or lastborn children. One reason for this is that parents have relaxed, and the later children are placed under less performance stress than the oldest. Also, since pressure and discipline are diffused among more children, the younger ones enjoy more freedom to interact with one another. Thus, they are more likely to accept quarrels and anger as passing, rather than permanent, features in their lives. They tend to be self-reliant (because less was demanded of them), and easygoing. This pattern often assures laterborns the ability to initiate school social encounters, and to succeed in adult life where human relations are more important than academic or professional pursuits. Sports and other group activities come naturally to the laterborn child.

A test of the belief that laterborns are more socially adept than firstborns was conducted at Xavier University in Cincinnati. The investigation was based upon a questionnaire which revealed how much a person was willing to disclose about him- or herself. It was given to 30 boys and 30 girls in high school. Laterborns scored higher than firstborns in breaking down interpersonal barriers, and girls scored higher than boys. The pattern among high-school students also corresponded with that found in earlier research among college students.[10]

Lest you, as a laterborn, accept these findings as a guarantee of easy friendships, remember that much depends upon the nature of the interactions within *your* family. Social achievement is as important as achievement in any other realm, and it is not possible to separate the two entirely. A firstborn's aloofness and superiority may turn off friends at work, and a laterborn's relations with brothers and sisters may color the nature of friendships in the professional world. One young man told me of his anger with a fellow worker who was a woman:

"She acts as though we're good friends," he said, "but

as soon as the boss asks her to do something, my ideas
are of no importance. She has sabotaged several situations
in which we were meeting with the boss. She had told me
before the meeting that she agreed with my plans, but as
soon as we're with the boss, she agrees with everything he
says and is silent when I talk. She gives me no support,
regardless of what she has said before."

This young man grew up as the third child in a family
of four. He had an older brother and sister, but most important to him was his younger sister, who was less than
two years younger than he. The girl formed a close tie
with him which almost excluded the rest of the family,
followed him around, and agreed with whatever he wanted
to do.

Of course, this man probably expected his female colleague to relate to him as his sister had. But his co-
worker had her own motives for relating as she did to
him and their boss. After the young man understood his
misconception of their relationship, he was able to accept
her limited friendship without expecting a devoted follower.

Another twenty-six-year-old man, second of two
brothers, consulted me because he was having difficulties
in work and personal relationships. He had grown well in
his career but was troubled about continuing progress.

Martin was a structural engineer. He was well liked by
his employers and peers, but felt they expected him to
improve his skills and be more assertive. He felt incapable of doing this. As we talked Martin confided that
his older brother had done well in school and he had
not.

"I really didn't care about studying," Martin said. "I
preferred playing ball with the boys."

It was not long before he saw that, as younger brother,
he had tried to achieve in areas where his brother did
not. He felt he could not compete directly, so he chose
other areas, although he was also very intelligent. Martin
was now learning that social and work relationships intermingle, and that he must strengthen his position with other
people. He enrolled in a class to improve his reading
ability, and joined a Toastmasters' Club, which gave him
the opportunity to speak before groups, to field questions,
and to become more assertive.

THE YOUNGEST

Youngest children join the social network according to the way they are treated by older members of the family. If given kind and gentle treatment, the youngest is kind and gentle with even those less powerful. Youngest children are often known for the gentle way they play with smaller children, and give excellent care to the family pets. If they are teased, roughed up, and laughed at when small, however, youngest children may develop a lack of trust and confidence in the kindness of others. They may also develop a fixation upon a favorite brother or sister which often inhibits later social relations.

This happened with a twenty-four-year-old man who came to me for counseling "because the world seems unreal." He worked as an accountant, but on weekends "I just sit in my room, either depressed or with this strange feeling of unreality. I just brood for hours at a time." He had no social contacts outside of work.

Leo was the last of four children. His father was a professional man, seemingly superior and distant, and frequently away from home.

"I can't remember that my father ever touched me," Leo said, "not even to spank me."

His mother was always busy in social and club activities or "out shopping for antiques," so Leo and his next older sister were often left in the care of a housekeeper, who paid little attention except to enforce edicts of their mother who demanded that Leo should "be a good boy, work hard, and behave properly at all times."

His only real companion was his sister, who alternately mothered him and fought with him. Her anger was sometimes violent, and the alternate love and hate she displayed toward him contributed to Leo's confusion about reality; she still remained his most reliable social contact.

Even though he had a fairly good job, Leo's crisis as an adult was triggered by the fact that he had moved away and lived alone near his work, and his sister had married. Although he resented his brother-in-law, Leo weathered the loss of his sister's companionship until she had a baby—then it seemed he had lost her to another rival.

This combination of usually normal events caused the

young man to withdraw, because he could not transfer the closeness he had enjoyed with his sister to relationships with other people.

In therapy Leo poured out his longing for warmth and closeness which had been denied by his parents and later by his sister. We worked through some of his problems relating to women, and then he was counseled by a male therapist, where Leo was able to release some of the suppressed anger he felt for his father. In the process, he developed a stronger male identity.

A boy who is the baby of the family may grow up with childlike feelings, unable to join easily in the boisterous world of men, and hesitant to approach women. If the youngest is a girl and is treated as the cute baby of the family, she may grow to maturity always expecting to be babied. In general, however, the youngest child in the family is often fun-loving and lighthearted—traits which he may use to advantage in life.

CHAPTER 11

Developing Sex Roles

What does it mean to be a female or a male?

The basic physiological characteristics are usually apparent even though unisex hair styles and clothing sometimes obscure the demarcation. Paradoxically, considering unisex, young people themselves often make use of naturally different symbols of identification: boys grow mustaches and beards and girls go braless for distinction.

The point is that there is much more to sexual differentiation than physical equipment or the outward show of clothing and hair styles. Each sex is expected to meet society's definitions of distinctive behavior. A proud father will bring his baby a tiny baseball mitt to hang in his crib to prepare him for the onset of Little League. If the baby has a twin sister, the same proud father will bring her a rubber duckling or a doll to cuddle and "mother."

Boys are expected to adopt a positive attitude toward work and earning a living. They are encouraged to like sports, beer, swearing, and ogling girls, and are expected to recognize any one of a thousand automobiles and know how to repair them and how to style them according to the latest fad.

Girls are expected to think about a career, but also to know how to cook, sew, and decorate a house. They are expected to talk rather nicely and let the boys enjoy looking at them. Men are supposed to be sexually aggressive and women are supposed to let men make the approach.

But is it that way now? Isn't everything changing?

If it *is* changing, I haven't found it so to any great extent, even among the very young men and women who tell me their most intimate thoughts and problems.

"I have a great job," one young woman said. "I love it. I feel like a liberated woman." But the next minute she added:

"There are some things you just have to wait for a man to do. I couldn't ask him out the first time."

And mentioning marriage—especially in a time when less formal arrangements seem easier—is still a no-no for most women.

"I know she's thinking about marriage," the man says, "but I'm not ready, and until I am it's not going to be mentioned by either of us." Many women still are concerned about the probability of scaring off a man even while they extol the pleasure and satisfaction of living a liberated life alone.

We hear much of sexual freedom—premarital and extra-marital encounters—but sex roles in the bedroom still have considerable definition. Most women wait for the man to make the approach. There remains a strong feeling, for both men and women, that women are to be "taken" or seduced by their men. A man feels that he must maneuver his date into bed, and a woman wonders if she can enjoy an evening of companionship without concern that she must pay for her dinner with sexual intercourse.

Who does what in sexual behavior remains almost as rigidly defined after marriage. Twenty years ago wives felt guilty because they were not always ready for sex at the moment their husbands desired it, and today twenty-year-old wives complain to me about the same thing.

Although great changes have occurred in adolescent and adult definitions of sex roles, much habitual automatic behavior of the two sexes remains at variance with the consciously accepted redefinitions. What vocal segments of societies sanction as the new mores is usually quite different from what the child learns in its adaptive struggles with parents and siblings. Despite cultural progress, childrearing generally conserves traditional values. It will be interesting to learn whether the children of those who have rejected old values will have developed truly different sex-role behavior in the future.

Many assume that these attitudes and forms of behavior are a natural way of life, but that is not the case. Life roles are learned through both conscious and unconscious pressures of the *family* group, and birth order plays a prominent part in the development of attitudes and behavior associated with gender.

ROLE FORMATION

Role is the word we give to a pattern of behavior and attitudes that a person displays in a specific situation which triggers a response. In school you are expected to behave in ways which add up to the role of *student*. If you deviate from the expected pattern—by not doing homework, let's say—you are in trouble. The same is true of living out sex roles. In each society somewhat specific patterns of behavior are expected of males and females, although societies differ enormously in the range of behavior allowed each sex role.

As anthropologist Margaret Mead sees it:

We know of no culture that has said, articulately, that there is no difference between men and women except in the way they contribute to the creation of the next generation. We find no culture in which it has been thought that all identified traits—stupidity and brilliance, beauty and ugliness, friendliness and hostility, responsiveness and initiative, courage and patience and industry—are merely human traits.

However differently the traits may have been assigned, however arbitrary the assignment must be seen to be (for surely it cannot be true that women's heads are absolutely weaker—for thinking—and absolutely stronger—for carrying loads—than men's), it has always been there in any society of which we have any knowledge.[1]

All of the traits assigned to one sex, the behavior expected of a person of that sex, form the sex role within the individual's culture. Differences in perceiving your sex role begin early in life. Although genetic factors are an obvious influence, you learn most of your sex-role characteristics from the parent of your sex. The psychoanalytic view of this concept is that you move through the Oedipal period of caring for the parent of the opposite sex (a boy for his mother and the girl for her father). When you recognize this parent can never belong to you, as he or she does to the other parent, you develop characteristics like those of the parent of your own sex, so you can at least be like the successful rival.

Another way you may learn a sex role is from your parent of the opposite sex, who may encourage, support, and validate its development. Father may reward his little girl for being feminine by his approval, and Mother may similarly encourage her son to be "manly." Some studies indicate that most children learn traditional sex roles even if the opposite-sex parent is absent much of the time. Brothers and sisters also train one another in what is expected according to the gender of each child.

Alfred Adler suggested that the sex of siblings, and to some extent the number of brothers and sisters, is important in the way a child adopts his or her sex role. A boy reared only with girls may feel different because he grew up isolated within his family. Such a child may develop characteristics of one extreme or another, and might feel that he must be strong and assert his masculinity, or he might be weak and nonassertive. A girl reared with male siblings may go through life feeling insecure and helpless.

An example of masculine identification is Rita, who came to therapy complaining she didn't have a chance "in a man's world." Although married and the mother of three children, Rita was fighting acceptance of her femininity.

There were two children in her family, Rita and a younger brother. Rita had tried to be gentle and passive like her father, while rejecting her mother, who was hostile and harsh to other members of the family, including her husband.

While in college, Rita had formed a romantic attachment for her roommate, a girl who was lame and obviously weaker than she was. In therapy (which came after Rita was married and had children) she recognized that the male part of herself identified with her protecting father, and that the female part was the tenderness she had felt for her roommate, which had kept her romantically attached to the girl, but with no thought of sexual contact.

Rita's confused sex role was further compounded by her marriage to a man who was in bad health and who had an occupation usually reserved for women. Even in this relationship, Rita was trying to fulfill some of her masculine identification by playing a protective role.

Western society has permitted few deviations from the patterns expected of men and women. Women cooked, sewed, and reared children, and did these things even if they worked outside the home. Men were the breadwinners, most often holding jobs away from home, and when they came home they mowed the grass, worked on cars, and read the paper while their wives made dinner. At least occupationally speaking, society now offers numerous options for both men and women to move across these lines. More women are finding niches in business and the professions with more satisfactory outlets for creativity; more men are sharing the housework and child care while their wives work. It is very difficult to break out of the stereotyped patterns, even when the inclination is there, without puzzling some friends and neighbors. Thus, sex roles still differentiate men from women in our society.

It should be clearly understood at this point that we are not talking about sexual *performance* or specifying preferences in sexual partners in this discussion of sex roles. A man who is masculine in interests, attitudes, and behavior probably will prefer making love to a woman, but this is not *always* the case. Some homosexual men are relatively masculine in their interests and overt social behavior, even to the point of marrying women and fathering children. Homosexuality, whether female or male, implies the physical and emotional need for physical sex satisfaction from a member of the same sex. In the next chapter we will explore sexual behavior in relation to birth order, but now we are interested in the extent to which the individual *fits into* the expected sex role concerning masculinity or femininity of behavior and interests only. Does birth order influence the way a person matches the masculine or feminine image encouraged by society?

SEX-ROLE PATTERNS

There is a man who works long hours, as a college professor or manager of a business. He drinks and smokes in moderation. According to his wife or girl friends, he doesn't care much for "snuggling," and they also complain: "He doesn't let me know if I'm a significant person to him."

This man had some friction with his parents while growing up. They opposed much of what he wanted to do, and he seemed headstrong. Now, however, he has a good relationship with them. They think he is responsible and are proud of what he has accomplished. His wife considers him self-sufficient and aggressive, "a very good man."

There you have the typical firstborn male—masculine —described through actual statements made by others about him. Here is the composite female firstborn:

She always did well in school, and teachers liked and encouraged her. She had problems with her parents as she grew up, particularly with her mother. Her parents were too strict, and when she reached adolescence her father criticized what she did or wore as "too sexy." She wished he would approve of her, and later felt most of her boy friends were dependent and perhaps that her husband was immature. She did well with an outside job and enjoyed it before she had a baby, but later ran her household on an efficient schedule. This is a typical firstborn woman followed by one or more other children.

From the patterns we have seen, it's evident that the firstborn boy has a greater opportunity to identify with the characteristics usually considered masculine than a girl has to find her feminine identity. This results, in part, from the fact that firstborns of both sexes often turn to father identification after a second child usurps the mother's attention once lavished exclusively upon her first baby.

The *only* child may adopt sex-role characteristics from both parents. One danger for the only youngster is the possibility of forming too close an attachment for the opposite-sex parent.

Male only children tend to be masculine in overt behavior, suggesting that they develop the manliness Mother expects of them. They are often interested in sports and business, but their behavior in close relationships—such as with children, close friends, or a wife—tends to be more like that expected of women in the mothering role. If there is a positive relationship with the father, the boy's behavior may be similar. If the father relationship is not close and the boy spends much of his time with his mother, he may grow to adulthood with a strong "mother within." Whatever hidden characteristics he may have, the only male is likely to fulfill society's expectations of a man.

A similar pattern usually follows for the only girl. Externally she may be quite feminine as the result of her father's pride in her femininity. But even if the father rejected her, she may present a feminine image to the world. Such rejection can lead to identification with the father and disdain of the feminine role.

LATERBORNS

The sex and relative age of siblings play an important part in the development of sex roles in the two-child family.

The combination of an older brother with a younger sister seems to cast the most clear-cut sex role for each according to society's view of males and females. These two, and their parents, confirm and corroborate each other's special sex role. Although this may appear to be an almost ideal arrangement for sex-role identification, the girl in such a family may feel that her brother was favored by their parents and then she is dissatisfied with her sex, believing she is weaker and therefore unattractive. She may develop a strong dislike for her own sex role, even while defending it, and she may be hostile and competitive toward her brother.

If the family contains an older sister with a brother, the girl may develop easily as a female, but the boy may not have a comfortable feeling about his masculinity because his sister seems stronger and more adequate. Such a pat-

tern may persist in later life, and was exhibited by a middle-aged man who came to me for help.

George displayed superior intellectual abilities, but
functioned only at an average level. While he was ambitious, he failed to throw his creative energies behind his
efforts. He could not establish close relationships with
other men, and complained that he could not understand
them. George envied the aggressiveness of mature males,
but felt incompetent to relate to authority: To him, a
boss was a "monster" rather than just another man.

George was the second of two children, and his father
died when he was two years old. Left with his mother
and an older sister, George grew up resenting female domination. Even in middle age he considered himself immature.

"I always feel dominated when I'm with my mother and
sister," he said, "and I can't seem to defend myself against
them."

George believed that men could be important and secure only insofar as they contributed to the welfare of
women. At the same time, he considered women to be
the stronger sex, because they seemed able to gratify their
dependent, aggressive, and sexual needs without guilt. He
envied them and wished he could be like them. His fear
of rejection by women was so strong that it inhibited open
expression or even recognition of his feelings of hostility
and anger toward them.

(This pattern of confused sex role is consistent with the
way many younger brothers of a sister develop, especially
if they do not have a strong and affectionate father for
identity and support.)

George married a woman who was passive and often
depressed. This gave him an opportunity to feel stronger
and to punish her. He withheld money, emphasized her
weaknesses, and rejected her by "blowing up" and moving
out of the house as often as twice a week.

This man used his wife as a comparison figure who
helped him to seem more mature and responsible than he
was. He pictured himself as a man who stayed with a
weak woman in sympathy for her love and dependency
on him.

During therapy it was important to provide George
with a relationship which encouraged the deep, warm response he could show another person if he felt *given to*

rather than *taken from*. Gradually he learned to stop punishing his wife with the anger and hostility he had felt for his mother and sister. As his wife felt more comfortable, she became a more adequate woman and there was less frustration between them.

Both clinically and statistically, the two-child family has been a fertile source of information about brothers and sisters in sex-role identification because there is such clear-cut differentiation between the first- and laterborn. Altus, at the University of California in Santa Barbara, found among undergraduate women that girls with brothers tended to be dissatisfied with their own sex roles.[2]

At the University of Chicago, Dr. Helen Koch, a professor emeritus in psychology, conducted a study of "sissyness" and "tomboyishness" among six-year-old children. She found that girls with brothers more than two years older than they, were relatively tomboyish, while secondborn males with sisters were relatively sissyish. Dr. Koch learned that the age difference between siblings is important in determining the way in which children fulfill their sex roles. Boys seemed to be less sissyish as the age difference between them and their older sisters increased.[3]

Other studies have found a tendency for an adolescent boy with one sister to be more masculine, and a boy with one brother to be more feminine.[4] Investigations have also indicated that men with older sisters are more interested in outdoor and technical activities, athletics, and have a greater desire for membership in all-male peer groups than men with older brothers—although I have observed the developmental pattern to be generally in the same direction in both cases.

Researchers believe there is an initial period in which a boy imitates his older sister, but then in later years he may behave differently in order to avoid parental and peer disapproval.

In families of two girls, many researchers have found both sisters to be relatively feminine with considerable interest in domestic occupations. The highest degree of conformity to the social feminine pattern is exhibited by laterborn girls with older sisters.

Although our observations agree with the tendency for both girls to be feminine in their general interests, we have found differences between two sisters that are simi-

lar to the differences between two brothers. The older
girl retains feminine interests and behavior, but she also
identifies with her father's achievement, and in this sense
may be more masculine than her younger sister. This
tendency sometimes causes inner conflict in adult years
between achievement outside the home and the wish also
to achieve along feminine lines: marrying, homemaking,
and rearing children.

Her younger sister frequently adopts a strong feminine
role, marrying and bearing children early. This is a
weapon which a younger sister may use to overcome the
intellectual achievements of the elder. I have seen many
cases in which an older sister felt downgraded in parental
esteem by the fact that her younger sister was first to
bring home a grandchild.

In families larger than two children, laterborn boys
usually display masculine interests and behavior, but are
sometimes unable to compete with the more achievement-
oriented and successful older brother or sister. In some
instances their masculine interests and behavior are associated with a lack of assertion and aggression. This can
happen especially with the middle of three children.

Marvin, a teen-ager, was born second of three boys. He
was sent to me for therapy several years after his parents
were divorced. His father was a passive person. As a
middle boy, Marvin was outwardly shy and inhibited. It
was his unconscious belief that if he kept quiet and did
not draw attention to himself, he might escape harm from
his brothers.

The boy was unable to accept the absence of his father,
who was not there to protect him from the two brothers.
He was afraid to express anger toward his mother, for
fear she would retaliate by withdrawing her love as she
had from his father. At the age of fourteen, Marvin was
at the usual pubertal stage, in which he was strongly interested in love between the sexes, and was also engrossed
in romance with his mother. He wanted her all to himself, away from the other two boys.

Marvin's responses in therapy suggested that he was in
the midst of a conflict over whether to identify with his
father or his mother. He was interested in feminine
apparel and make-up, but apparently not to show them off
himself. Instead, they seemed to be invested with sexual

interest because they symbolized his mother. He also confided that his favorite game was sexual exploration which he played with several male friends.

What seemed most dangerous in this period of crisis was that Marvin had never had an adequate father figure with whom to identify. His father was rather effeminate and had often been absent. As Marvin grew, he seemed to turn toward his older brother as a model for identification, but an interview with the brother brought out material that suggested he might take advantage of Marvin by acting out the homosexual yearnings.

After working with the boy for a short time—during which he expressed his need for dependency on a mother figure—I referred him to a male therapist. Marvin genuinely needed an association with a strong man with whom he could identify and on whom he could depend for protection from other members of his family.

Another example of difficulty in establishing a comfortable sex role was nine-year-old Matthew, a middle child with two sisters. He was sent for therapy because his parents were concerned that he liked to dress in girls' clothing and was interested in his mother's and sisters' cosmetics.

Matt's father was a businessman who considered himself devoted to his children but actually spent little time with Matt. The boy tended to identify with his elder sister, who was five years his senior and was kind to him. His parents forced him to give up things in favor of his younger sister. ("While my mother was in the hospital, I told my older sister a new baby would be a third pest.")

Matt told me how his father worked at the office all day and then came home to do housework for the mother, who told me: "I can't do physical things. Since my first daughter was six months old and I lifted her, I've had pain in my hip and leg. I live with pain all the time."

Matt said: "Father is not the boss. My mom is."

It was easy to see the causes of this boy's confusion in trying to achieve sexual identity. It was necessary to counsel all members of the family except the younger sister before they were able to see what this boy needed.

Later-middle children in larger families generally find their sex-role identification in the give-and-take among brothers and sisters. Much depends, however, upon the mix of boys and girls, their relative positions within the family, and parental attitudes toward them.

One twelve-year-old girl was brought to me for help because she was not doing well in school and fought bitterly with her mother and two older sisters. Pamela was the third in a family of five. The first three children were girls, the last two boys.

"This is my boy," Pamela's father said, apparently with pride, when he brought her in for therapy. He explained that when she was born as the third girl, he "gave up on" having boys. He encouraged Pam to be his companion and to become interested in sports he liked: golf, tennis, and horses. They had become close companions.

Her mother was a distant and unaffectionate woman. "I find it hard to be close to any of them," she said wearily. "There are so many."

In my sessions with Pamela it became apparent that she had an entirely different view than her father of what she wanted. Her ego ideal was a grown-up seductive woman who could conquer men by her appearance. She was depressed because she thought she was unattractive and could not compete with other girls, including her sisters, in getting a boy friend. Because of her mother's distance, the relationship with her father took on excessive importance.

Pamela did not want to give up the satisfactions of affection she received from him, so at early puberty she was struggling between maintaining the masculine interests which pleased her father and the search for femininity which she prized. Though her father didn't know it, it was his interest in her which stimulated her wish to be attractive to him as a female.

Revealing these factors and presenting them logically to Pam and her parents gave them a better perspective of the problem. Hr father gradually withdrew his insistent demands for her masculine activity and turned to his two younger boys. Her mother struggled to show her middle child more affection and understanding. As a result, Pam's inner conflict was reduced and she was able to improve her relations with people.

In general, when considering the larger family and sex-role formation, the first two children tend to follow a pattern similar to that described for the two-child family. The later-middle child in a family of more than three has a variety of opportunities to develop sex-role characteristics which mostly depend upon the nature of relationships within the family. The last child in a larger family is likely to be rather masculine if a boy, or feminine if a girl.

Our observations support Adler, who found that if one child is isolated by sex from the other children in the family, that child may develop very strong traits in either a masculine or feminine direction.

In considering how well any individual fits into standard patterns of sex-role development, it might be interesting to summarize the primary differences between men and women in our society as reflected by studies of birth-order effects:

Males display more need for achievement than females.
Males are more *motivated* by the need to achieve.
Men are less moralistic than women.
Men are less conforming than women.
Women seem more motivated by the need for approval than are men.
Men are less likely than women to seek the company of others when anxious and frightened.
Women tend to be less independent than men.

None of these behaviors is genetically determined. They are set by the way girls and boys are influenced as they develop. With changing social values for men and women, we can expect to see greater similarities between males and females. Perhaps the importance of these birth-order studies, which show the differences between men and women in our society, is to indicate where changes must be made if there is to be equality between men and women.

Obviously, women must be given more opportunities to have freedom and achieve. Those who now tend to be more moralistic and conforming may need encouragement to expand their views about acceptable human behavior. The indications that women are generally less independent than men reflects their historically encouraged dependency and indicates that they must develop their abilities to become self-sufficient. Women's stronger need for approval suggests that they—and society—must provide conditions which allow them to develop their own self-esteem.

HOMOSEXUALITY

Homosexuality in both men and women may be considered an extreme condition in the misidentification of sex roles. This statement should not be construed as criticism or disparagement of the person who prefers another of the same sex as the source of sexual gratification. Our consideration here is strictly limited to some of the ways birth order and the interaction of family members may contribute to such development.

Theories regarding the causes of homosexuality range from genetic factors to social pressures and relations with parents and brothers and sisters. As with other aspects of human development, there is probably no single cause. It appears that many different conditions must be present and combine to bring about this deviation from the usual heterosexual behavior pattern.

From data and clinical experience I believe that either a boy or girl who is an *only child* and who displays strong characteristics of the opposite sex may move toward homosexuality in adulthood and should be helped to accept the sex role which he or she is rejecting. This is based on the observation that continuing "sissyness" or "tomboyishness" in childhood does seem to be a forerunner of homosexuality. Homosexual men who were "sissies" in childhood are often only children or only sons, and an even larger proportion of lesbians are found to be only children.

Since the only child has no brothers or sisters, we may be able to isolate causes within the parents' relationship that seem related to developing homosexuality. Discord in the marriage is a frequent condition. Whether because of this discord—or a cause of it—the father is often physically or emotionally absent. This brings the only child, male or female, into close contact with the mother. War, work, death, or divorce may be reasons for the father's absence, but the most important condition is that in which the father seems disinterested in the home or his child. He either permits the mother to be dominant or she assumes this role. The male homosexual tends to identify with his mother. Some lesbians tend to identify with the mother, others with the father. For many of these girls, the father is less important than their preoccupation with living out various aspects of the mother-daughter relationship.

Male homosexuality, according to Dr. Bertram Forer, appears to have its roots in the relationship with the mother as the major model and source of gratification as well as frustration. This may also apply to lesbians. Although there may be a more intimate relationship with the father during childhood, it is the mother whom the lesbian describes as interested in her while less loving than the father. The girl may receive the impression that her mother would have preferred her to be a boy or not to exist at all. The attitudes and feelings which parents transmit to their children may be a transference of their own childhood feelings about parents and siblings.

The causes of homosexuality are too interwoven and complex to limit the likelihood to only children. Dr. Forer has found a lack of friends in school and childhood for both female and male homosexuals.[5] Thus, the developing world of the homosexual seems one of isolation with an ambivalent mother, one who is not only experiencing dissension with her husband but also dislikes men (in the case of the homosexual son) or dislikes her own sex role (in the case of a lesbian daughter).

A pair of examples illustrate how homosexual development may relate to birth order.

Sally, at age eight, exemplified the develompent of masculine behavior and interests in a girl, behavior which might move on to adult homosexuality. She was the older of two children, with a brother four years younger.

Psychological tests revealed that Sally disdained any reference to girls' things. She could not deal with a problem that related to dolls, for instance, but could handle it successfully when the word "ball" was substituted. As young as she was, she recognized her interests in boys' things and seemed to like it that way. "I do things mostly in a boy's way," she said.

A few months before she came to therapy, Sally's parents had separated—her father left the family. She showed her anger by the way she disposed of him symbolically, imagining him falling, dying, or "flying away." The person who most disturbed her, however, was her small brother. She felt he had pushed her away from the gratifying affection of her mother, and literally hated him. She belittled him by calling him stupid and talking about how weak he was.

At the same time, Sally was trying to identify with the male whom she saw as superior in intelligence and strength. Her goal was to make a home for herself and her mother. (Her father and brother would be excluded.) Most older sisters of brothers tend to identify with their fathers, but this girl who felt rejected and deserted wanted to take her father's place and become her mother's protector.

Because she could not change her basic nature, Sally was frustrated and angry, especially in school, where she was confronted by situations where her physical and intellectual superiority was challenged.

Therapy was recommended for Sally, because it appeared that if she did not receive help, she might develop into an adult incapable of warm relationships, identify with the masculine role, and perhaps even become a homosexual.

The second example was a boy named Harry born in the middle of a five-child family. The oldest was a brother, a sister immediately preceded Harry, and he was followed by two brothers. The mother was strong and moralistic, while the father was easygoing and away at work much of the time while Harry was approaching adolescence. He was close to his older sister, and shared her drive for intellectual achievement. On the other hand, he was grouped with the two younger boys as their leader in play situations.

Harry formed a close attachment to his mother, who admired his craftmanship and artistic tendencies. His father paid little attention to him because the boy was doing excellent work in school, and had trained himself to be quiet and undemanding in order to gain parental approval among the other children, particularly the two noisy younger brothers.

This boy achieved well in high school, accepting positions of student leadership. He also performed well in individual sports. Throughout these years, Harry allowed other people, parents and teachers, to define the person he would be. Thus, he never gained a strong image of himself as an individual, although his areas of excellence were well recognized by his brothers and sister.

Harry was shy and unassuming, and found it difficult to approach girls, confiding later that he always felt more comfortable with other boys. This included physical interest in the locker room, although he did not permit himself to attempt homosexual acts in high school.

Identifying with his moralistic mother, Harry was torn between his homosexual urges and religious teaching that this behavior was wrong. It was not until late in college that he experimented with homosexual relations and, after an emotional struggle, came to grips with what he considered to be his true nature.

The general evidence for male and female homosexuals is that both tend to come from smaller families. Several studies have revealed that a preponderance of homosexuals are either only children or come from two-child families. Also, both male and female homosexuals tend to have fewer sisters than brothers.

Correlation of these conditions suggests that the male homosexual who is not an only child is more likely to be the older of two brothers. If the father is physically or emotionally absent, the mother may turn to her older son, who will attempt to meet her needs. He may try to be like his mother rather than his father, the male she resents.

As for lesbians—if not an only child—the tendency seems to be even stronger in the direction of coming from small families. Lesbian women are more hostile to younger brothers than non-lesbians. Some women wish to be male, and their fantasies may include having a penis or wanting a sex change, often accompanied by terror of being "penetrated" as an admission of femininity.

Combining these factors suggests that the older sister of a brother is more likely to be a lesbian than a girl in any other birth position except the only child. The girls' mother indicates her dislike for her own sex role, values male qualities, and wishes her daughter were a male. The daughter tries to please her mother and replace the father who is absent. The advent of a younger brother may very well accentuate the older sister's hostility toward males and intensify her attempts to meet her mother's values by stressing identification with her father.

We have suggested here that the older brother of a brother and the older sister of a brother may be more likely than any others, except the only child, to become homosexual if other important conditions prevail. However, it may be that changing social attitudes resulting from the women's movement may change the values placed by parents upon the significance of having a girl or a boy. If each is valued equally, then the pressures which tend to distort sex-role identification may be relieved.

CHAPTER 12

Sexual Adequacy

Monty was thirty years old when he came to me to discuss several problems. Some had to do with uncertainties and lack of assertiveness in his work, but the primary symptom was sexual impotence.

Although his sensual feelings were strong, Monty often found that in his first intimate contact with a woman he was completely impotent. There was some improvement as relationships deepened, but he frequently lost erection just before penetration even though erection had been achieved in foreplay. When such a "failure" occurred, he was never physically able to have intercouse during the same evening or sexual episode. Sexual inhibitions of this kind are very common.

It was puzzling that this relative sexual inadequacy had not broken up Monty's love affairs until he himself terminated them. He told me that most women with whom he had been involved said they cared about him.

As therapy proceeded, other patterns began to emerge. Monty was sensitive to the impression he made on other men as well as women. He allowed them to make decisions for him and did not trust himself to cope with present or future situations.

We traced much of this back to the fact that Monty had an older sister who had dominated him from his earliest years. Their mother was also domineering with all members of the family. This led to sharp quarrels between mother and daughter, so that Monty, in order to avoid the line of fire between two dominant women, got along with his mother by being nonassertive and subservient. Thus, he was subject to two strong female forces, a mother much older than he and a sister who was several years his senior. Ultimately, both relationships complicated Monty's sexual performance.

Most of his love affairs were with women much older than he, who, like his mother, accepted him as he was. He came to understand that consciously or unconsciously he selected women who would relate to him this way. Monty complained that he could not be aggressive or dominant, yet he chose women who were aggressive and dominant.

Although Monty's older women seemed unconditionally accepting at first, eventually they tended to take control. As he said, "They put me down a lot." As with his mother, Monty concentrated on being "lovable" in all adult relationships. This seemed to mean that he had sex appeal, especially for older women, but he could not get what he wanted in ways normally considered masculine.

Before we could delve very deeply into his sexual problem, Monty had to come to terms with the strong attraction he felt for his older sister. He had been sensually excited and curious about her, but his parents had suppressed these inclinations when he was small.

"It seems like I always knew I was not supposed to be interested in that kind of thing," Monty said.

So he grew to adulthood feeling he should not be sexually aggressive toward a girl his own age. A normal sex drive caused him to seek out partners, but his tendency was to fall passively into the arms of women who would lead him, as his mother had. In therapy he learned that he resented both older and younger women because it seemed "they have too much power."

Monty's resentment was expressed by his penis, which is often the victim of unconscious attitudes: He was not aware of his feeling as he approached the sex act, but in effect he was punishing his sex partners when his penis became limp just at the moment when it was supposed to gratify the "domineering" woman. The resulting vicious circle was repeated again in his affair with a woman who became more aggressive as he became less sexually adequate.

Monty recognized his resentment of his partner's behavior but did not, until late in therapy, associate it with his limp penis. As he began to feel more free to assert himself in other aspects of his life, Monty's body went along with him and permitted him to be sexually aggressive.

The symptom of impotence, like any other sexual symptom, may express vastly different feelings in different individuals. In firstborn males it often accompanies anxiety about adequacy of performance. In onlies it may express concern about degrading the woman who represents the idealized mother.

SEXUAL EMPHASIS

You may question—in this time of growing permissiveness of sexual expression—whether we are overly concerned with sexual adequacy as related to birth-order effects. The fact is that counsel and therapy are sought more often than ever before by men and women concerned about sexual behavior. This increase is a function of the greater openness about sexual behavior and the reduced shame, guilt, and embarrassment associated with it. It is also a function of increasing knowledge in treatment methods, but the most important cause is probably the greater challenge for highly efficient sexual performance.

Sexual problems, however, are part of the interpersonal complexities experienced when one person relates to another. It is only in masturbation that a person can feel completely comfortable in what is now being proclaimed as the "need to be one's own best lover." Theoretically, individuals might couple as the lower species do, concerned only with the sensual experience. In practice, however, sexual intercourse involves *all* aspects of being human. The difficulties of such interaction appear to be leading more men and women to disenchantment with the whole sex scene. Increasingly, we hear:

"I'm tired of trying to make sex pleasant for another

person. Sooner or later their feelings or mine get involved. If nothing else, there's always the ritual of courting or being courted, short as that ritual may be. It's masturbation or nothing for me in the future."

The freedom to masturbate is basically important in achieving a reasonable amount of autonomy. Lack of this freedom can place people, at least in feelings, at the mercy of another person. Since sex still remains an interpersonal experience for most people, it is inevitable that all aspects of relating to another person become involved in sexual interaction as in all social situations. Since birth-order effects are most likely to influence an individual's manner of relating intimately with others, the influence of family position can always be traced in a person's sexual attitudes and performance.

Case studies, such as Monty's, describe ways in which adjustment can go wrong. Persons who need therapy often have developed to an extreme degree the characteristics which may be typical of a person in a certain place in the family. Monty's problems do not mean that every younger brother of a sister or every oldest boy will be impotent. There are often many environmental and genetic determinants, not just one such as birth order, which contribute to such conditions. What we have initially labeled as sexual inadequacy in Monty's case turns out not to be inadequacy, but *purposeful* behavior.

Sexual effectiveness is one of the more crucial adjustments necessary for men and women to live comfortably. Difficulties for men usually cluster around homosexual fears, anxieties about masturbation, premature ejaculation, and various levels of impotence measured by a man's ability to achieve and maintain a penile erection to gratify his partner. The male concern about the adequacy of his penis is rooted in the simple fact that without erection he cannot engage in sexual intercourse in the manner society generally considers to be normal. His problems are accentuated by the increasing pressure by society for performance. Women, of course, have the almost infinite capacity to receive the male, even if not aroused sexually, so that female difficulties of sexual adequacy often are measured in terms of achieving orgasm.

Homosexuality in both men and women, as we have seen, is a different order of sexual expression, and not necessarily symptomatic of sexual ineffectiveness.

BIRTH-ORDER EFFECTS

In describing male sexual problems, Dr. Bertram Forer says:

"Those who express functional sexual difficulties, significantly more often than the non-sexual problems, are only children or firstborns. The firstborn male child seems peculiarly susceptible to the development of sexual problems."

Dr. Forer's observations are borne out by a number of other studies. One found that first and only children have a high tendency to fail sexually, and the greatest proportion of young patients with initial difficulties in heterosexual intercourse were firstborn sons. Another study found that 85 percent of such cases were firstborns.

One man in his early thirties, a firstborn, said that although he loved his wife, he was tempted by extramarital sex.

"When I was growing up," he said, "I felt guilty about my sex urges and tried to avoid such experiences. I was also working because my family was not in good circumstances, and I just never had a change to screw girls. Now everybody seems to be having a great time, and I find myself tempted constantly."

Dr. Forer suggests that "the lack of older siblings as a buffer between the child and his parents makes him the focus of whatever neurotic traits they may have. The comfort of the parental adjustment is expressed particularly in their children's sexual lives."

The firstborn male's anxiety about achievement in all areas may contribute to sexual failure, at least in his estimate of himself. Many men have told me they never feel comfortable unless their wives reach orgasm each time they engage in intercouse. Such a high level of self-expectation is almost certainly doomed to failure, because physical love constantly changes and is different according to time, place, and circumstances. Furthermore, the man's *self*-evaluation in terms of sexual performance victimizes his wife as well as himself. He is relating to his role rather than to her as a person.

We have found homosexual patients more likely to have living parents, though separated or divorced, with the homosexual living with his mother. Other male difficulties, however, such as homosexual fears, masturbation anxiety, premature ejaculation, and impotence most often seem to be complaints of men reared in stable families.

Male only children are likely to express guilt about their sexual behavior, although some studies have shown (as in the case of Monty, cited at the beginning of the chapter) that the men who are most disturbed about sex are likely to be those with older sisters. While investigating two-child families, one researcher found that men with older sisters are more likely than men with brothers or younger sisters to reveal homosexuality, sexual repugnance, and avoidance of heterosexual relationships.[1]

One younger brother of a sister told me that in childhood they played a game of "Operation," in which his sister assumed the role of a physician who cut off his penis. Understandably, this man later had a problem with impotence. He was able to relate sexually only to girls who were much younger and boyish.

Other younger brothers seem to suffer impotence stemming from a failure to assert themselves. Often such boys were told by their parents that they must protect females, especially their older sisters.

Mike, for instance, who had been reared with two older sisters, found he was attractive to older women. During high school several women teachers were interested in him. As he grew older he had sexual relations only with girls several years his senior. Finally, at age twenty-one, he became impotent, and this problem brought him to psychotherapy. The impotence began when he had relations with a young woman much like one of his sisters.

As he talked about his childhood, Mike remembered that his parents had been permissive about their children engaging in sex play and exhibiting themselves to one another. In this open atmosphere the children learned much that probably was beneficial, but Mike's older sisters often made fun of his immature sex organs. He had no way of understanding that their ridicule was based partially upon competitiveness and envy of his male organs, so he accepted their disparaging evaluation.

This childhood play apparently left him with a lingering fear of physical inferiority. Mike's impotence began when he asked his sex partner if his penis was as large as others she had experienced. She told him that it wasn't.

Mike continued to find new, and older, sex partners,

but his impotence occurred more and more frequently. His problem was not easily solved. Only after some years of therapy did he begin to look for women his own age, and his impotence was alleviated but never completely cured.

It is our observation that firstborn men seem more likely to struggle with premature ejaculation and anxiety about sexual performance, while younger brothers have problems achieving and maintaining erections, a condition related to their conflict with aggressiveness and assertiveness.

Burke, for example, was third among four children, with two older brothers and a younger sister. At age twenty-two he found himself shifting from one job to another and from one woman to another.

He was the third consecutive boy in his family, and complained that his father seemed to dislike him because he was "just another boy."

When he came to see me, Burke had just ended a "living in" arrangement with a woman who miscarried his baby. Two years before, this woman had had a miscarriage while living with Burke's next oldest brother.

In our discussions he came to realize that he had turned to his older brother as a model and substitute for the father who seemed to reject him. In picking up his brother's former girl friend he felt he had achieved equal status. As he looked more deeply into the brother relationship, he also recognized an incestuous wish, the desire for physical contact with his brother, which Burke satisfied by having intercourse with the woman his brother had slept with.

Burke also examined two of his strongest motivations. He was torn between being dependent or independent, between being the protector or the protected. He later saw this as movement between his role as the protected little brother and being the protector of his little sister. With men, including employers, he related as a little brother, and did not accept responsibility. With women he tried for a relationship in which he could dominate.

FEMALE CONFLICTS

Women indicate an opposite trend from men in sexual adequacy where the firstborn is concerned. Firstborn women are least likely to be virgins at marriage, and their ability to achieve orgasm is generally higher than that of women from any other birth position.

A Czechoslovakian team of gynecologists studied 655 women for orgasmic ability during sexual intercourse. All were under forty-five years of age, and each had been married at least one year. They were divided into three groups, including 316 who reported no difficulty achieving orgasm, 279 who experienced orgasm infrequently, and 60 who said they never had achieved orgasm. In the first group the investigators found a majority of firstborn women followed by brothers and sisters. Lastborn women were below average in orgasmic capacity, while middle and only children showed an average ability to reach orgasm.[2]

Some sexual problems, especially for only and firstborn girls, may be related to the absence of the father from the family. We have found that firstborn adolescent girls seldom deviate from traditional sex-role patterns, but it may be difficult for them to interact with men.

Mavis Hetherington, at the University of Virginia, studied the effects of father absence due to divorce or death on personality development of 72 firstborn thirteen- and seventeen-year-old girls. Daughters of divorcees sought male attention and engaged in heterosexual activity at an early age. By contrast, the daughters of widows were often sexually inhibited, rigid, and restrained around men. It was found that early separation from a father caused a more severe effect than later separation.[3]

In general, firstborn women usually enjoy good orgasmic capacity, although a woman may need practice to learn to have an orgasm. If she has a history of masturbation or premarital sex, and particularly premarital orgasm, she is likely to have marital orgasms as well.[4] This relates indirectly to the pressures placed upon the firstborn child for high achievement. Most sex researchers have associated higher education and professional careers with good orgasmic capacity in women.

SEEKING SEXUAL PARTNERS

Erotic and other love feelings are born in the family, between brothers and sisters and parents. Much of history is marked by the intermarriage of siblings or other close relatives, but beyond perpetuation of royal bloodlines (most often the subjects of history) lies the interaction between brothers and sisters in the average family. This interaction often sets the pattern when a man or woman seeks a sexual mate.

How many women look for a replica of Father or brother, while men seek "a girl just like the girl who married dear old Dad"? This is not to say everyone will seek a mate resembling a member of his or her family. The opposite often is true, but a portrait artist commented to me that he often finds great similarity in the appearance of husbands and wives.

One woman, who wished to marry but had difficulty maintaining relations with men, concluded that her problem was related to the fact that her father was short, thin, and dark, while her brother was tall and blond. She was attracted either to short, dark males or tall, thin ones.

"Even in the first grade," she said, "I remember liking the short, dark boy who sat on one side of me and the tall, thin boy who sat in front. I couldn't decide which I liked better. I think that all my life I've been avoiding getting too closely attached to either of the physical types which attract me."

(The only physical type she could choose without having some kind of incestuous feeling would be a fat redhead, and there aren't many of those readily available.)

This woman finally settled for a man much like her father. This is considered by psychologists to be a healthy choice, since it means that a person marries one like the parent who was so highly valued.

Dorothy Thompson, the journalist wife of Sinclair Lewis, made this comment: "In the end, I translate all my emotional states into replicas of an earlier family relation." She spoke of the child she bore with Lewis as so much like herself that "I played with my son in my own nursery." [5]

Although association with an opposite-sex sibling may familiarize you with the opposite sex and make you feel more comfortable with it, the same association may arouse feelings of guilt about sexual relations with a person like your brother or sister. Disturbed sexuality in marriage can often be traced to a similarity between a spouse and a brother or sister.

One woman with a brother five years younger (whom

she resented) married a man four years younger than she. From the beginning she was uncomfortable with his sexual advances, and finally all sex between them ceased. She then moved into a "big sister" relationship with him. The marriage ended in divorce when she learned her husband had found other sex partners.

We see many indications that childhood experiences with brothers and sisters make differences among adults in their attitudes toward the opposite sex. One study found that college students with opposite-sex siblings showed more curiosity (an intellectual quality) than students who did not have such siblings. One woman complained that she had been the unwilling object of her brothers' sexual curiosity when she was young. The older brothers frequently caught her in an isolated spot and insisted on examining her to find out where a female body could carry a baby and how it found its way out.

Physical contacts between brother and sister are important in learning differences and similarities between men and women. These contacts may be limited to looking, some physical touching, and a little tussle and play, but they also may extend to actual sexual activity (usually short of intercourse). Brothers and sisters give each other many opportunities for showing tenderness, warmth, and comfort. One man, an only child, complained to me that he had no opportunity to learn about girls as he was growing up.

"People who have brothers and sisters," he said, "have a chance to develop relationships that aren't necessarily tinged with sex."

Many sexually blocked adults have histories of insufficient childhood sex play. Lack of comfortable childhood sexual exploration often handicaps adult sexuality.

LOVE ATTITUDES

There are many hidden aspects in sibling interaction as it relates to sexual adequacy, but the cradle of love offers the following *possibilities* for formation of love attitudes:

1. *Understanding the opposite sex*, how they think and behave. For example, the only child is often disadvantaged in that if the love partner in adulthood does

not relate as a parent, there may be problems in the relationship.

2. *Developing attitudes about yourself as a love object.* One girl told of teasing by her three brothers.

"They called me puny and a carrot top," she said. "If they said anything nice to me, they were trying to get something from me."

As an adult this woman still reacted to kind words as if the person wanted something from her. She had a low opinion of her appearance and responded negatively to compliments.

"If my husband compliments me," she said, "I wonder if he wants to go to bed with me or throw a party for all his friends."

3. *Learning about physiology.* This probably is not as important now as in the relatively recent past. However, there remains a difference between viewing bodies on the movie screen and actually being with them in the intimacy of the home.

4. *Conditioning, or experiencing sexual stimulation.*

Sex play in childhood is educational, and such experiences often carry over into adult sexual fantasies and behavior. Siblings in certain birth-order positions are more susceptible to domination than others. Younger boys or girls forced to submit to older brothers and sisters may have problems as adults.

I've known several young men who were forced by older brothers to submit to sex play, and had homosexual fantasies during sex with women. An example on the feminine side was Susan, a youngest child and the only girl in her family. Sex for her as an adult, she said, was never more than "a painful duty." Her attitude was that she must do what others wanted, and she was as resigned and acquiescent as she had been with her brothers, who demanded to examine and fondle her sexually.

When she married, Susan's husband demanded frequent sex, on the grounds that it was needed to keep him physically healthy. Despite her distaste, Susan was required to submit to his sexual needs so that he "wouldn't have a headache." She complied, as she had with her brothers, and never complained, although her anger often surfaced at other times.

5. The fifth hidden aspect of having lived with brothers and sisters is that a person *may seek substitutes for them*

in adult love relationships. For, outside of the parents, brothers and sisters are the most important people in a child's environment. It is only natural that these persons be among the first objects of a child's developing love and hate. In the personality of the adult love object there often lies the buried image of a brother, sister, or incestuous affection in the past.

6. As we have emphasized, individuals often attempt to *relive in adulthood the patterns of behavior learned earlier* in relating to parents and brothers and sisters. Such behavior was learned as the result of experience which offered security if the boy or girl responded in certain ways to brothers and sisters. That security is still experienced in adulthood, although the behavior may result in other discomfort because it is not acceptable to another adult with whom the person comes in contact.

One older sister always looked for men with whom she repeated a confused relationship with her younger sister. She allowed these younger men to take advantage of her, sexually and otherwise, just as she had allowed her sister to take advantage of her in childhood in order to maintain the image with her parents of being the more adaptable of the two girls.

Younger brothers of brothers and younger sisters of sisters often emphasize sexual behavior at an early age, but for a different reason than older siblings. The young brother tends to emphasize physical conquest and not be as guilt-ridden as an older brother, while a younger sister seems to be stimulated to compete with her elder. In the process, this younger sister often distresses her parents, who see her growing up too fast and getting involved in sexual situations she cannot handle.

Since sexual adequacy and marriage are closely linked in developing comfortable adult relationships, in the next chapter we shall examine more closely the roles played by birth order in selecting and living with a marriage partner.

SECTION

V

---

*Marriage
and
Parenthood*

CHAPTER 13

Marriage

Jan was the oldest of three children, with a brother and sister. She came to me for help after she had been married five years to her third husband. Each of her husbands had been younger than she, and her comments about her current mate related to conditions which had led to her two previous divorces.

"My husband is immature," she said. "I'm afraid to trust him about anything. I'm not sure he's going to hold down his job. I don't know what he would do if he didn't have me to depend on. I certainly can't depend on him."

Jan's dreams, as she related them, were full of situations in which she and her children were attacked by animals or vicious people. Her husband usually was in these dreams, but he gave her no help. Her cries for assistance were always directed toward her father.

During therapy Jan came to understand that her first-born drive for excellence and her need to feel stronger than her younger brother had been relived in her adult relationships. She refused to regard any man to be as strong as she was or even capable of protecting her when she needed it.

Later she recognized that her husband was willing and

able to care for her and their children. A marriage which had been relatively good became much better, as Jan learned to respect her husband's abilities.

Although many factors contribute to the success or failure of a marriage (including less formal living arrangements preferred by some couples), this case illustrates how understanding of personal characteristics derived from birth order can help resolve dissension and irritation.

Since we have discussed sex-role identification and sexual adequacy, two basic questions remain regarding the effects of birth order on mating and marriage:

1. Are men and women drawn to each other in terms of birth order?

2. Does success or failure of a relationship relate to ordinal position of the two?

There is persistent curiosity about whether like attracts like, or the opposite, in choosing a marriage partner. Do we try, when seeking a mate, to recreate the conditions that we experienced with brothers and sisters in our childhood home? The answers cannot be precise or absolute, because your choice of a love partner is limited by necessity to the finite number of people you meet in a lifetime.

Considerable evidence confirms that like attracts like in terms of environment and socioeconomic status. Persons are more likely to marry if they share similar religion, age, ethnic origin, class position, education, and background. Yet there are many who select mates from radically different backgrounds. Research does not always agree where birth order and sex of siblings is concerned.

One poll of 200 men and women found no significant birth order correlation between mates, but another conducted by Dr. William Altus did reveal a connection. He found a tendency for firstborns to marry firstborns and laterborns to marry laterborns among the parents of 452 undergraduate students at the University of California in Santa Barbara. He surmised from this that since there are fewer children on the average in upper-class families, there is a greater opportunity for like to marry like from similar economic and social backgrounds.[1]

Dr. Walter Toman, formerly of Brandeis University, sought to learn whether enduring social relationships have better chances of happiness the closer the partners dupli-

cate the sibling patterns of their families. He found that
oldest brothers of brothers tend to choose youngest sisters,
and youngest brothers of brothers to choose oldest sisters.[2]
The theory is that we all learn roles in relation to the
age and sex of brothers and sisters and may wish to continue in marriage the roles that correspond to those of
childhood. If so, men with younger sisters are more likely
to marry women with older brothers, while women with
younger brothers are apt to marry men with older sisters.

Some people are driven, often with no awareness, to
duplicate their childhood sibling position. One lesbian,
reared as the youngest of three, invariably selected girl
friends who were firstborns. A professional man, also
youngest of three, always married older sisters—four of
them. Therapy revealed that both these people had reacted similarly in their love relationships—each began as
infantile and dependent on the partner. Then, as the
partners assumed more dominance, they turned defensive,
and each accused the other partner of being bossy. Next
they assumed the role of "hurt little child," as they had
felt in childhood when it seemed other siblings took advantage of them. Finally, both the lesbian and the professional man rejected their current love partners, who
seemed to suppress, stifle, and mistreat them. Therapy in
both cases required development of insight so that new
relationships would not arouse their reactions as little
brother or little sister.

If marriages are happier when the union approximates
the childhood pattern, an older sister should be more comfortable marrying a younger brother. We have observed,
however, that it is specifically the renewal of the childhood relationship which reawakens guilt about incestuous
feelings toward a brother or sister. This guilt, often unconscious, can disturb a marriage.

"I know what the trouble is," said one man who had
been married and divorced twice. "I am attracted to red-
heads like my sister. But I find myself marrying blondes
brunettes—anything to stay away from a girl who re-
minds me of how very much I loved that sister of mine
when we were small."

Others try to avoid duplicating a childhood relationship
which was hostile and punishing.

"I can't get interested in a man who looks anything like
my older brother," a woman said. "We fought constantly."

AGE AT MARRIAGE

"Only children long for someone to sleep with," one man said. "They see their parents sleeping together and feel lonely in their single beds. But they think of sleeping together as something that should be limited to married couples, and sex, of course, is included in 'sleeping together.' Children with brothers and sisters pair up with each other and just see companionship in sleeping together or in the same room."

We have often observed that female only children long for husbands and often marry young. Once married, they believe strongly in marital fidelity. Male onlies also tend to marry young and to remain chaste until they do. If they have premarital or extramarital sex, they may view the outside affair as "profane." In fact, the tendency to view mothers and wives as sacred, but sex partners as profane, sometimes causes conflict in the male only about sex with his wife. This may be one reason why only males are separated and divorced more frequently than other men. Therapy for male or female only children must often focus upon releasing inhibitions toward having sex with wives and husbands who represent parent figures and are therefore sacred, not to be touched.

Dr. Peter H. Murdoch of the University of South Carolina studied the marriage age of 93 men and women faculty members. He found that firstborn men tended to marry earlier than laterborns, but detected no difference for women. Puzzled by this apparent discrepancy, Dr. Murdoch changed his question in polling 71 unmarried coeds. He found that firstborn women *preferred* a lower age for marriage than laterborns. From this he surmised that if firstborn girls marry later, it is only because they must wait to be asked.[3]

Similar results were found by A. P. MacDonald, Jr., of Cornell University, who questioned 93 couples. The average age of marriage for firstborn men was 23 years, but 24 for laterborns. No significant difference was found between the ages of women at marriage. Dr. MacDonald was interested in the possibility that firstborns, in courtship and marriage, might adhere more rigidly to accepted norms and ideals, a difference frequently attributed to the two groups. He found no such difference, but discovered that firstborn more than laterborn women preferred June weddings, a preference which is in keeping with observations that firstborns are more conventional in their behavior patterns.[4]

COMPATIBILITY

Are there certain combinations of persons who may produce a more successful marriage, or conversely, doom it to failure?

The answer is a qualified "yes," but much has to do with sibling *rank* and *gender*. Some studies indicate a marriage is likely to succeed if the partners each had siblings of the opposite sex, perhaps because a boy or girl becomes accustomed to the opposite sex and thus may accept a partner more easily.

Dr. Theodore D. Kemper at the University of Wisconsin investigated 256 business executives and their wives, searching for the best marital combinations. He found no evidence that the men or women sought partners similar to brothers and sisters, but he did find greater compatibility in certain birth-order pairings. Those marriages in which couples expressed greater satisfaction include:

Husband with younger sister(s) and wife with older brothers.

Husband with older sister(s) and wife with younger brother(s).

Husband youngest married to wife who is oldest.

Less preferred marriages are:

Husband with older and younger sisters married to a woman with older brother(s).

Husband with older sister(s) married to wife with older and younger brother(s).

Both husband and wife oldest.

Both husband and wife youngest.

What quality is associated with good marriages but absent from others? Dr. Kemper believes it is the relative power of husband or wives. Older siblings appear to exercise more power *within* the family group and laterborns more often use power *outside* the family. In Kemper's study husbands were most content with marriages wherein the power structure compared with childhood sibling patterns. In the first instance cited—the husband with younger sisters and wife with older brothers—the man was more powerful in relating to his sisters than the wife was in relating to her brothers. At the opposite extreme is the marriage in which both husband and wife were oldest in their families. This pattern almost guarantees a severe power struggle.[5]

Firstborns often are not confident that they can be loved. The man, especially, may be concerned that he harbors weaknesses, which would include loving the wrong person. This attitude limits his opportunities for successful relationships. When he feels he is not loved he reacts with anger, which insures its own rejection. He likes to be the aggressor.

In another study of 593 couples, a researcher found that in male-dominant pairs the wives were more often youngest or only children. In female-dominant couples the wives were most often oldest or middle children. In equalitarian couples, no relationship with birth order was found.[6]

The following is an example of a marriage which probably was doomed from the beginning:

Sallie and Ray met in high school. She had an older brother and younger sister; he was the older of two boys.

Sallie remembered always trying to "be a good girl" to please her critical and hostile mother and to gain some reaction from her father, who seemed to be emotionally absent. She learned not to say what she really felt, and developed migraine headaches. Later, in her marriage, the headaches were occasionally replaced by emotional outbursts, of which she was ashamed.

Ray was cool, withdrawn, and preoccupied with physical activities, such as driving motor vehicles on rough terrain.

Tensions grew worse after they had three children. It was Sallie who sought marriage counseling, to help control her temper and extract some warmth from her husband. Ray had felt so unloved and distrustful that he had no notion of how to elicit warmth from anyone. He had few friends, and no knowledge of how to make a friend of his wife.

Sallie soon withdrew from conjoint therapy, leaving her husband to struggle by himself. She became aware of her childhood inability to find warmth or approval. She also recognized that the price she thought was required of her—that she always be good and hide her own needs—was doing her a disservice, and led to rage rather than constructive ways of obtaining warmth from her husband.

Ray's passivity in work led him to virtual unemployment for a long time while he made no effort to support the family.

At this point, Sallie became more independent and began to value herself. Dissolution of the marriage and her expansion into the outside world occurred after she ended her brief episode of psychotherapy.

She had entered therapy struggling with her guilt about deserting her husband and his despair at being rejected. I helped her maintain her stand and build her growing sense of self-worth. She was still periodically hostile to her children, but the episodes became less frequent. Finally, she understood that she had related to domineering men who depreciated her as her older brother had done, and realized that she must be on guard against this tendency in the future.

SUCCESS OR FAILURE

In a 1965 study of 742 marriages which had endured for fifteen to twenty years, the highest rate of divorce and separation occurred among the men who were only children. Next highest were youngest men. Male oldests had a relatively low divorce rate, as did the middles of three or four children. The pattern was different for women. Here the highest divorce rate was among youngests, while the rate for firstborns was lower. Middle children were next, and female onlies had the lowest rate of all.[7]

Our clinical experience supports this difference between men and women. Female onlies are concerned primarily with financial and emotional security. They put up with severe frustrations and strains in order to hold a marriage together, but once they decide the marriage is no longer for them, little can be done to change their minds. Male onlies are also likely to cling to a marriage, but if the situation becomes too difficult they may turn to outside sources for their primary need—emotional satisfaction.

If you are a youngest male, you are more likely to seek divorce if you are the younger of two than if the youngest of three or more. Sex of the older sibling is important. If you have an older sister, you are almost twice as likely to be divorced than if you have an older brother. Next among youngests in the incidence of divorce is the youngest girl of four children. For the youngest of three, the incidence is near average.

In this 1965 study, the divorce rate was low for middle children of both sexes. If you're a middle child, you are less likely to look for a parent substitute than the only or oldest, perhaps because you never were as close to your parents as to your brothers and sisters.

Among oldest children, the man is least likely to break up a marriage, while the woman is second only to the youngest in incidence of divorce. This seems clear in terms of power or dominance. In our society the male-dominant marriage most often succeeds, since it appears easier for a wife to adapt to this situation. If a male oldest marries a woman who adjusts to his need for achievement, responsibility, and the tensions which accompany such drives, he is likely to have a successful marriage. The female oldest child unconsciously seeks a partner like her father, but when her stance clashes with her husband's, a struggle is inevitable. The larger the family, the less likely the oldest male is to be divorced, but the *more* likely the oldest woman eventually will seek separation.

Investigators have found, in large families, that fewer of the children marry than among the population at large, and this tendency is stronger for women than for men. Men from large families have a better record of marital happiness than their sisters do. Firstborns in the large family, especially women, have a relatively low ratio of marital happiness.

Now it may be helpful to look at some specific marriage combinations from the viewpoint of birth order.

FEMALE ONLY + MALE ONLY

As we have seen, only children tend to marry early. If you're an only child, you will seek a close relationship, like that of your parents, to ease the loneliness you felt during childhood.

Steve and Sarah, for example, were married when she was eighteen and he was nineteen. Both sets of parents were pleased with the marriage, and gave their children a honeymoon in Europe, a house, two cars, and a part-time maid. (Only children are often so indulged even in adulthood.) The young couple had no economic worries, because Steve was "learning the business" with his father.

The two had lost their virginity to each other three weeks before the wedding, but it soon became apparent that sex was more important to Steve than to Sarah. She enjoyed the warmth and affection of the experience, but orgasm eluded her. This was not a problem during the year, because she soon became pregnant. (Male onlies often are disinterested in children, but only women look forward to bearing children.) Their excitement, plus their parents' pride, buoyed them up until a son was born. Two years later they had a daughter.

Sarah now was twenty-two and Steve twenty-three. She found that being a mother and housewife was absorbing but arduous. A full-time maid was provided by the parents, and Sarah turned her attention to philanthropic activities.

As the years passed, she saw less and less of her husband, as he was absorbed in his work and a new home. His sexual advances, because of her half-hearted response, almost ceased. She had conditioned him as surely as Pavlov's dogs. Then Sarah panicked. She needed a secure emotional relationship and demanded companionship. While she wanted her husband's affection and attention, she was reluctant to engage in sex and still could not reach orgasm. Steve tried to meet some of her demands but became impotent with her. Her rejection had also trained his body in the art of restraint.

Sarah retaliated by finding a lover. When Steve learned of this, his own emotional security was threatened. He sought counseling to help decide whether or not he should try to save their marriage.

I explained that only daughters usually permit their husbands to dominate, and only sons prefer a position of strength. Female onlies usually fulfill the feminine role for both husband and children, while the husband expects the care from his wife that his mother provided. The wife expects her husband to provide the good things of life, as did her parents. He has a high drive for achievement, while hers is only moderate. Since there is little struggle for dominance, it may seem that neither is in charge, perhaps because in childhood they worked alone or were controlled by their parents. Both tend to be self-indulgent.

Sarah had indulged her desire to be an economically protected mother and wife. Steve's disinterest in fatherhood did not become evident until the children were older and she needed help. He drifted away, spending his time entertaining customers and playing golf and poker. His needs did not include being a devoted father and husband, especially when his wife's preoccupation with domesticity bored him. He justified outside sex on the ground that "those girls had nothing to do with" his home relationship. Sarah indulged her own need for attention in someone else. She bolstered her self-esteem, wounded by her inability to achieve orgasm, by finding another man.

Both Steve and Sarah were drawn into therapy. Her motives were soon clear to everyone, including her lover, who found another partner. Steve had difficulty accepting his wife's infidelity, but both learned they might achieve the same sexual pleasure and affection from each other. As they learned the similarity of their needs, they rearranged their lives to indulge each other more. With sexual education Sarah was able to achieve occasional orgasm, and their marriage improved.

FEMALE ONLY + MALE OLDEST

The factor of self-indulgence also became apparent in the case of Jean, an only daughter, who married Jim, an oldest son. Both sets of parents were wealthy and delighted with the marriage. Jean had never had sex except with her husband a few months before they married.

"I didn't think much of it then," she said, "but I was afraid he wouldn't marry me if I didn't appear to like it. My parents made me think marriage should be just romance and enduring love. I expected him to be an understanding and interesting companion. That's how it seemed with Father and Mother, and I expected my husband to control his sexual desires in a gentlemanly way."

Jim didn't see it that way. With the oldest need for dominance, he demanded sexual relations, but Jean could not accept the sexuality or other responsibilities of being a wife. With the firstborn male's sense of duty and reluctance to seek a divorce, Jim left home temporarily "to give the marriage a chance to work itself out." At age twenty-five, Jean came to me for help. She also had a drinking problem. Her parents had gratified her wishes so fully that she had a naive faith in the goodness of things. She felt there was no necessity to experience frustration or to cope with it. Parents of only children frequently substitute material things for the affection, attention, guidance, and discipline that is needed.

Jean's therapy was difficult, because her parents resumed their protectiveness and supported their baby's viewpoints. The marriage improved, but its survival would be uncertain because of the severe restrictions built into Jean by her parents.

Most marriages between female onlies and male oldest children have a better chance of survival than this example. The wife usually permits her husband to assume the dominant role, which is natural for him, and she enjoys the parent surrogate he provides. The oldest male usually is a good provider, conscientious and desirous of holding a marriage together. Oldest males may be demanding, but women tend to stay married to them. The husband appreciates the charm and optimism of an only-child wife. He envies her optimism, because he is likely to be pessimistic and anxious. Problems may stem from his drive to achieve and his assumption that his wife knows how much he loves her. Female onlies frequently see their husbands' work as a rival. They want a partner who belongs ot them wholly as their parents seemed to belong to each other.

"I wanted him there all the time," one wife said, "so I got bitchy when he came home late. I would sometimes go to his office and find something to do, just not to be lonely."

"She won't let me work," the husband complained. "She calls me at work seven times a day. She wants me to be loving when I'm tired from a hard day at the office."

If you're a wife in a marriage with this birth-order combination, you must resolve the difference between your need for a good provider and a man who gives frequent reassurance of his love. The oldest husband may not be as tender and affectionate as you might wish. For the marriage to work, you must learn to accept some limitations in the tradeoff for a man who will devote his highest efforts to you and your family.

FEMALE ONLY + MALE SECOND

This match may be egalitarian. The wife is not concerned with power or domination, but wants a comfortable, satisfying relationship. A male second may feel uncertain about his masculine power, but his wife gives him the right to dominate without question. The following illustrates some problems that may arise in this marriage:

Cerise was indulged by her parents. She had no career ambitions, but expected leisure and a high standard of living. Her husband Claude's older sister had been a strong achiever in school, so he had concentrated his efforts in other directions. He was a businessman, but refused to place hard work before enjoyment of life. His low level of ambition frustrated Cerise, who expected to be indulged by her husband as she had been by her parents. She found that if she wanted expensive clothes or furniture she would have to go to work for them.

Claude needed her acceptance and support, so he became unhappy also. Since neither was willing to change attitudes, their marriage ended in divorce.

If you're a male second from a family of three or more, your drive for success may be similar to that of an oldest boy, especially if you were the first or only boy in the family. Problems in marriage with a female only may be similar to those facing the female only and oldest male.

FEMALE ONLY + MALE LATER MIDDLE

It is difficult to generalize about men and women born from third to next to last in a family of four or more children, because their development depends upon so many conditions which may vary according to family circumstances. If the children interrelate normally, the later middle usually finds a balance of behavior in marital and other relations. If there was excessive aggression and competition, he or she may feel squeezed into a defensive corner and be less comfortable in adult relations. A younger boy with older sisters usually enjoys higher self-esteem than an older boy with younger sisters or a boy with brothers.

Dwight was an example of a later middle deprived of self-esteem by two older brothers and a sister (he also had a younger sister) and a stern, rejecting father.

When he came to me for help, Dwight was a professional musician and a successful one, but he drank and used marijuana excessively. His wife tried to hold the marriage together, but finally threatened to divorce him. She had remained with him only because of their three small children and the financial support he provided.

His wife ran the house competently during his absences on the road, but resented the danger of his using drugs and alcohol, and interpreted his low sex drive as lack of interest in her as a woman.

"I don't think we would ever have sex," she said, "if I didn't take the initiative and talk him into it."

While in therapy Dwight revealed that during his first fifteen years he was passive and dependent. For four years before his younger sister was born, he was the baby of the family and felt incapable of protecting himself against aggression from his father and older brothers. He saw his mother as a saintly figure badly treated by her husband. Dwight suppressed his sexual urges to meet the high standards of this saintly mother, and also to escape criticism and harm from the older siblings. Above all, he felt that if he expressed sexual feelings he would lose his mother's respect.

"I'm shy with women," he said. "I blush when people talk about sex. I feel inferior when I'm making love."

After marriage, Dwight's drinking and drug use increased each time a baby was born, as though the birth of his own children reawakened competitive feelings caused by the birth of his younger sister. He regarded his wife as he had his mother, as a protective and saintly woman. He saw himself as the evil one who did nothing but hurt his wife and family.

Therapy was aimed primarily at improving Dwight's self-esteem. Through hard work and practice he had achieved excellence in his profession, and I tried to get him to see the value of this. Also I supplied some of the admiration, care, and attention once provided by his mother and older sister. He felt he had lost his wife when she turned toward mothering their children and then became angry with him.

As he felt closer to his own ideal of being an adequate man and father, Dwight related more warmly with his wife. She gave him more attention, and finally helped him control his use of alcohol and drugs, which he used mainly to relieve depression and loneliness while away on business.

If you are a later-middle child, you are less likely than others to be separated or divorced. Marital satisfaction for a female only and a later-middle male may often depend upon the woman's unwillingness to compromise.

FEMALE ONLY + MALE YOUNGEST

This marriage combination may be comfortable, because there is little basis for a power struggle. Also, if the man is from a large family, he may be as achievement-oriented as an oldest son without the anxieties and tensions common to firstborns. This husband, especially if he has older sisters, may have developed charm and gallantry to achieve status. When Leonid Brezhnev of the Soviet Union was paid a compliment by Madame Pompidou on his attentiveness at dinner, he said:

"Thank you. I was the youngest in the family, so I had to be nice to the ladies."

Gallantry by the youngest male may satisfy the only-child wife's desire for appreciation of her femininity. If problems arise, they will probably center upon the reluctance of both to assume responsibility.

FEMALE OLDEST + MALE ONLY

Both male only and female oldest children experience high rates of separation and divorce. What are their chances of happiness married to each other?

Remember that oldest women are responsible, self-directed, dependent on others' approval, and often sexually adequate. Theoretically this woman could be an excellent partner for a male only child. She may supply mothering and care, which he needs. She may also supply motivation when he lacks it, needing a push by a significant woman in his life—wife or mother—to act constructively. In return, he may give his wife confidence and self-esteem, and his optimism may counteract her anxieties. This woman, however, may dominate her husband so severely that he turns to others for pleasure and gratification.

FEMALE OLDEST + MALE OLDEST

Although oldest women have a high divorce rate, male firstborns are the opposite. The wife in this marriage will appreciate her husband's drive and responsibility. These qualities, plus his high self-esteem, may ease her anxieties and insecurity. This combination, however, promises an all-out power struggle. One may attempt to impose values on the other, and it may be difficult to compromise. One partner in such a marriage commented: "We both wanted to be top banana."

These two also may compete for attention. One observer of such a conflict said to the wife: "Look, your husband is more intelligent than you are, but you're prettier!" The wife did not forgive the remark for years. She wanted to be seen as prettier *and* more intelligent.

FEMALE OLDEST + MALE SECOND

If you are the second male of two children, relations with your wife will depend to a degree on whether you have a brother or a sister. In either case you may suffer from a lack of confidence. If you had an older brother, you may appreciate your wife's serious attitude toward responsibility while you are more relaxed about achievement. If you had an older sister, however, you may harbor resentment and anger toward women. This may surface if your wife is domineering.

If you are second of three or more, your attitude toward achievement and responsibility may be similar to that of an oldest male. In this case, much of what has been said about the marriage between an oldest male and female may apply, although the power struggle is not usually so severe.

FEMALE OLDEST + MALE LATER MIDDLE

The later-middle child may be ambivalent about exercising power. Since men prefer marriages where there is a clear definition of power—even though they do not hold it—a later-middle male may adjust well in a marriage to a female oldest. Problems could derive from the husband's lack of emphasis on achievement, which may frustrate his wife. Later-middle males demonstrate a generally good record of marital success.

FEMALE OLDEST + MALE YOUNGEST

The self-esteem and achievement of a youngest man depends upon the proportion and number of girls and boys in his family. If he was in a male minority, he will probably have high self-esteem and ability to cope with his wife's domination. If he was youngest of many boys, he may inherit their ambitions plus their help in achieving them. This pattern should fit in well with the aspirations of his oldest-child wife.

If this husband is dependent and submissive or fails to assume responsibility, there may be great tension in their marriage. If the question is no more than dominance, the male youngest may be more content with a female oldest than with a woman from another birth position.

FEMALE SECOND + MALE ONLY

The second-child wife's orientation depends on whether she is the second of two or was followed by other children. If the second of two, her attitudes toward her sex role and men depend largely on whether she was preceded by a brother or a sister. If she has only an older brother, she may be ambivalent about being feminine. If she has an older sister, she may be more content with her feminine role, and have higher self-esteem than the girl who grew up with a brother. Like her male counterpart (younger of two), there is a considerable risk of divorce.

If this wife is second of three or more children, she may develop like a first child but be more openly competitive.

Like the male second of three or more, she may be ambitious. The female second looks for a partner who will upgrade her and her children in every way. Her marriage to a male only is similar to that between a female oldest and male only, except that the secondborn woman will be more tolerant than the oldest, and not as likely to engage in a struggle for dominance.

Any marital conflict in this pair may have to do with competition for dependency and self-indulgence. If the wife is second of three or more, she is likely to appreciate the easy confidence and self-esteem of her only-child husband. Her drive and initiative will meet his need for help from a strong female as a substitute for his mother.

FEMALE SECOND + MALE OLDEST

Conditions of this marriage depend upon whether the wife is one of two children or second in a larger family. Both men and women who are second of two tend to have a high divorce rate. A brother with a younger sister and a sister with an older brother usually develop conventional sex roles. They may be comfortable with each other. A brother with an older sister and a sister with younger brother, however, both develop conflict about sex and sibling roles, and the chance of marital problems with each other is therefore greater than in some other marriages.

A female second from a family of three or more might be impatient wtih a husband who was second of two, especially if she is ambitious. Some second males from two-child families disdain achievement which was stressed by the older brother or sister. Success of marriages between second children depends greatly upon the relationship each had with siblings.

FEMALE SECOND + MALE LATER MIDDLE

The male later middle has a good record of marital happiness. The subtle ambition of the female second may cause disagreement if her husband does not meet her needs for progress. If she is second of three or more, she may tend to dominate, but her husband may willingly concede this role to her.

FEMALE SECOND + MALE YOUNGEST

The nature of this marriage will depend upon whether the wife was the latter of two or second among three or more. Again, if she was the second of two, her marital comfort with a youngest husband may depend upon whether she had a brother or a sister. If she had a sister she accepts her feminine sex role more easily. She may be less domineering than her husband and not demand achievement, which sometimes places youngest husbands under pressure. In this case, each may push the other to assume responsibility.

If the wife was second of two with a brother, she will probably struggle with her need for dependency and with her sex role. Her dissatisfaction will make her husband uncomfortable, because youngest males seek peace in their personal relationships.

If she was second of three or more, she may have a conflict between dominance and dependency. If she is comfortable with competitiveness, her husband may be relaxed in permitting her to pursue her goals. However, female seconds who marry youngest husbands often vacillate between mothering them and forcing them to assume greater responsibility. One such woman saw her husband as less intelligent, able, and independent than she, despite the reality that he was working at a high-level job.

FEMALE LATER MIDDLE + MALE ONLY

Later middle children generally achieve good marital adjustment, perhaps because they retain the childhood ability to adapt their moods and needs to older and younger siblings. They have a wide range of behavior at their disposal. Perhaps the main tendency for the later middle is to submerge her needs to please others, which can cause resentment and dissatisfaction. The female later middle tends to be "parental," depending on the sex of her siblings. A girl reared with brothers is inclined to be either motherly or little-sisterish with her husband, depending on whether she had older or younger brothers.

Between a female later middle and male only there usually is no struggle for dominance or power. This marriage is likely to feature equal status in decision-making. The wife probably will permit her husband to assume dominance while helping him to be comfortable in a role with which he is uncertain. As a child he was both the center of attention and the object of discipline from two powerful parents.

FEMALE LATER MIDDLE + MALE OLDEST

As with the male only child, the female later middle tends to be a satisfactory marital partner. There is no conflict about dominance unless the husband is over-bearing. The later middle wife may be too subservient.

FEMALE LATER MIDDLE + MALE SECOND

This marriage has a strong chance for comfortable adjustment. The male second is apt to assume the more dominant role without conflict, and is better prepared to assume responsibility than is his wife.

FEMALE LATER MIDDLE + MALE LATER MIDDLE

If there is ever an opportunity for equal assumption of decision-making—and an opportunity for conflict over assuming responsibility—this combination is it. However, the specific conditions of marriage between persons from these birth positions depend upon their childhood roles. If the wife identifies strongly with the female role, she will probably adjust to a man from any later-middle position.

FEMALE LATER MIDDLE + MALE YOUNGEST

Later-middle wives have good records of marital adjustment, and youngest husbands have low divorce rates.

Any problems that arise are not likely to involve a domineering wife, because the husband won't be concerned about domination. There may be some conflict about assuming responsibility, but this wife is generally well equipped to meet her husband's dependency needs.

FEMALE YOUNGEST + MALE ONLY

If the power struggle is important, marriage with a female youngest promises the greatest happiness for a man from any family position other than youngest. One study, however, showed a high divorce rate for youngest women, which related to the number of siblings in their families. For youngests of three, the incidence was average. For youngests of four, separation and divorce were more frequent. The last child who is treated affectionately by parents and siblings usually makes a good marriage. If she is teased or ridiculed, her marriage may suffer from her low self-esteem.

A female youngest and an only-child mate should be able to avoid conflict over dominance and responsibility. Since the male only often combines achievement and high self-esteem with joy of living, the two can be happy together. If conflict develops, it may relate to daily questions of managing the home and supervising children. The motive for divorce of female youngests may stem from their disinterest in responsibility, and their desire to have a good time.

FEMALE YOUNGEST + MALE OLDEST

In this combination there should be no dominance conflict, yet there tends to be a problem. A male oldest plays the parental role with a youngest wife. She encourages this by depending on him for aid and care, but may also resent it, because she feels she is not being treated as an adult.

FEMALE YOUNGEST + MALE SECOND

Power conflicts are not likely in this marriage. Any problems may originate from the wife's attempts to depend on her husband. Even this may only enhance the male second's feeling of dominance, which he unsuccessfully attempted to achieve as a child.

FEMALE YOUNGEST + MALE LATER MIDDLE

This marriage should be quite satisfactory, since the husband is likely to hold the dominant role he prefers. Problems may arise because of the wife's disinterest in responsibility and this same tendency among some male later middles.

FEMALE YOUNGEST + MALE YOUNGEST

This marriage could work well if each partner brings ample financial resources to the wedding. They'll need it to support their tendencies to live the good life. Two youngests usually find some way of making it possible to play together. Whatever problems arise are likely to be about which partner can force the other to assume responsibility.

In this discussion, remember that you are an individual with your own traits and attitudes, many of which do *not* come from birth order. In marriage, consider yourself and your partner as unique people, partially molded and trained in special ways of relating to others by the accident of your birth position.

CHAPTER 14

Parenthood: I

Birth-order effects are crystallized by family conditions which prevail during the earliest years of a child's life. Adults and young people already past the formative years will hopefully find tools in this book to reaffirm or change their life patterns. Infants or children not yet born will benefit even more if their parents understand and apply this knowledge to guide sibling interaction, so that each child may appreciate and develop his or her maximum potential. No single birth position holds a monopoly on talent or value. As with any preventive medicine, a measure of parental wisdom and attention may save expensive hours of psychotherapy later on when the adult needs to unwind tangled personality threads.

Birth order enters the equation of parenthood both when a couple is planning a family and after children are born.

In this chapter we shall explore how birth order may help determine a person's readiness and desire to have children and what sort of parent he or she may be. Because family planning is changing rapidly under the influence of new birth-control techniques, abortion, and population control, these trends will be considered in a later chapter. At this point, we will consider the young married couple and how they may relate to their children in terms of their birth-order combination.

PYRAMID EFFECT

Relating to children in terms of the parents' birth order may be termed the *pyramid effect*, by which characteristics developed in a birth position are passed on to children and even grandchildren.

Stanley, for example, was a later middle with two older sisters, an older brother, and a younger sister. Such a boy often grows up protected by his mother and older sister but in conflict with his brother. A younger sister, in this context, seems to encourage a man's tendency to be gentle and concerned about the females in his life.

Stanley was subservient to his wife, at home and in his business, where she shared the work and decision-making. He was concerned about his wife's needs, but obsessed with protecting and caring for his daughter. Frequently he was caught in the middle of disagreements between mother and daughter.

"He would side against me when I argued with Mother," the daughter said, "but then when I had gone crying to bed because I didn't get what I wanted, he would slip a five-dollar bill under my pillow."

Gradually the conflict between mother and daughter (intensified by Stanley's vacillation in trying to please them both) became so violent that when the daughter reached age sixteen they sent her to a boarding school in Europe. Stanley sends her money without her mother's knowledge. He hopes she will return from Europe prepared to work and live by herself, away from the maternal conflict.

"I'm just jelly when either my wife or daughter want something from me," Stanley said, "whether it's affection, money, protection, or care." The daughter's development was obviously influenced by characteristics her father derived from his birth position.

A more complex case is that of Timothy, a middle child between sisters. The most important factors here were the older sister and the fact that Tim was the only boy. His parents idolized him. As an adult, Tim leaned on women as helpers or employees, but never related closely to them. It seemed that in order to maintain his male identity, he would not concede too much to women.

Tim married an older sister of a sister. His wife was not intellectual, but she identified with her father while growing up. She quickly assumed dominance in her husband's business. There were a few flurries in which he asserted his masculinity in outside flirtations, but his wife tolerated this so long as he did not take them seriously and worked closely with her as a business partner.

Their main problems concerned parenting their two daughters. Tim was overprotective and anxious about them, as though repeating his relationship with his younger sister. There he could turn from being dominated by his older sister (now represented by his wife) to dominating and protecting the younger (now represented by his daughters).

Tim's wife resented his closeness with their girls. She competed with her daughters as though they represented her younger sister, who had arrived when she was used to being the only child in her family.

In therapy Tim's wife came to understand that he cared for their daughters because the children belonged to her as well as to him, and that he and the daughters wanted to share their lives with her. She became more objective and, in fact, enjoyed a richer relationship with her daughters as well as with her husband.

THE DESIRE FOR CHILDREN

Two gross generalizations about having babies—which may or may not be supported scientifically—are that many first children are not planned, and that men are less willing than women to accept parenthood responsibilities. In choosing a mate, it helps if we know what to expect in the partner's attitudes toward children.

One study of small families revealed that men who were only children, along with youngests of two or three, are least likely to desire parenthood. One explanation may be that male onlies and youngests have no practice in the role of being older than anyone else in the family. They are accustomed to being cared for rather than *caring* for. Such men often are close to their mothers and enjoy maternal care. Identification with fathers is less strong than it is for boys who are oldest, older, or middle.

In clinical practice we have found male onlies to be overwhelmingly disinterested in having children *before the fact*, but their interest often picks up after a child is born. Women onlies are ambivalent. Our experience indicates that less than one-third of only-child women are strongly interested in rearing children, although they may value producing a baby.

The situation changes for oldest children in families of two or more. Here a majority of men wish for children, and oldest women are almost unanimously strong in desiring motherhood. The power they felt during childhood years, when they served as mother surrogates to younger brothers and sisters, may influence this desire.

Among the second of two children there is a sharp division between the parenthood desires of men and women. In men, the second of two and last of three are among those least desirous of having children. However, the woman who is second of two is even higher than the firstborn in her positive approach to motherhood. Why is there such a difference between men and women in this birth position?

The man who is second of two, of course, has no experience playing the parent role during childhood. His power usually is outside rather than within the family; thus, he may not value family roles as much as the older brother or sister who achieved some of *their* satisfaction by dominating *him*. Younger sister, however, identifies with her mother, in opposition to her older sister or brother, who identify with attitudes and values of their father. The younger sister competes with either an older brother or sister, but she still accepts the feminine sex role. One way of competing with an older sibling is to move at an early age into marriage and parenthood. We have observed that younger sisters marry young and have children as soon as possible, often before their older sisters do.

Men or women middles, especially the second or third among four, often want children. However, we also find that in families of six or more the in-between women, as a group, have fewer children than their older and younger

sisters. This may not reflect disinterest so much as a reluctance to expose their children to disadvantages these
women may have experienced as middles in a large family.

We have seen that youngest and only males express low
interest in parenthood. This is also generally true for
women who were the youngest of three or more and thus
were accustomed only to the dependent role. It is interesting, however, that when a woman is youngest of
three or more—but then is followed after a long period
of time by another child—she becomes more interested
in motherhood than other youngest women. This suggests
the importance of the mother-surrogate role in developing
the desire to have children and the competence to raise
them.

QUALITY OF PARENTHOOD

THE ONLY CHILD

Although both men and women onlies rate low in
desire for a family, once a baby is born both react with
strong concern and responsibility. They may continue to
be ambivalent, but women onlies often show great effi-
ciency in mothering two, three, or more babies. While her
children are young this woman may be more satisfied to
stay home and handle the responsibilities than women
from any other birth position. Her anxieties are more
likely to concern relations with her husband than the demands of motherhood.

There are some parenting problems, however, for both
men and women onlies. They consistently complain about
the noise and confusion their children create, and this
distress stems from the fact that there was a minimum of
disturbance in their childhood homes. If an only male
marries an only female, they may recognize their need
for quiet and solitude in advance and opt for no children
at all. However, the mate-selection process does not often
present such choices, and an only child may pair up with
someone who has a strong desire for children. The resulting confusion may strain the marriage.

This was true of an only son who married a woman
with an older sister. Mort's wife was vivacious and often

spoke of wanting children, although he was less enthusiastic.

"She was warm and affectionate, and I sensed she
would make a great mother," Mort said. "So I thought
there must be something wrong with me for not wanting
children. After all—before this talk about the population
explosion—having children was the thing to do, and I
didn't mind the idea of having a boy to carry on the
family name."

The decision was soon made for him. Mort's wife became pregnant a month after the wedding. Even before
the child was born, Mort was disturbed.

"Vivian became more distant as the months went by,"
he said. "I didn't enjoy seeing her lovely figure stretched
out of shape, but more than that, she seemed to turn
inward, as though the baby was the only thing in the
world and I wasn't there any more." (This is a common
reaction of only sons who were accustomed to the full
attention of their mothers.)

After his son was born, Mort was proud, but he left all
the care to Vivian.

"What got me," he said, "was the utter confusion in
the house after that. Diapers all over the place, milk
bottles, and the kid crying at all hours. Maybe I was
selfish, but it was a shock to step into that atmosphere
after a quiet day at the office. Besides the noise and confusion, Vivian seemed totally focused on the boy and
seldom had time for me."

The situation grew worse after the birth of their second
child, a girl. Several evenings a week Mort found an
excuse to go to a meeting or "out with the boys." Vivian
sensed that her husband was drifting away, and discussed
it with her mother. Fortunately, her mother was a per-
ceptive woman, and advised Vivian to pay more attention
to her husband.

One night when the children were asleep, Vivian approached Mort, and they discussed the entire situation.
Both were mature about it, aired their feelings without a
blowup, and were able to achieve a renewed closeness.
As his son grew out of infancy, Mort enjoyed him more,
and finally they had a happy family of four children. But
this would not have happened if Vivian had not understood and respected her husband's needs.

Not all marriages progress so pleasantly. Only-child

mothers often react to the noise and confusion with impatience and nervous tension which causes them to scream at their children. This sets up a cycle of tension which does not end until either mother or child breaks the pattern. The mother must often take deliberate steps to prevent the buildup of tension. She needs quiet time, and some mothers hire baby sitters who allow them to go off alone shopping, to the library, or for a drive in the park. Others send the children to nursery schools or day camps.

Only-child fathers also need quiet time. Usually they can find refuge in places like the office, but it is important to recognize their need so that something can be done before they begin avoiding home, wife, and children. The spouse of an only child should recognize the other's need and help arrange family life so that the father has time alone to recharge vitality and interest in the family.

Only-child parents sometimes react in special ways according to the number and gender of their children. The father may be devoted to daughters but struggle with sons, especially an only son. If the son is also an only child, the conflict between the two may be great, because of their competition for attention from the wife and mother. Similarly, an only-child mother may be devoted to her sons but in conflict with her daughters.

A special situation may occur for the only-child father. He may seem jealous or resent all of his children if they take too much of his wife's time. He may be indifferent or hostile, disturbing his children's self-esteem, and especially their assumption of sex roles. If father is indifferent to his daughter, she wonders if she is valuable as a female. If he ignores his son, the boy questions his manhood because his father does not seem to value him as a male.

Child discipline is also a difficult task. Only-child parents may vacillate between strictness and overindulgence. Usually the parent is strict, because he grew up learning traditional morals and behavior. Many only children, having been indulged by *their* parents, take the opposite tack and are strict with their own children. Such parents find it difficult to maintain consistent discipline, and may bewilder their children by giving or denying permission which seems out of character. Only-child parents tend to be overprotective, as were their parents, and supervise their children closely. But they may also be permissive in granting "things," or giving their children freedom to make their own decisions about such issues as selecting friends and going to college.

THE OLDEST CHILD

The qualities of seriousness, a strong conscience, and need for achievement which mark the oldest child, also carry into parenthood in other ways. If both parents are oldest children, their child may find itself in a stern, harsh household. Fortunately, birth order is often different for the two partners, serving to soften the harshness that two oldests might bring to parenthood.

In general, the oldest child welcomes children and is a responsible parent. Size of the parent's family may make a difference. Some research indicates that in families of more than six, the firstborn man enjoys parenthood more than the firstborn woman does. This may be because she was taking on so much responsibility for brothers and sisters that she resents the burden her own children impose. Male oldests are more likely to experience the father-surrogate role in childhood as one of power rather than servitude. Thus, they retain less anger about child-rearing responsibilities.

Firstborn men take parenthood seriously. They may be moralistic, disciplinarian, and perfectionist in the requirements they place upon their children. They often demand more adult behavior than should be expected of an immature child.

Firstborn mothers may be fearful and anxious. They usually are competent, but sometimes are unable to accept their own adequacy unless it is confirmed by others. At the same time, they resent any implication that they are less than perfect mothers. Both men and women from this birth position often fail to understand or empathize with others' feelings. This is often a lack of tolerance, and they may also appear cold and intellectual to their children.

The firstborn mother is likely to press her own firstborn to early achievement, particularly in learning to talk. The child may learn to talk excessively or, because of stress, develop a speech impediment. Firstborn women also fear uncertainty. One described an experience she had as a child.

"I was with friends at a carnival," she said, "and we came to the end, which was a spot where we were expected to go down a slide, but the bottom was hidden from view. I could not get on. Despite the gibes of friends and assurances by the attendants, I could not get on that slide. An attendant finally took me down a stairway.

"It has been like that all my life. Anytime I couldn't see the outcome of a plan or situation, I was anxious and afraid."

Going to prenatal classes, which firstborn expectant mothers do more often than other women, may help them "to see the bottom of the slide."

SECOND CHILDREN

A second child is more often relaxed, tolerant, humanistic, and considerate of the needs and feelings of his or her children.

The man probably will stress masculine pursuits and be more attentive to sons than to daughters. Clinical experience shows that the second-child father, if he grew up with an older sister, may remain distant from his daughter if she is the first child. This father may not press his children toward academic efforts, since he himself achieved in ways opposed to his intellectual older sibling. He may depend too much on his spouse to discipline the children because he is reluctant to do it himself.

The second-child mother is usually considerate. Problems may depend on whether she had an older brother or older sister. If she had a brother, she may have difficulty accepting daughters because of her own sex-role ambivalence. If she had a sister, she may be dependent, conforming, and need help in rearing her own children.

One woman, the second of two girls, had felt inadequate competing with her sister during childhood. After marriage she inexplicably felt hostile toward her first child, also a girl. As Tess explained it: "I simply could not give anything to her."

The mother resisted and resented the care her baby required, and she limited her attention and help during the little girl's early school years. After she had entered therapy for other reasons, Tess was shocked to realize that she actually tried to make her first child fail, just as she had tried unsuccessfully to thwart her older sister.

Another woman transferred feelings toward her sister to her daughter. During childhood Yvette had been mothered by her older sister. Then, as her own daughter grew older, she often called the daughter by her sister's name.

It was the daughter who finally sought help in untangling her guilt-tinged feeling that she was responsible for her mother's welfare. Yvette had instilled the notion that the daughter was to be responsible for caring for and protecting her mother, just as Yvette's older sister had done. When this transferred burden was understood, the daughter was able to overcome it. Yvette, however, died still demanding her daughter's care and trying to make her feel guilty when she did not give it.

The secondborn mother usually accepts a son warmly. According to psychoanalytic theory, producing a male child is how a woman acquires a penis. Strange as this theory may sound, it does seem to apply to women who struggle with their feminine sex roles. After producing a son, they will often settle down and devote a great deal of effort and care to that child for this reason.

Secondborn males followed by other children are likely to react somewhat like an oldest child in encouraging their children to compete. The secondborn woman may combine competitiveness and feminine interests in mothering. Having both older and younger siblings, she learned to compete with the elder while exercising power over the younger. Her main problem may be that of demanding too much of her children, and criticizing them if they do not produce.

LATER MIDDLES

These children develop unique roles in their attempts to achieve identity and stake out a claim for power and status. Since later-middle women have fewer children than others and tend toward happy adult adjustments, they usually cope well with their own families. Male middles of four express a desire for children, and the women usually are devoted mothers.

The most common problem for later-middle parents is

probably conflict over which one will exercise authority. If a later-middle male marries a woman from an earlier position, he may be ineffectual in controlling and supervising their children, and everyone may suffer as a result. Such parental conflict sometimes produces one or more rebellious children who are hostile toward the father because he did not protect them against a stern, demanding mother.

YOUNGEST CHILDREN

Men and women who were youngest are usually not enthusiastic about having children, yet they may be delightful parents. Since youngest children enjoy helping others, especially weaker ones, they are often kind and gentle to their offspring. They show great empathy and understanding toward them. Since they themselves can be playful, vivacious, and spontaneous, youngest parents may establish a pleasant family atmosphere in which all enjoy one another very much. On the other hand, youngest parents may be overprotective of their children, just as they themselves were overprotected.

For example, a mother who was the youngest of four girls had a fear of water, lightning, and heights. She had difficulty understanding and relating to her two sons, particularly the younger, who was athletic and seemed to always live on the edge of physical disaster.

There are also cases in which youngest children were subjected to unpleasant teasing and handling by brothers and sisters. This may carry over into the parental role.

Terry, for example, was the youngest of three. Her mother worked outside the home and gave her baby little time and attention as she was growing up. Often left alone with her brother and sister, Terry was teased, tickled, and otherwise tormented. As an adult she shrank away from physical contact and had few close friends.

This withdrawn reaction carried over into her marriage. When she had a child, she wanted to care for it, but found that she did not like to touch or cuddle her child. As a result, Terry's baby went through childhood deprived of warmth and affection.

PAIRING PARENTS

We are often asked which combinations of parents may be the healthiest from the standpoint of birth order. The following should be interpreted with care, as it contains broad generalizations and attempts to isolate only the most distinctive individual characteristics and interactions.

Only-child mother and only-child father
Mother plays dominant role in parenting while the father avoids the irksome details. They must negotiate to insure equal responsibility.

Only-child mother and oldest-child father
This couple must take care that discipline does not become the sole responsibility of the father.

Only-child mother and second-child father
If the father is second of two, he and the mother need to reassure each other that they can capably fill the job as parents. If the father is second of more than two, he may dominate the child's discipline. Mother may require extra effort to ensure full participation in direction and discipline.

Only-child mother and later-middle father
This combination should be comfortably egalitarian. The wife may see her husband as too lenient with the children.

Only-child mother and youngest-child father
These parents may need to reassure each other that they are not too lenient and indulgent with the children, and make sure that both take on responsibility.

Oldest-child mother and only-child father
The father may be disturbed by the serious intensity the mother puts into parenting; she may need to become more tolerant.

Oldest-child mother and father
Father may be like an only child: strict but also indulgent. Both parents need to become more tolerant with

the children. The parents' power struggle must incorporate some way to achieve a more peaceful home atmosphere.

Oldest-child mother and second-child father
If the father is second of two, he may seem too relaxed and withdrawn in rearing children. If the second of three or more, marriage may be similar to oldest-child mother and oldest-child father, but the father here will bend more to his wife's opinions.

Oldest-child mother and later-middle father
Father may seem too indulgent with the children, and the mother may need to become more tolerant both of her children and her husband.

Oldest-child mother and youngest father
Parents will need repeated reevaluation as to whether the father is bearing his full share of guidance and discipline.

Second-child mother and only-child father
If mother is the second of two, the couple is likely to share equally in parenting. If she is the second of three or more, what has been said about oldest-child mother and only-child father is likely to apply.

Second-child mother and oldest-child father
If mother is the second of two, the husband may dominate the discipline and guidance. If she is the second of three or more, the parents may struggle over severity of discipline. Mother may want the children to behave and achieve, but she is likely to be threatened by the father's severe standards.

Second-child mother and second-child father
The quality of the marriage relationship will be important in determining the quality of the parenting. If parents get along well, all will be well with the children. If not, the home atmosphere will be difficult for all.

Second-child mother and later-middle father
If mother is the second of two, parental harmony should prevail. If she is the second of three or more, she may

believe the father is not carrying his share of parental duties.

Second-child mother and youngest-child father
If the mother is the second of two, both parents may be reluctant to take responsibility for rearing children. If she is the second of three or more, there will probably be no conflict.

Later-middle mother and only-child father
The parents here enjoy relatively equal status, but the father may consider his wife too indulgent with the children.

Later-middle mother and oldest-child father
It is likely the father may assume too much responsibility in disciplining the children.

Later-middle mother and second-child father
If the father is the second of two, this may be an egalitarian situation with equal assumption of parental responsibility. If the father was second of three or more, he may seem too severe in child discipline.

Later-middle mother and father
Usually there is no conflict here, but if there is, it will concern which parent is to assume the responsibilities of child-rearing.

Later-middle mother and youngest-child father
This is usually a harmonious combination. If conflict exists it will be over the father's reluctance to take on responsibility in the home.

Youngest-child mother and only-child father
The mother may vacillate between being stern and over-indulgent with the children and need more participation by the father.

Youngest-child mother and oldest father
Uncertainty which this mother often feels about her adequacy as a parent may lead her to resent the father's confidence in the parenting role. He may feel that she is too indulgent.

Youngest-child mother and second-child father
If the father is the second of two, there may be conflict over who is to assume responsibility. If he is second of three or more, he may willingly assume a large share of the tasks, and thus they may handle the parent role harmoniously.

Youngest-child mother and later-middle father
This may be a comfortable parent relationship with no power struggle except occasionally over who is to take on the major part of the child-care responsibilities.

Youngest-child mother and father
Both may be reluctant parents, and conflicts may arise in the area of assuming responsibility. If all goes well, they will probably make a relaxed and pleasant home for their children.

CHAPTER 15

Parenthood: II

Most couples (and this may include some unmarried mothers) look forward with pleasure and enthusiasm to their first child, natural or adopted. As prospective parents, you may feel deep joy anticipating your first baby, but this feeling is often mixed with anxiety.

How will the child affect your lives?

Will you be able to continue the pleasures you enjoyed as young marrieds?

What new responsibilities must you assume?

If pregnancy and labor are difficult—as it is likely to be with a first birth—you may be overwhelmed by parenthood before the task shifts from physical to psychological.

With the first child, two attitudes generally prevail:

1. Both men and women still wish for a son more than for a daughter—although we might wish the masculine bias did not exist, it remains a fact in most societies—and

2. the first child has a greater chance of being accepted, *regardless of sex*, than any later child in the family.

Whether the baby is a boy or girl, the first challenge is feeding. The firstborn's mother will be more anxious about this task than she will be with later children. Evidence has shown that with first children, mothers try harder, devote more time, and are less effectual in feeding two-day-old babies than mothers of later children. So at the beginning a firstborn youngster finds that he must try harder to get what laterborn children obtain easily. The mother often relates nursing ability to competence, and may suffer a loss of self-esteem with her first child. This often increases her determination to "shape up" the child as he grows older.

Sleep poses a similar problem. If feeding is difficult, the baby may be uncomfortable, sleep poorly, and cry often. Again, the mother of the firstborn may interpret the child's discomfort as her own incompetence, and try to force the infant into conforming sleep patterns. Because of experience, this struggle is usually less intense with later children.

Many babies reward their parents by eating and sleeping well and cooing instead of crying. They also develop motor and sensory skills, a natural process which seems miraculous to the new parents. The observation of infants from one to fifteen months old has found motor and sensory performance higher for first children than later-borns, probably a result of greater mother-child interaction with the first born. This superiority does *not* suggest higher intelligence, but it may gratify a mother's ambition for a firstborn who promises a great accomplishment.

An infant, of course, is not interested in achieving anything except a reward from his parents. Relief from hunger, cold and wetness is associated with the presence of mother or father, and as the child grows older he learns to obey parental wishes because obedience is rewarded with acceptance, warmth, and praise. Girls often respond to care with fewer demands and greater relaxation than boys. They seem to be more cuddly and less active.

Because of the close rapport between a mother and her first baby, firsts and onlies are anxious when separated from the person upon whom they depend for comfort and pleasure. This separation anxiety was manifested by a small-child actor who in one of his scenes was directed to cry. He refused.

"All right," said the director in desperation, "we're going to take your mother away."

The boy promptly cried loudly, and refused to stop even when the scene was completed. The film company proceeded with other work, but suddenly the boy ran behind the director and kicked him.

Since mothers talk with their firstborns more than later children, firstborns learn to talk and think in adult ways more rapidly. Firstborn babies are also isolated. They are generally more fearful than laterborns and more sensitive to pain, a condition associated with anxiety. Any child may learn to use anger and aggression to get what it wants, but first children do so more than others. This may be one reason why they are more inclined to quick and long-lasting anger as adults. When only children learn to obtain gratification in this way, they may have begun to establish a lifelong habit of quick, intense anger which loses friends, lovers and spouses.

Consequently, new parents should do what they can to be more relaxed with their first baby and not use love or its withdrawal as a weapon to force achievement, such as toilet training. It is not easy to translate this advice into action, because the first experience of parenthood challenges a man and woman to do the best possible job. It will be better for the whole family if the parents can relax and enjoy this child as a new human being who will expand and enrich their lives, rather than as a measure of their competence.

Now we will see how knowledge of birth order may lead to more effective parenthood.

THE ONLY CHILD

Whether a boy or girl, the only child tends to remain closer to the mother than the father. This attachment influences the adult need for close relationships, emotional dependence, self-esteem, and also sex-role development. Mothers tend to be overprotective, supervise all activities, and permit few outside contacts. The child becomes dependent on one person.

Only children may be less self-starting than others, because they have fewer opportunities to develop ideas and make decisions. They are often lonely and compensate with fantasy play including make-believe companions. While seeming content, they actually resent being left out of the relationship between their parents. One mother of a six-year-old boy was troubled by his behavior.

"Joey sits in front of the television set every evening and constantly masturbates," she said.

She revealed that she had taken a part-time job after the boy entered school, and when she was home she was busy with household tasks. His father watched television, and Joey was exiled to another TV set in his room. Thus the boy learned to entertain himself. He received stimulation and human contact from the television screen and, through masturbation, from his body.

Once this pattern was explained, his parents understood why Joey needed more of their time and attention. They disconnected his TV set, and required him to watch the family set with his father. Whenever he began masturbating, they gently but firmly explained this was not an acceptable practice when other people were present. The masturbation stopped, and father and son found TV programs to share, and soon their companionship increased.

Another complaint was voiced by the mother of an eleven-year-old daughter:

"Leslie always has her nose in a book or she fiddles around and daydreams," her mother said. "It takes her hours to do anything, because her mind's in the clouds. She makes good school grades but always seems to have her mind on something else when she's home."

Only children often must learn to live in fantasy. Overprotected and limited in outside activities, they read and daydream to keep occupied. After Leslie's mother understood this, she began a social program for the girl, and made special efforts to entertain relatives and friends. Leslie soon became less withdrawn. In cases such as this it is essential that parents help their children experience social contact with peers at an early age, such as nursery school, clubs, or other activities.

Another problem is the "Oedipus complex," which may develop with special intensity in the single child. Son and father may compete for Mother's attention; Mother and daughter for the father's. Although some rivalry is inescapable, parents must be careful to avoid interference with their own relationship. The period from roughly three and a half to five and a half years are when the child makes special Oedipal attempts, and parents may contribute to the intensity of the child's feelings by permitting him to sleep with Mommy and Daddy. Loving and cuddling a child is good, but taking him into the parents' bed must be handled carefully.

One family came to therapy with their only daughter, Rosy, age four and a half. Earlier, father and daughter had begun a fun routine of wrestling for a few minutes each morning in the parents' bed before they arose for the day. This continued for almost a year.

One night Rosy screamed and brought her parents running to her room. She said she had a bad dream and was afraid someone would hurt her. Each time her father tried to leave the room, she cried so loudly that the parents allowed her to sleep the rest of the night with them. A week later the nightmare occurred again, and once more Rosy was permitted to come into the parental bed. The following week, Rosy cried at bedtime and insisted she was afraid to sleep alone. Her parents decided they had a problem.

I explained how little girls often need special attention from their fathers, but that the stimulation and physical contact in the parental bed could excite the child without her understanding the reason. I also explained that only children have a special longing for the comfort offered by sleeping with someone. The father was advised to stop stimulating her, but *not* to withhold normal affection. Rosy's nightmares began to subside.

I also advised Rosy's mother to ease her distress during the night. A couch was placed in the girl's room, and whenever she seemed very frightened, her mother spent the night there. This schedule quickly helped Rosy to stop the behavior calculated to attract her father's attention. At the same time, she was reassured that both parents cared, and that she need not face her problem alone. Rosy's parents wisely headed off a situation which could have resulted in family jealousy and dissension at a later time.

Mothers often favor only boys more than girls. The boy may be aggressive but still conform to the mother's wishes in order to maintain the relationship. Only girls tend to adopt extreme patterns of either overcompliance or refusal to comply with the mother's wishes.

Parents should be on guard against the only child's propensity to homosexuality. The father's absence seems to be an important predisposing condition, placing the boy or girl fully under the mother's influence. The boy identifies with her, but fears his sexual feelings toward her. The girl may take a masculine role to replace the missing father but remain dependent on her mother for affection.

An only child is usually popular with peers, does well in school, and learns positive ways of getting attention. He or she may be lonely and quick to anger if frustrated, but most often is charming and engaging in personal manners.

THE FIRSTBORN

As soon as another child is born, perhaps even before, firstborns sense the change in status with their parents. The effects may be less if they are under eighteen months old or over six years when the second is born. If younger than eighteen months, they are not yet firmly entrenched as sole owner of the parents; if six years or older, they have already established the only-child pattern. Many children feel jealous when a second child is born or arrives as a stepchild, even though the rival appears when they are in their late teens. Each new child changes the status of the firstborn, but none so much as that first brother or sister.

One forty-year-old man sought therapy because his wife wanted a divorce but he did not understand her hostility.

Perry had a sister two years younger, a compliant father, and a dominant mother. He was his mother's favorite, closer to her than to his father, and distant from his sister.

"She was a pest," he said. "She couldn't do much, playing baseball and such. I felt sorry for her because she was a girl and so helpless." Later his wife complained that he belittled her as he had his sister in childhood.

"He considers me helpless," his wife said, "and yet he constantly demands that I help with heavy jobs like mowing the lawn."

His wife had a younger brother and had identified with her father. It appeared that Perry valued the masculine part of her personality, but considered the feminine side weak.

Parents must keep in mind that the first child has been an only child for a period of time, and expects undivided help and attention. He has begun to talk, act, and think as they do, and feels he is an important member of the family. Another child forces the first to develop new ways of maintaining and enhancing himself. Because the new infant is helpless, parents see their firstborn as more mature, and press for rapid changes in his or her behavior. He is bewildered by the change in the parents and anxious about the new things expected of him. The fact that first children are easily angered and slow to regain composure may result from the parents' divided attention. Parents with more than one small child are under special stress, and use corporal punishment more on their first child than upon later children.

Patience is one key in dealing with the firstborn child after another is born. This is difficult, but subsequent problems may be avoided if parents are able to see both children in perspective, as human beings with the first needing as much love and guidance as it did before the second was born. Another key is to recognize the abrupt deprivation of the first child's dependency at the birth of the second. One manifestation is rage; another is regression to earlier behavior such as demanding a nipple bottle. Parents should talk with the first child *before* the second birth, and consciously indulge him after the second baby is born.

OLDER GIRL OF TWO

An older girl feels less stress if the second is a girl rather than a boy. In either case, she develops ways to handle the situation. If the newborn is a sister, the older girl uses her age, strength, and intelligence to compete. She may mother her sister but be disappointed in her mother for producing a rival and then move closer to her father.

Although the older girl may appear to adjust, this may be her only way of coping with feelings of rejection and loss of dependent satisfaction. She tries to hold her parents' respect by being good, but she feels uncertain of her worth. She may reject her own longing for affection. One older sister told me that she wiped off the kisses of relatives to show them and her parents how little she cared for their attention. She denied her own need. By remaining close and affectionate with the older daughter, parents may easily overcome such self-distorting tendencies.

In trying to meet parental standards, the oldest girl may put up with hostility and aggression from her baby sister. She may suppress her own feelings so much that she becomes unable to assert herself later in life. When younger sister is a charmer, the first is likely to reject others and become stridently assertive.

OLDER SISTER OF A BROTHER

A new brother poses a serious challenge to the firstborn girl. Her security depends upon continued closeness, especially with her mother. She has been "good," has achieved to please her parents, and is content being a girl because most parents welcome their firstborn regardless of sex. Then a brother comes along who is most welcome because he is the first boy in the family.

Here is the root of women's struggle with feelings of inferiority. Most parents are a bit prouder of a boy than of a girl, and their daughter recognizes this attitude instantly. Because she senses that she is valued less, she cannot escape feeling jealous. *The burden upon parents is to make certain that their daughter feels valued for herself just as fully as their son.*

Often the older sister compensates by seeking her father's attention and assuming his values. She may become an excellent student as a way of doing what little brother cannot yet do. This girl may be curious, ambitious, and tenacious, but also jealous, competitive, exhibitionistic, aggressive, talkative, and quarrelsome. Parents need to help her cope with her brother and support her self-worth as a girl. Her father can reflect her value as a feminine person and encourage her capabilities. Her mother can support her feminine interests and be fair in judging quarrels.

OLDER BROTHER OF A BOY

The older boy becomes more dependent upon his mother when a brother is born, but with preadolescence he turns toward independence.

Birth of little brother spurs the elder to verbal and intellectual accomplishment. While this boy may *seem* to conform, teachers find him quarrelsome, insistent upon his rights, and slow to recover from anger. After age ten or eleven he may become less truculent and more independent with his peers, but he always tries to dominate his younger brother.

The first boy fears losing status with his mother. He tries to please her by conforming to her values, and may seem dependent because he seeks her advice, assistance, and company. If that relationship is not comfortable, he may become hostile and rebellious. From ages nine to twelve, this firstborn may seem more interested in being with peers than with parents, but after puberty he again desires closeness with his mother. He is masculine, but in trying to become closer to his mother he may also develop some feminine traits.

One boy's father was an impatient man with a violent temper. His mother was cool and distant. When Patrick was two, a brother was born.

Patrick became anxious about being separated from his mother. He refused to play out of her sight, and was so hostile to his brother that she feared for the infant's safety. Patrick's father offered no refuge or companionship. Before the brother's birth Patrick had been "probably the best child in the world." His mother was unprepared for his clinging (desperate dependency) and hostility at a time when the baby required so much attention.

The older boy developed allergies—eczema, hay fever, and asthma—each new symptom eliciting more of Mother's attention. Finally, when he was four, she had to be with him night and day so that he would not scar himself by scratching, or suffocate from asthma. His symptoms represented a psychosomatic way of asking for attention that he was unable to express verbally.

Both Patrick and his mother required intensive therapy. She gained self-confidence and encouraged her husband to spend more time with Pat. Fortunately, the boy made good progress as soon as he started going to school. This, plus insight gained in therapy, helped him to satisfy his need for attention and self-esteem, and his allergy symptoms diminished.

BROTHER WITH YOUNGER SISTER

This boy reacts to his sister's sex by emphasizing his masculinity. He is more comfortable than the older brother of a brother, because his mother still puts a special value on her only son. His sister never develops the prowess to keep up with him in play, and because he need not compete with her, he becomes less domineering and quarrelsome and more independent during preadolescent and adolescent years. Caught between two females, however, he may be a bit anxious when he is developing sexually.

An older boy sometimes tries to avoid his sister. One young man, with a sister two years younger, said:

"My sister is of no importance to me, but if I had to take some tack other than ignoring her, I would put ground glass in her sugar bowl. I have no interest in anything she does. We have never been friends. She acts like a baby and gets everything she wants from Dad by acting that way." (This last statement helps to explain his hostility.)

Older brothers stress masculinity and deride their sisters. This resolution of their lost special attention may cause them problems in later relations with women. Parents can ease this conflict by encouraging communication, understanding and tolerance. Mother, especially, should not favor one child to the detriment of the other.

PARENTING A SECOND CHILD

By the time a second child arrives, parents have learned from the first but are unable to give as much attention to the second baby. Second children are not subjected to the same attitudes that encourage the firstborn to achieve. While they remain second of two, they enjoy a special relationship, particularly with Mother. First babies teach parents not to demand excessively mature behavior from their seconds, so parents tend more to protect their second children from illness and injury.

The secondborn receives less pressure and is often less irritable and provoking. Mothers sometimes say, "I wish

I'd had my second child first," but they also have remarked: "If I'd had my second child first, I wouldn't
have had another."

If parents discipline their first boy or girl too harshly,
the second may become quiet and withdrawn to avoid
punishment. Sometimes he may rebel, or become passive
if he has lost fights with his older sibling. The elder will
use verbal aggression while the second attacks physically,
withdraws, or finds more subtle ways of enlisting Mother's
aid. The secondborn is often well accepted by peers and
teachers as easy-going and friendly.

YOUNGER OF TWO GIRLS

This child may seem independent while small, but becomes more dependent later. She feels closer to Mother
than to Father, and identifies with Mother's values. She
may be rebellious in adolescence and aggressive with her
sister while assuming a "hurt child" stance. She usually
has good relations with her peers, and may value their
opinions over those of family members. Initial fear of
failure may cause disinterest in school.

A special problem for the younger of two girls is the
possibility of sexual overstimulation too early in life. One
girl said:

"I've always wanted to be like my older sister. She met
a boy when she was thirteen and is still going with him.
I wanted to do that. That's why I hold on to boys so
much."

Later she understood other ways she had envied her
sister.

"I've always been frightened of Father," she said. "He
understands nothing of how I feel. He has bloodied my
nose and beat me up. He has never touched my sister.
She orders me around, but I've always wanted to be like
her. I've seen how my parents think she is so perfect."

When this girl came to therapy, she was pregnant by a
fourteen-year-old boy and had been arrested for aiding
him in stealing hubcaps. Her baby was aborted. Later she
married, still at an early age, but she has had a satisfactory
life since then.

YOUNGER SISTER OF A BROTHER

This girl may be nonconforming as an adolescent and envy her brother's maleness. She feels dominated and less powerful, is quarrelsome and vengeful. She may be a tomboy, but is confident, enthusiastic, popular, and a leader outside the home.

One twelve-year-old girl with an older brother told me that she hated him and felt her mother was on his side. She was disdainful and hid his possessions for revenge.

"He hides behind Mother's skirts," she said. "I don't."

An eighteen-year-old girl sought my help because she thought she was ugly and couldn't hold contact with a desirable boy.

"When I was a teen-ager, my older brother said only derogatory things about me," Peggy said. "Even now he never talks to me as though I'm an equal."

They quarreled often. She became concerned about her appearance when she noticed her brother was unusually good-looking. She felt he had better skin, hair, and eyes than she did.

As she talked things out in therapy, Peggy sensed some decrease in her animosity and tension. She finally understood her brother's behavior in terms of sibling competition. As her hostility diminished she also felt more confident with other men. She began to appreciate her appearance once she stopped comparing herself with her brother.

Perhaps the greatest thing parents can do for a girl in this position is to help her gain her brother's approval. Father may be tender and admiring and Mother supportive, but her older brother can crush her self-confidence. She cannot know that one reason why he puts her down is that he may be attracted to her.

"I grew up on his telling me how ugly I was," one girl said. "I never thought I'd have a boy friend. Even now my satisfaction in having one is showing my brother that I can."

YOUNGER BROTHER OF A SISTER

This boy is often nonconforming, dependent, and his parents' favorite. He quarrels with his sister and in later childhood may try to dominate her. As the only boy he receives so much family warmth that he may be excessively family-centered, and low in social participation and leadership. Although the favorite, this boy may not develop self-esteem and confidence because of inability to compete intellectually with his sister.

Parents should be careful not to throttle his competitive spirit "because you're a boy and boys should take care of their sisters." In one family the parents so firmly instilled the idea that their son should not hurt his sister that later he was unable to assert himself with any woman.

SECOND OF TWO BOYS

This boy may seem conforming when actually he is non-communicative. He may be independent from age five to nine, dependent during preadolescence, and then show a surge of dominance after age fourteen. He is overshadowed but also impressed by his older brother. He may be unfriendly to adults and nonconforming in school, but popular with his peers. His drive for achievement may be less than his brother's, but he will not fear failure. This boy often excels in athletics and other masculine endeavors.[1]

As a way of outmaneuvering his brother's top position in the family, the second boy may use babyish dependency to gain attention. One mother brought her seven-year-old second son to therapy because of poor enunciation and infantile speech.

"He doesn't try and he doesn't care," his mother said. "It's more important for him to be a baby. He's impossible with both his father and me. He tells me to shut up when I try to help him speak more clearly."

Tracing back, we found that the mother had devoted her attention to the older boy, who was seriously ill just at the time the younger was learning to speak.

"Our second originally was an easy child, and healthy," his mother said. "I was more relaxed with him. I let him take care of himself. I didn't neglect him on purpose. I had to be with my older son."

Prolongation of infantile behavior was this second son's way of getting his mother's attention. Now, at age seven, he could no longer succeed with baby behavior and had become aggressive to get his way. Speech therapy was helpful, and play therapy resolved some of his feelings of being ignored and eased his aggressiveness.

The following are some suggestions for parents of the two-child family:

1. *Be careful about comparing the children with each other.*

A firstborn girl was devastated when her mother told her that her brother's I.Q. was higher. A second boy complained:

"My mother always said: 'I never had to tell your sister to do her homework. Your sister always makes good grades. Your sister always does her chores.' But I'm not my sister, and I have to do things my own way."

2. *Don't expect the same behavior or achievement from the second as from the first child.*

3. *If they are of different sexes, encourage each to develop according to his or her potentialities, regardless of society's definition of sex roles.*

4. *Prevent the firstborn from dominating the second.*

A second boy, unable to assert himself with his sister, said: "When we were alone she would make me get down on my hands and knees, touch my forehead to the floor, and say, 'Allah, Master.' I think I'm still doing that with women."

5. *Encourage intellectual development in the second-born.*

6. *Do not assume all is well because you do not hear complaints.* Either child may take an opposite stand from the other to appear stronger. If the older complains, the younger will not, and vice versa.

7. *Either child may be aggressive in complaining.*

Parents tend to favor the complainer. Try to uncover the real situation and be fair in discipline.

SECOND CHILD FOLLOWED BY OTHERS

The middle of three or second in a larger family is often considered the most difficult birth position of all. This boy or girl grows accustomed to competing with an older sibling for parental favors and after another baby must regroup defenses to compete with the new child.

Parents should be forewarned that after a third baby is born, their second will make greater demands for help and approval. Mother and Father, occupied with caring for all three children, and especially the infant, may react to the middle child's demands with anger and rejection. The best advice I can give is: *Don't* reject your secondborn just because he suddenly seems more difficult. The child will react aggressively and sometimes negatively in order to recapture parental love and attention.

There are several things to watch in the way the middle child reacts with others. He may become bossy, taunting, and insulting both with siblings and other peers. Sometimes this child's problems are more visible to teachers. School observation often reveals the middle youngster to be more vulnerable to poor personal and social adjustment.

Many adjustments relate to the sex of siblings. Here are examples:

BOY BETWEEN TWO SISTERS

Kevin's parents became alarmed when he persisted in wearing his mother and sisters' make-up and clothes. At age ten the boy spent most of his playtime with girls or in his room dressing as a girl.

The father considered himself devoted to all his children, but the mother said that he was "all business" and spent no time at all with his son.

Kevin had many fears. After seeing a frightening movie, he "threw up all night." He was afraid his mother would die. He said "other kids don't like me." His parents drew a pathetic picture of the boy often sitting on his front porch watching other children. When encouraged to join them, he said: "I don't want to, they don't want me."

Family therapy revealed that Kevin had been constantly dominated by three females: his mother and the sisters who surrounded him. He was forced to give up things for them, and his mother was fearful and overprotective. She allowed none of the children to own bicycles for fear they would get hurt. Kevin was even sent to the same summer camp with his sisters.

As a major resolution in therapy, Kevin's father came to understand how little attention he had given his son. Both parents began to control the sister domination, and allowed the boy to assert himself and develop a male identity. Counseling and family cooperation were so successful that at age sixteen Kevin had learned to drive, had a girl friend, and dressed stylishly.

MIDDLE OF THREE GIRLS

This attractive twelve-year-old's behavior had brought her mother "to my wits' end." Phyllis was stubborn and refused to obey. She lied, and the family was in constant turmoil because she was rebellious and fought with her sisters. "She usually starts the quarrels," her mother said.

Phyllis had school problems, too. She dressed flamboyantly and wore too much make-up. She was jealous of other girls' clothes and the attention they received from boys, and she often engaged in hair-pulling bouts. Both parents saw her as "the bad one from the beginning." Her father called her a "monster who gets into everything, breaks everything, and breaks every rule." Phyllis herself wished to get along better with her sisters. She did not like the trouble she caused, but "something gets into me and I just can't help it."

During family therapy it came out that Phyllis never had received, from either parent, the attention given the other two girls. Her father had been disappointed when Phyllis was not a boy. Then, when the third child was also a girl, he was charmed by the baby and paid even less attention to Phyllis.

I encouraged the parents, especially the father, to give Phyllis more attention and affection. His change in attitude probably prevented even more difficult problems by removing the motive for her aggressiveness and boy-chasing.

SECOND OF FOUR CHILDREN

This secondborn girl had an older sister, a younger brother and younger sister. At age fourteen Lorraine was, she said, "the only virgin I know."

Lorraine's mother had divorced the father after the

four children were born, then entered a mental hospital for treatment of depression. While she was there she had frequent and promiscuous sex with male patients. Later she was released from the hospital.

The three younger children were held in court custody. Lorraine was sent for psychological counseling because at that point she had shown no great problem of personality adjustment. It was hoped she could be "saved" despite the unsavory environment she would face when she returned home.

At first Lorraine was defiant and spoke tersely. Later she became more trusting and revealed that, like any younger sister of a sister, she had learned her own ways of obtaining status in the family. In her case, the opposite path gave her a strong sense of responsibility and an unwillingness to be sexually promiscuous like her mother, her sister, and her aunts, who also had produced illegitimate babies.

Therapy supported Lorraine's already strong ego with information and advice. Her interest in school improved, and she graduated from high school. She is now married and working as a stenographer.

Parents are least likely to recognize the needs of the second child in a larger family. Careful observation and listening will help isolate problems and locate the roots of unacceptable behavior. Above all, parents should appreciate their children's needs—all of them—for attention, interest, approval, and companionship.

PARENTING LATER-MIDDLE CHILDREN

Later-middle children learn many ways of gaining attention and competing with brothers and sisters. Since there is a tendency to get lost in the crowd, later middles often do not trust their ability to get what they want by direct approach to the parents, and may develop devious techniques to gain individual recognition. This struggle works to their advantage in most cases. In larger families, later middles tend toward better adjustment than other children. This may be why so few of them seek psychological counseling.

Parents are usually less pleased when these later-middle children are born—still another child is not as welcome as the first or second may be. Older children place them at a greater distance from their mother and father, and later children see their elders as more powerful. Since the middles are thus thwarted in exercising power within the family, they may find it elsewhere, raising problems with peers and teachers.

One advantage accrues to the later middle if he is the first or only child of that sex. An only boy in a batch of girls (or girl among boys) will find special opportunities for individuality.

Later middles tend to make lower school grades, partially because they are not pressed to achieve. Also, the threat of rejection, used to obtain obedience, may not be effective, because later middles have always coped with some level of rejection. One girl, the third of four, was referred to me by school authorities because she was doing poorly in school.

She described herself as "the one who gets blamed for everything and punished," and was not interested in accomplishment. At age fourteen her aim was simply to find a man who would take care of her. She had failed to construct feelings of self-worth and competence, which prevented her from trying anything she considered of value. She was "lost in the middle" as one of four children, all the same sex.

As we progressed, this girl identified with me because I gave her some of the attention and advice she had been lacking. Two years later she was making good grades and planned to become a paramedic.

Another woman was third among four children, born fifteen months after the only son. Myrtle never had good relations with her parents or brothers and sisters.

"I have hated everybody all my life," she said. "I've always been a miserable person."

A child born so soon after another, especially if the former is favored, as was Myrtle's brother, may not receive the mothering that encourages self-esteem and the good feelings that are reflected in cheerfulness. Nevertheless, Myrtle married three times (perhaps seeking someone who really cared), and had a total of four children. She worked hard to maintain the family.

When she came to me, she had developed a reaction against all the efforts she had made. She wanted to leave her husband and children to escape her responsibilities.

She felt unable to work, and spent her days in bed or watching television.

Such symptoms may often be eased by support from therapy, and objective examination of the relationships which contributed to the depression. Soon Myrtle was functioning again as a mother.

Suggestions for parents:

1. *Encourage the later-middle child toward achievement.*

2. *Help this girl or boy to feel as adequate and important as earlier children.*

3. *Support the development of special interests and skills.*

4. *Give the laterborns measured responsibility at appropriate ages.*

5. *Be on guard against domination by the older children.*

PARENTING THE YOUNGEST (AMONG THREE OR MORE CHILDREN)

This boy or girl must cope with being the smallest and weakest of all persons in the family. He or she may not develop a drive for achievement, because it isn't necessary to obtain parents' approval and indulgence. This child may capitalize on smallness and use crying and tattling to compete with siblings.

On the other hand, this youngster (particularly in a large family) may become a high achiever because of help from parents and brothers and sisters who serve as pacesetters and guides. He expects help and uses personal contacts in a pleasant way to reach a goal. The youngest child receives everything the parents have learned, and also the wisdom of brothers and sisters who have already tested the outside world. Relations with parents vary: They may be close, since this is the baby, or distant, because parents are weary of solving problems for the older children.

One youngest girl was so close to her widowed mother that, as she said, "I slept with my mother until the day I married." In her case, the closeness seemed to help develop a firm level of self-esteem and confidence in the warmth and generosity of others.

In other cases, parents may be overprotective while resenting the burden of another child. One such example was a boy, welcomed because his mother wanted a son after two daughters. For the first years the mother was warm and giving, but increasing demands upon her time by her husband and daughters caused her to grow weary of the youngest.

"I urged him to go out and play," she said. "Sometimes I locked the door so he couldn't get back in until I let him."

The boy's upset from this treatment, which he experienced as rejection, was not apparent until he entered school. The first day he left the playground and ran home. He developed a school phobia and would not stay there unless his mother sat with him, reflecting his fear of separation from her. Finally the family sought help. With play therapy and acting out relations with his mother, the boy's anxiety diminished and he was willing to go to school by himself.

THE CHILD WITH "TWO SETS OF PARENTS"

Other conditions may prevail if the youngest is born a number of years after the other children. Such a youngster may feel that he has two sets of parents. The mother and father of an eight-year-old boy, for example, were perplexed when he ignored their guidance. Patrick was born when his brother and sister were five and seven.

Insight came when the father took Pat and his brother, then thirteen, to a father-son campout. After a day or two, father observed that when he told Pat to do something, the boy checked it out first with his brother: "Do you think I should? Is it all right?" As his father commented, Pat had two sets of parents, his father and mother and his brother and sister. The situation was easily resolved through a series of family meetings at which the problems were talked out and individual roles were clarified.

Problems with the youngest child may include excessive dependency. If the child succeeds in getting what it wants through crying and tattling, these practices may develop into lifelong and limiting methods of relating to others. Lastborns may cling to their parents and parents may cling to them. One mother became aware, when her youngest was a teenager, that he had never gone far from the nest. He came home after school and immersed himself in television. At nine he went to summer camp, but had to be sent home early because he refused to eat, sleep, or leave the tent. His mother finally realized that she had enjoyed having him depend on her to this extent.

A special problem is that the youngest child, more than others, experiences keenly the loss of a parent by divorce, separation, or death. An older brother or sister can sometimes act as a substitute father or mother, but loss of a parent when a child is small creates a lasting effect and requires help from caring friends, relatives, or therapists. A small child may blame himself for the apparent abandonment. Later in life this translates to fear of losing another loved one, such as a wife or husband.

On girl, for example, struggled with a feeling that men would always reject her because her father left home when she was ten. She turned away from men on the basis of her childhood expectation of receiving no help or attention from them, thereby forestalling their meeting her needs. She married "because that was the thing to do," but her life was marked by repeated psychosomatic illness that represented her hopeless denials of her wish for attention.

Evidence has shown that the youngest child is more likely to become an alcoholic than older brothers or sisters, especially if a parent has been lost in that child's early years. Such a loss may have many meanings to a child which may cause him or her to feel *unusual* tension and depression later. Alcohol is an easily obtained drug which relieves such feelings, at least temporarily. In clinical situations, youngests with similar problems have turned to other drugs.

Suggestions for parents in raising youngest children:

1. *Make sure the youngest is not dominated by older siblings.*

2. *Keep teasing by older siblings within careful bounds.*

3. *Provide opportunity and encourage the child to achieve.*

4. *Stress experiences that lead to self-reliance and direction.*

5. *Encourage decision-making and independence.*

6. *Watch that the youngest does not tackle situations over his head, as repeated failure will lead to feelings of inadequacy.*

7. *If there is a special problem, such as illness or loss of a parent, provide outside help if necessary. Such help may be valuable and ease emotional distress even if no serious symptoms seem to be present.*

GENERAL RECOMMENDATIONS FOR PARENTS DERIVED FROM BIRTH-ORDER STUDIES

1. Do not hope to eliminate all jealousy between children. This is a healthy emotion expressed by all higher species of animal life. It emerges from recognition of a wish to improve one's status by obtaining and keeping something of value which also is sought by someone else.

Like nations, individuals must learn to compete with one another in a constructive way rather than employ techniques destructive to themselves and others. The most important task for parents is to help family members compete in cooperative ways (not necessarily a contradictory statement). The greatest responsibility is to develop children who can fit into a cooperative society.

A beginning step in minimizing futile ways of expressing jealousy is to help each child see other children as improving his condition rather than detracting from it. A new baby can be presented as a source of richness for the entire family.

Help other children participate in caring for the new baby. Talk to them about him. Explain why so much time and care are needed, and what to expect in the baby's development.

2. Try to "civilize" each child in a way that allows him or her to retain confidence and self-esteem. Constant criticism and belittling can destroy or prevent development of self-confidence and initiative. Such treatment may drive adolescents or young adults to drop out of school and to exhibit other antisocial behavior.

3. Harsh discipline can instigate rebellion. Even though a parent is concerned and loving, excessive demands and strictness can drive a young man or woman to seek other ways of alleviating tensions, anxieties, and feelings of guilt. These may include indulgence in alcohol, drugs, unhealthy sex, and destructive behavior.

4. Teach your children, by example, the benign use of power. Do not use the new baby as a club to force more mature behavior from the older children.

One woman, before her third child was born, asked for help in achieving more maturity in her second. (This approach may be very good, addressing a problem before it becomes critical.)

"She isn't toilet-trained yet," the mother said, "and she insists on having a pacifier. She even wants a bottle now and then. What can I do? I think she's just spoiled rotten and I'm furious with her. I don't know what I'll do with her when the baby comes if she goes on acting like this."

Although this mother probably should have been less relaxed in training her second child, it was not the time to force it. I advised her to let the older girl continue with her infantile ways until the new baby had been accepted in the family, and then use birthdays and other milestones which the older girl could see as points of pride in becoming more mature in her habits. Punishment can only fixate childish behavior more rigidly.

Do not use a new baby as an excuse for forcing more responsibilities upon an older child. Feelings of inadequacy and lack of confidence can result. Keep in mind the ages of your children, and that what you may expect from each will be different at any point in time.

Different methods will be needed to motivate first and laterborn children. Firstborns are motivated by success, but may stop trying after repeated failures. Laterborns need parental support to motivate them. However, if they achieve success too easily, they tend to stop trying.

5. Be sensitive to the ways your children relate to you. Do they like you, value your approval, talk to you and see themselves as having similar values? Encourage children to tell you how they feel and think, as their behavior may be a cover-up.

Firstborns usually learn to accept parental values after some preliminary flurries of rebellion. Laterborns may require a conscious effort on the parents' part to nurture closeness and to make sure parental experience and wisdom help them develop high standards of behavior.

6. Family interaction conducive to constructive development of personality and behavioral traits for all members of the family includes:

• consistency in parental attitudes and behavior.

- encouragement of democratic attitudes; discouragement of authoritarianism by both parents and siblings.
- approval and trust by parents, with encouragement of these attitudes among siblings.
- consistent, firm, and moderate discipline.

SECTION

VI

---

*A Look
into
the Future*

CHAPTER 16

Using the Information

Knowledge of birth-order effects is by no means an automatic formula for curing emotional ills. Experiences you enjoy or suffer as the result of growing up in a certain position in your family are only a part of the overall environment contributing to maturity and personality development. Birth order thus becomes one of several signposts we may use in identifying the roots of emotional difficulties, just as a blood-pressure check is one of many tests a physician may require for diagnosing physical health or illness.

Research results, although still far from complete, suggest ways you may apply the information in your own lives. I have shown how it may help you better understand yourself and the people around you—friends, relatives, children, husbands, and wives—and relate more happily and successfully to them. It can help also in vocational pursuits, sexual relations, in planning families, and in rearing children.

This knowledge can help the practicing clinical psychologist formulate theories about individual clients. When indications are clear that birth order is pertinent to the problem, this information can help patients become aware of and overcome what they are doing that is not effective in adult life as the result of roles learned in childhood. Since many parts of the learned life role are constructive, knowledge of birth-order effects may help a person understand, accept, and use the constructive aspects more effectively.

Perhaps most important, social scientists may examine the possibility that interaction within the childhood home develops interpersonal skills that may apply to solutions of great social problems. Sociologists may find relationships among people that will contribute to more rational answers to world problems.

As a psychotherapist, I find that birth-order information helps me to do what I believe every therapist should do: understand so well what is going on within patients that you almost get into their skin, as it were.

When people come to talk to me for the first time, I automatically acquire information about their early families from a recounting of their lives. Learning whether they were reared as only children or one of several, and where they ranked in the family hierarchy, causes me to wonder what pressures were exerted upon each person in his particular family. What did he do to meet those pressures? What behavior was learned to compete with other members of the family to obtain parental attention or adjust to a lack of attention? What are the results of this treatment in the present? Even though I must work with the client's present behavior and personal relationships, my understanding of birth order helps me to reach into the past where the child was reared in the family.

It is equally important to learn about other essential people in a client's life. I am often asked to interpret these people to a patient, and the knowledge of *their* birth order helps in this. A person struggling with a psychological problem not only requires insight but "outsight" as well. A patient needs to understand what is happening between him and other people, what is happening *between* people outside himself, and what is happening *within* people outside himself.

For instance, knowing that a patient's boy friend or husband is an only child permits some theorizing about what is going on inside that person and how he can be expected to interact with the client. My patients themselves are not naïve about these relationships. One man, for example, said:

"Well, she's an only child, and that's why I'm having trouble with her."

But what is there about being an only child that troubles this specific relationship?

One young man, the oldest of five children, was in love with a girl but he was disturbed because she indicated no interest in serious activities, such as work.

Learning that his girl friend was an only child helped me to explore her background for possibilities of change and maturity. This oldest-child client wanted to settle down in a comfortable home and have children. His only-child lover did not. As we examined her attitudes more deeply and carefully, he gradually came to accept that her values and attitudes were so widely divergent from his that she would not make a good wife for him. He could also understand her behavior as *hers* (impersonal), not directed specifically at him.

Knowing how birth order may affect a situation sometimes helps to shortcut the therapeutic process. A dramatic example of this was one of the few emergency cases that have come to my attention.

Norma was referred to me by a physician because she was suffering from deep depression and threatening suicide. Her doctor considered her case so serious that I saw her within hours after he called. Information I possessed about birth-order effects helped me relate to her immediately.

Early in our conversation, Norma revealed that she was the oldest of seven children. She now had three of her own, ranging in age from eleven to twenty years. Without delving at once into the reasons for her depression and suicidal feelings, I turned instead to the more positive aspects of *her* birth position.

Realizing that a firstborn woman usually feels strong responsibility for those in her care, I told her that she must feel great concern for her children and related it to her firstborn position. She accepted this thought readily. Then I told her some of the consequences to her children if she should kill herself. She became increasingly thoughtful as the session progressed, and by the end I felt I had diverted her temporarily from her suicidal intent.

The next day Norma called to ask me if I knew of a

place where she could be protected against her self-destructive tendencies.

Meanwhile, I learned more about what had driven this woman into a deep depression. Her husband had foolishly told her about his fantasy desires to indulge in sex outside their marriage. He said he had fallen in love with a girl half her age (and half *his* age) and wanted his wife's permission to spend every other week with the other woman. He was quite serious about the suggestion, citing the wave of sexual freedom which seemed to be sweeping the country as a justification, but at the same time he emphasized that he wanted to remain in his marriage.

His suggestion was a special shock to Norma because, as a firstborn, she had been deeply saturated in traditional morals and values. Needless to say, her security, her self-esteem, her values were all threatened by her husband's proposal. What had been a lifelong precarious emotional adjustment insured that the shock would have very serious effects.

Obviously much deeper therapy was required for Norma before she could make any genuine adjustment, but at least the knowledge of birth-order effects helped to prevent an immediate tragedy for the family. (Her husband, of course, also needed to be drawn into the therapy situation.)

In less critical situations, the effects of birth order may be clearly pertinent in one case, but only conjectured in another.

A therapist must be sensitive to the danger of jumping to conclusions that are not valid in a specific case, or even making suggestions to a patient. I have always tried to be careful not to suggest birth-order relationships until there is a great deal of evidence to support them. Then I find that mentioning the *possibility* (and it cannot be more absolute than that) is often enough to clarify personal relationships for a patient.

CHAPTER 17

Which Birth Position Is Best?

Before suggesting some implications that birth order holds for the future of our society, we cannot ignore the question which seems to begin and end every conversation on the subject:

"Which position is best?"

It would be convenient if we could list them in a neat hierarchy from best to worst, but that is not possible. As foregoing chapters have shown, each role imposes specific challenges, offers specific opportunities, and fosters special skills and attitudes. When used constructively, these challenges and opportunities permit a child from any birth position to develop a life style or role equal in value to that of any other place in the family.

No birth position is intrinsically better than another, and none poses more problems than another—they are simply different.

I believe my greatest contribution may be to help each person to recognize advantages and disadvantages deriving from his or her birth position, and to make maximum use of this knowledge. As Alfred Adler said, it is not important where you were born in your family. What is important is that each position offers a different environment for development. Parents and other family members can *alter* this environment if change is needed. An adult who recognizes his own characteristics which originated from the environment of birth position may take action to emphasize the good traits and ameliorate the bad ones.

My repeated emphasis on these points is intended to break down the general feeling that firstborns and only children automatically have the best of everything, and to encourage others to feel that they enjoy equal opportunity to live satisfying lives. My motive also, while not detracting from the high esteem enjoyed by boys (especially firstborns), is to promote equality for girls in parental esteem and with their brothers and sisters. As one young man observed:

"Whether or not you consider first best depends upon whether or not you hold in greatest esteem scientific and other academic success as compared with other areas of achievement. Perhaps there are other areas of life which are more important than these, or just as important, and perhaps laterborns are doing well in these areas."

His remarks are pertinent, especially when related to social changes since the late 1960s, when young people began to reevaluate America's preoccupation with the Puritan work ethic and the concept of material wealth and achievement as the most valued goals of existence. In our society we have tended to place the highest value on competitive, scholastic, and professional abilities, but now the emphasis is shifting to other aspects of living: humanitarian values, harmonious social relationships, and achievement along lines other than those loaded with educational skills. Parents of the future may value a son who retires to a commune in the woods as highly as another who becomes a famous scientist. They may cherish a daughter who follows a professional career as deeply as one who takes up the role of wife, mother, and housekeeper and produces grandchildren. The family is the basic social unit, and its attitudes, values, and interaction will reflect the future requirements of the larger society in which it exists.

Before I predict the future, however, let's look for a moment at how some individuals view their own birth positions and subsequent adjustment to personal and professional values. Dr. Bossard,[1] in his study of large families, found that nine out of ten children who were *fourth* born among six were seen by others as having made comfortable emotional and vocational adjustment, while firstborns of large families were seen as having the poorest record. By contrast, the evidence for smaller families points to better adjustment by firstborns, at least so far as achievement is concerned.

In Bossard's study, adults reared in large families tended to believe that brothers and sisters in the fourth and fifth birth positions had the best of it. They thought the oldest child most often was given too much responsibility, was the practice child for parents, and was exploited. Only one-third of the firstborns were satisfied with their own positions.

Most adults from large families also did not see the lastborn as a favorable position. They saw this child as indulged, overprotected, and self-centered in adulthood. The youngests themselves, however, were more satisfied with their own positions than either oldest or middle children. More than 85 percent of the youngests liked their birth position. About 80 percent of the in-between children also were content with their own birth rank.

The following are some comments which we have gleaned from persons born in various birth positions regarding which is best:

Only Child, Male: Successful engineering director in a large organization:

"Since I was the only child, I received many benefits my parents would not have been able to give me if there had been other children. I was always well dressed and well fed, something not true for other kids I knew who were from large families and were reared during the Depression.

"I was able to go to college. My parents were very sociable, so there were always lots of parties and dinners going on in our home. They welcomed other kids. In fact, my mother was never happier than when I had a lot of kids there and she could fuss around in the kitchen cooking pies and cakes for them."

Oldest Child, Male: A doctor from a family of three children:

"I really liked being oldest. I felt wise and strong relative to my younger brothers and sisters. All through our growing-up years I considered myself their teacher and protector. I even felt that I kept our parents from being too strict with them.

"I think having that position helped me develop self-respect and that I learned something about taking responsibility for other people."

Second Child, Female: College professor, wife, and mother from a family of four children:

"I'm glad I wasn't first. My older sister was given a great deal of responsibility because my father died when the youngest child was a baby and my mother had to go to work.

"I had responsibility, but it wasn't restrictive the way it was for my older sister. She was in charge of us and the house, and it kept her busy, while I was able to spend more time studying and going to school functions."

Second Child, Male: A biologist from a family of two children:

"My sister was five years older than I, and I think the fact that she was that much older was good for both her and me. She acted like a little mother for me. Since she was very bright and liked school, she kept me interested in school and in learning.

"I think she had a much more difficult time than I did, though, because she had more responsibility. I suppose part of her problem was related to her being a girl. More housework was expected of her while, as a boy, I was given greater freedom."

Middle of three, Female: Home-economics teacher, wife, and mother:

"I loved being in the middle, even though I've heard that many people don't. My older brother bugged me when I was small, but when I was an adolescent he brought around some very interesting friends for me to meet.

"I think I learned at an early age to be comfortable with men because there were so many of his friends around. My younger sister seemed to be put at a disadvantage by having so many older people around."

Youngest of four, Male: Member of city council:

"I had all the advantages. Everybody took care of me and saw that things went well for me. Fortunately, neither my parents nor my older sisters and brother thought I should be babied. They were anxious to see that I learned to take as much responsibility as I could.

"They all probably think as I do: that they were reared

in the best position. But I *know* I was! I don't think I could be as successful as I am in politics this early in my life if I hadn't found it necessary to learn diplomacy in getting along with all those older people."

CHAPTER 18

Implications for the Future

Awareness of family relationships and the effects of birth order may become increasingly important as this knowledge is integrated with other changes in the society. It promises a new quality, and quantity, of people with women's growing freedom to assume independent roles and more control over the size of their families.

"Two factors promise a profound change in the role of women in society during the decades immediately ahead," author Lester Brown commented in 1974. "One is the desire of the world's women to have social and political rights and economic opportunities equal to men. Second is the pressure of population on the earth's resources, approaching a point where it may not be feasible for all women to bear children." [1]

During the past ten years we have already witnessed a profound change in the childbearing patterns of Western society. In the United States—stirred most deeply by information about the population explosion, resource depletion, and environmental degradation—we have seen a declining birth rate, which, if it continues, will bring us to zero population growth within a generation. The goal (not necessarily advocated by the author) is for parents to have only enough children to replace themselves. In one brief decade, society's attitude has turned abruptly.

Large families are "out"; small families, or none at all, are "in."

As one middle-aged father commented:

"I used to be proud that my wife and I had six sons. If we were at a cocktail party I would find some way to call attention to our family and enjoy the admiring responses, especially since my wife still appears young and attractive. Sure, it was the *macho* thing. Having six children proved my manhood.

"But now, since all the propaganda about how a person in America consumes twenty to thirty times as much as in India or some other country, I'm embarrassed to tell people how many children we have. All it really proves is that my wife was fertile and that we had sexual intercourse at least six times in twenty years. Now I'm pleased that my six sons so far have produced only three grandchildren. They're not all married yet, of course, but if they all do get married I hope they'll hold the total of my grandchildren to twelve, enough to replace themselves and their wives."

(The replacement level, taking into account births, deaths, and infertile women, is actually an average of 2.1 children per woman of childbearing age. It should be acknowledged also that the birth rate can turn upward again, just as it has turned downward during the past decade.)

There are several reasons why American women stopped reproducing at their accustomed level. One was emergence of new contraceptive techniques and information in the 1960s. Another is the widening area and conditions under which abortions are legal. As has been said before, these provide tools by which women can control their bodies. In America, in the immediate past, it has been estimated that 20 percent of all babies born were unwanted children. Widespread use of contraception and abortion should help to reduce that figure. However, contraception and abortion could not have created the sudden decline in childbearing without the broad change in attitudes which has occurred throughout society.

Factors contributing to the new attitudes include the high cost of living and education, widespread use of adequate contraceptives, concern about crowding and over-population, more liberal abortion laws, and changing life styles reflected by women's liberation.

A Gallup poll conducted in 1974 showed that the proportion of Americans who favor large families had declined from 41 percent in 1969 to 19 percent in 1974. The median response was two. In 1945, 23 percent of the people considered two children to be an ideal-size family. In 1974 this had grown to 46 percent.[2]

Another indication of what may be expected came from senior women surveyed at Stanford University in 1973. Only *1 in 25* of these young women expected to become full-time housewives within five years of graduation. Although Stanford students represent a high level of intellectual capacity, it is from this kind of source that the changing attitudes are spreading.

If these trends continue, most children of the future will grow up in small families. How will the small-family ethic affect the children? What will it mean if most youngsters of tomorrow grow up as only children, or first or second among two?

LARGE-FAMILY VALUES

We might first consider what has been the value of large families. We are frequently told by people who favor big families that there are many advantages for children in this environment. Bossard's excellent studies of large and small families may give us some clues. What does he see for parents and children in large families?

Some of the benefits accrue to parents. Older children help discipline the younger ones, and much of child rearing depends on what the children do for and with each other. Younger children accept their elders as disciplinarians. Bossard came to believe that there was an advantage for the children, in that sibling rivalry was often trivial and short-lived. The children themselves reported that growing up in a large family helped them to solve social problems as adults. There also seem to be advantages for some older children from large families who learn to serve as leaders and protectors, and develop habits of responsibility and service. On the other hand, the fact that these roles are forced on the children may limit their opportunities for personal development. Many oldest girls reported feeling exploited by parents who made them surrogate mothers for the younger children.

SMALL-FAMILY VALUES

Bossard found the following advantages and disadvantages for children reared in small families:

1. They enjoy greater material advantages. Family resources are not diluted among many people, and thus the child may receive an automatic head start in the world.

2. They receive more individual attention from parents.

3. They have greater opportunities for advancement in social and economic status.

4. They occupy the center of the family stage.

5. A disadvantage is that their early orientation to the small group may limit their ability to fit into society with large-scale organization and bureaucracy.

James A. Sweet, a University of Wisconsin sociologist, pointed out in 1974 [3] that in the U.S. births are actually falling most rapidly among the poor, the blacks, and Mexican-Americans. From 1960 to 1970 the fertility of urban whites fell 27 percent. Blacks declined 37 percent, while Indians and Mexican-American births diminished 45 percent and 30 percent respectively.

The implication of this pattern of decreased fertility in all cultural groups, according to Sweet, is that "a smaller share of American children will be growing up in impoverished settings with large numbers of brothers and sisters."

This trend is significant for predicting birth-order effects among future children. The achievement records of first-borns have depended greatly upon the economic resources of families which allow firstborns to obtain education and professional training to the detriment of later children. When considerable wealth is present, all children in a family show equal interest in obtaining college degrees. Thus, we expect that smaller families will permit more children to receive the educational training best suited to their potential.

We anticipate that mothers of small families will work outside the home, and that their desire to do so will be one reason for the small number of children. They will also have less time available to spend with their children. Bossard told us that in small families children receive more individual attention from parents, but is this true in families where both parents work?

There seems to be a correlation between the close contact of the firstborn with parents and his advantageous position in verbal development, academic achievement, and motivation for accomplishments. Firstborns are often successful in occupations heavily loaded with verbal demands. Frederick Wyatt of the University of Michigan, James T. Fawcett of the East-West Population Center in Honolulu, and Nancy Russo of Richmond College, City University of New York, suggest that fewer children and less sibling interaction could have an adverse effect on verbal intelligence quotients. Is this prospect good or bad?

We believe that any possible deleterious effects will be offset by the improved *quality* of parent-child relationships, especially with mothers. Parents of small families *want* their children, which implies that they are motivated to give those children as much time and guidance as good child-rearing requires. Working parents of the future may look forward to hours with their children without the ambivalent resentment of many mothers who feel trapped into remaining home with their children.

Thus the interchange between parents and children may be enriched with the communication of ideas and information.

Television can also be a tremendous force in developing children's verbal intelligence, vocabulary, ability to use good judgment and abstract ideas, and supply a wide range of information. We say "can" because few of the programs now on television direct their programs to aiding children in these ways. All too often the producers prostitute themselves by seducing children into their programs (and persuading Mom to buy advertised products) with material that may entertain the children but fails to stimulate thoughtful speech and ideas. Most programming uses words and concepts that children hear on the playground or that they know are disapproved of by adults and teachers. In fairness, there are *some* good programs, and it is a tribute to the desire of human beings to better themselves and their children that these fine programs have a large audience of children and parental approval. Our changing society needs to look very closely at this powerful source of intimate communication.

The fourth advantage of smaller families, cited by Bossard, is that those children have a greater opportunity for advancement in social and economic status. It is anticipated that this trend will continue. Economic support and other advantages should exist in small families of the future, especially since society at large now seems to be accepting responsibility for much of the education of its poorer and minority groups.

The last two characteristics of small families (as seen by Bossard) are not likely to apply to families of the future. Children are *not* likely to "occupy the center of the family stage." Women who work outside the home, while also holding primary responsibility for what occurs inside it, are not likely to permit their children to be the center of their lives. A psychologist can see the possibility of a real advantage in this for child development, if parents manage their lives, their homes, and their occupations successfully.

Although I have cited advantages for children who relate closely to parents in the family circle, I have been limited to considering family life as it *has been* and continues to be in many homes. I have shown how each child's effort to achieve status and strength has caused him to utilize the opportunities of his place in the family.

I have not had the need to delve into the much deeper questions about the place the child, in general, holds in the family structure. I believe that being the center of the family stage—as has certainly been the place of children in the past thirty to fifty years of American family life—is NOT advantageous for the child, for parents, or for society.

What I mean is this:

Human beings have always been and always will be oriented to group living. The individual can be comfortable only if he or she comes to value and relate to the needs of others as well as oneself. The Puritan ethic, which regulated American society during its years of existence as a colony and then as an independent country, emphasized subjugation of individual impulses to the requirements of a developing society. The large famiiles of that day supported this point of view, in that each child was required to react and contribute to the welfare of every other child in the family as well as to the parents. Out of this childhood responsibility and social interaction grew adult ways of contributing to the society.

During the decade following World War II, and accelerating thereafter, the family became progressively more child-oriented. Parents, especially mothers, saw children as their most important product. What was happening to society directed what was done in the home. Society was recovering from depression, war, and, perhaps most of all, from a long period of economic development in which what happened to society as a whole was more important than what happened to the individual.

With the surge of improved economic conditions, it became possible for all children to aspire to better things in life than their forebears enjoyed. Many parents saw the possibility of their own increase in status and security through the prowess of their children. The child, indeed, became the center of the family stage.

Society offered parents support and encouragement in concentrating on their children. "Togetherness" became the subject of thousands of articles and lectures after World War II. Millions of dollars were spent developing parent-education courses and programs. Much of this was valuable, but one aspect of the concentration on children is suspect. Children grew up seeing themselves as "center stage." Among the deeper personality processes involved was an emphasis on immediate gratification—a child was encouraged to develop narcissistic concentration on himself.

A natural outgrowth is our current preoccupation with existentialism (concern with individual experience in the immediate present), the development of "growth" movements, and the use of drugs devoted to intensifying the individual's sensory experiences. The popularity of these movements comes from the tendency of persons reared in child-centered families to carry into adulthood the perception of themselves as the natural center of action.

It has also risen out of a trend away from subjugation of the individual to society. This movement must be seen as healthy recognition that human beings need to live comfortably with themselves as individuals as well as interact effectively as members of society. The pendulum has been swinging back from concern with the person as a worker, important mainly for his contributions to society, toward a point where individual human needs are also allowed expression.

Society tends to extremes in overcoming what were seen as disadvantages of the past. When you have the tremendous energies and resources of the American people, a movement can become an avalanche.

The emphasis on self-gratification can be viewed as moving pathologically toward obsession with gratification of immediate impulses that is of doubtful value to the individual or society. Preoccupation with inner experiences has resulted in the prevalence of drugs that seem (to many susceptible and suggestible people) to promise hope for special experiences and emotional growth. The much-needed acceptance of natural sexual impulses, desires, and human interests has expanded to condone individual gratification to the exclusion of the concerns of others ("I am my own best lover").

The insistence on gratification of individual needs has also ignored the effects on society as a whole of tasteless printed and visual material which may not be *calculated* to influence the susceptible young, but cannot help reaching them. It influences their attitudes toward sex and the role of others in gratifying their sexual needs.

The emphasis on expressing one's feelings, especially hostility and aggression, has led to a proliferation of films and TV shows depicting violence in its most primitive aspects. Public acceptance of this material is counter to what thousands of years of civilization have shown us is the need of human beings to protect each other.

Small families of the future could increase this emphasis on self-gratification, as opposed to the needs of other individuals and society, if it were not for other concurrent movements. One of these is the probability that parents will insist upon children serving the needs of all (including parents, who will be further inclined to insist upon this because they were reared under a system which emphasized *their* rights to gratification). Children in these small families may have to participate in the family's work. Outside help is difficult to find, usually fleeting, and expensive. Children who see that they have obvious value to contribute are children who will grow up to feel responsible, whether from large or small families.

Along with the need and approval for women to work ouside the home must come some provision by society for care of the children. They will have opportunities to go into society outside their homes much earlier than they have in the past. In fact, they go into society now without leaving home, through the medium of television. The obvious dilemma for society and those who produce television programs is how to balance free enterprise with the social requirement of presenting material that is informative and beneficial to the millions who watch. This is of such importance for the development of society that it is difficult to speak of it without anxiety. For the moment, it is good to find that some intelligent parents are acting as home censors of television fare for their children.

Community child-care facilities probably will improve and increase. There are already many opportunities for parents to take small children to community music, dance, and swim classes which permit children to interact with others at an early age, and with adults other than their parents. It seems likely that an increasing percentage of infants and very young children will be placed in day-care centers where they will have the same opportunities.

Will birth-order differences disappear under these conditions of more interaction between the family and society at large? Absolutely not, although the effects will change.

Parents are always likely to welcome a first child in a different way from any later child. Mother, father, and child will continue to interact according to Freud's precept: In the struggle to find power and sexual adjustment in the intimate home environment, young and old will interact in the familiar Oedipal conflict. A later child will always find a first with whom to compete and parents to be won. Requirements of living in a family where parents cannot take on all household responsibilities, coupled with early contact with persons outside the home, may make sibling rivalry less intense. Ways of relating to other individuals may be learned earlier and probably more effectively than they are now. But the differences between onlies, firstborns, and laterborns are likely to exist in the future, even though there may be a growing proportion of first and secondborn children in society at large.

THE ONLY CHILD

If the future portends a growing percentage of one-child families, what problems could this bring to adult relationships?

First, brothers and sisters help establish a well-rounded sense of identity for one another. They admire, criticize, and tell one another who they are. In transactional terms, this means that as only children grow up they do not experience with peers the gradual process of developing what we term an *adult within*.

This effect is more severe for a girl than for a boy, apparently because parents protect girls from outside contacts more than they do boys. The girls, as adults, often tell me they *feel* like children.

"But I just don't feel grown up," one said. "I don't feel that I should be accepted as an adult by other people, and I'm surprised when they do accept me that way."

A second psychological hazard is that the single child has no one with whom he or she must compete for the attention and acceptance of parents. The only child is not stimulated to develop skills that will be admired by brothers and sisters; hence, many only children grow to adulthood with little sense of competence and skill. This, again, is more serious for a girl than for a boy, who usually learns to do things as he goes along, partly to please his mother and gain her approval.

A third hazard, paradoxically, is that the only child feels almost *too* secure. A child with brothers and sisters feels, consciously or unconsciously, that if he goes too far in aggravating the parents, they may "throw him out" and keep the others. The only child rarely feels this way. I believe that is why only children sometimes develop extreme anger and bitterly criticize others in their lives such as husbands, wives, or children.

Parents often say of an only child:

"I never was able to do anything with him [or her]."

This suggests that from a very early age the child learned to dominate the parent (especially the mother) who gave up trying to discipline or control. Thus, only children, especially girls, may develop nasty ways of getting what they want, such as tantrums, screaming, striking, scratching, or violent criticism. Only girls have told me:

"If my mother wouldn't give me what I wanted, I would go to my father. If he wouldn't give it to me, I would scream and complain until they finally gave in."

Needless to say, such habits will carry over into adult relationships with husbands and wives. The reason this causes more trouble for girls than for boys seems to be that wives of male only children will accommodate their idiosyncrasies in order to insure security and maintain peace, but husbands of only girls who behave in this manner may simply refuse to continue the marriage.

Another social hazard for only children is that because they are constantly cared for by their parents, they often do not learn to do things for themselves. This again causes more difficulty for girls than for boys, because the things most girls are expected to do for themselves (such as keeping room and clothes neat) are the kind of things they will be expected to do as married adults. Only girls not only evade responsibility for their own things, but are also not urged to develop career ambitions. Such children are often interested in little but loafing. As one woman remarked: "I'm really just a bum at heart."

Male/female equality may cancel out some of these problems in the future, with domestic duties sometimes shared by wife and husband, but one other social implication may be drawn from the increasing number of one-child families. Only children should fit neatly into the accelerating tendency toward single (one-person) residences. Because only children are accustomed to solitude, and less emphasis is being placed on marriage now, they could move into and out of love relationships quickly because of their inability to tolerate the frustration that comes from long, binding relationships.

In dwelling upon the psychological hazards inherent in the single-child family, my purpose has been to show parents where they can head off problems in advance. One thing to do, if you plan to have only one child, is to provide that boy or girl with as many social experiences as possible beginning in the very early years. The need for this may be illustrated by an only male speaking for himself:

"Here I am, age thirty-two, never been married, very few friends. The girls I like don't like me. I get only the dogs. I think I've been afraid all my life to relate to the girls I find attractive. My mother always made sex such a forbidden thing. She criticized any girl I liked, and I couldn't like the girls she recommended for me.

"Mother always said 'I'd be ashamed' about anything I did connected with sex, reading a dirty book or turning to look at a girl.

"At the same time," the man continued, "I saw my

father working his balls off to take care of my mother and me, while she seemed to do nothing. I got the impression that men just work and take responsibility while women get all the good parts of it. So I've always resisted taking responsibility for a girl, because I didn't want to be put in the same position as my father.

"And my mother was always taking care of me. As a result, I was never left without anything I needed or wanted, and I got attention to anything I needed done. I didn't learn how to do a lot of things myself, and I didn't look elsewhere for someone who would take care of some of those things for me.

"I really can't reach out and make friends, even men friends," the only child added, "because they're always doing something that bothers me, and I can't stand that kind of frustration. I didn't have a chance to feel lonely when I was a child, because my mother was always there, breathing over me. Now I feel as though I'm looking on all the time. I don't feel lonely enough to reach out and try to be with people. At the same time, I feel left out of everything.

"I think it would have been so much better if my parents had been separated. Even if I had lived with my mother, I would have been able to have some time with my father. Surely he wouldn't have had to work all the time then as he did to take care of us. Now I'm the only one left to take care of my mother, which she expects me to do financially. Because I don't enjoy being with her and her 'girl friends,' I usually have to spend family days, like holidays, by myself. She didn't give me a brother or sister whom I could visit now and then."

These are the deep complaints of an only child. We might visualize a future world in which a large minority of adults are only children threading their lonely ways through society, never able to form the long-term satisfying relationships they need so vitally. At the same time, this male only child acquires many assets from his family position. He has a high level of self-esteem. He has financial help, care and attention from his mother, and a good economic and educational start in life, because family resources were not spread among many children. His problems center mainly upon establishing intimate relationships. The difficulty is that of finding a person who will give him the undivided attention, esteem, and care that was provided by his mother. These problems may be easily solved or forestalled if parents who plan to have only one child take the necessary steps to help that child develop as a social human being.

THE TWO-CHILD FAMILY

Many couples in the future will have one child. Some will choose none. Some may have three, which promises to become the large family of tomorrow. It is likely, however, that most parents will have two children, wishing to reproduce themselves and hoping their second will be opposite-sexed from the first. Such a trend also may lead to more girl-boy than boy-girl families, because many couples will stop having children if they get a boy on the first try.

The main implication the two-child family holds for society lies in the discrepancy between the two children. If, as we have found, the firstborn emphasizes intellectual achievement and hard work, while the secondborn shuns such development, our future world might be divided between persons having widely different characteristics and interests. The ultimate extrapolation might be a division of the world into two classes, workers and drones. We doubt, however, that this will come to pass. Hopefully, it will be avoided by parents who take care to give both children a full opportunity to develop their abilities, and birth-order information can help to bring this about. Parents who realize the effects of giving more attention and applying achievement pressure to their first child can learn to give the same encouragement to the second. On the other hand, the first child can be helped toward more comfortable social adjustment with a potential for relaxed and happy living.

An important factor is the fact that fewer parents in the future will be burdened with caring for large numbers of children. Many adults are not capable of spreading their love, attention, and economic resources evenly among many children. While future youngsters may lose some advantages gained from sibling interaction, they may gain more from parents who are aware and capable of giving fewer children what they need. This applies especially to girls. With less emphasis upon outmoded and archaic attitudes regarding male superiority, coupled with the prospect of having only one or two children, parents of the future are likely to bestow equal love, esteem, guidance, and attention upon their sons and daughters.

Overall, knowledge of birth-order effects can be of greatest value in helping parents help their children—all of them—achieve their fullest potential. In the long run, you can do the greatest good for your child by helping him or her learn that the greatest mutual benefit will come from peaceful competition. You can encourage your children, and yourself, to move toward cooperation, tolerance, and caring about others—attitudes and skills that will help all of you live comfortably with other people the rest of your lives.

Notes

Introduction

1. Alfred Adler, *What Life Should Mean to You* (New York: Capricorn Books, 1958), p. 154.

Chapter 1   A Place in the Family

1. Sir Francis Galton, *English Men of Science* (London: 1874).
2. Adler, op cit., p. 154.
3. Gertrude Stein, *Everybody's Autobiography* (New York: Vintage Books, 1937), pp. 70–71.
4. Margaret Mead, *Blackberry Winter: My Earlier Years* (New York: William Morrow & Co., 1972), p. 19.

Chapter 2   Why Birth-Order Effects Occur

1. Ashley Montagu, *Life Before Birth* (New York: New American Library, 1964), p. 187.
2. Marlene Cimons, "Program to Reduce Mongolism," *Los Angeles Times,* Part X, Oct. 12, 1974, pp. 1–4.
3. I. S. Wile and Rose Davis, "The Relation of Birth to Behavior," in *Personality in Nature, Society and Culture,* edited by Clyde Kluckhohn and Henry A. Murray (New York: Knopf, 1949).

Chapter 3   Special Circumstances

1. Stein, op. cit., p. 134.
2. Roberta R. Collard, "Social and Play Responses of

Firstborn and Laterborn Infants in an Unfamiliar Situation," *Child Development*, 1968, 39(1), pp. 325–334.

3. Robert Helmreich, Donald Kuiken, and Barry Collins, "Effects of Stress and Birth Order on Attitude Change," *Journal of Personality*, 1968, 36(3), pp. 466–473.

4. J.H.S. Bossard, *The Large Family System, An Original Study in the Sociology of Family Behavior* (Philadelphia: University of Pennsylvania Press, 1956), p. 165.

5. Mead, op. cit., p. 61.

Chapter 5 Personality Patterns: II

1. Harry McGurk and Michael Lewis, "Birth Order: A Phenomenon in Search of an Explanation," *Developmental Psychology*, Nov. 1972, Vol. 7(3), p. 336.

2. *Life* magazine, May 12, 1972, p. 22.

3. Kathleen Norris, *Family Gathering: The Memoirs of Kathleen Norris* (Garden City, N.Y.: Doubleday, 1959), p. 228.

4. Bossard, op. cit., p. 36.

Chapter 6 Achievement

1. Peter Dubno and Richard D. Freedman, "Birth Order, Educational Achievement and Managerial Attainment," *Personnel Psychology*, Vol. 24(1), Spring 1970, pp. 63–70.

2. E. E. Sampson, "Birth Order, Need Achievement and Conformity," *Journal of Abnormal Psychology*, 64(2), 1962, pp. 155–159.

3. E. E. Sampson and Francena T. Hancock, "An Examination of the Relationship Between Ordinal Position, Personality and Conformity," *Journal of Personal and Social Psychology*, 5(4), 1967, pp. 398–407.

4. Bernard Baruch, *My Own Story* (New York: Henry Holt & Co., 1957), p. viii.

Chapter 7 Vocations and Creativity

1. Mark I. Oberlander, Kenneth J. Frauenfelder, and Helen Heath, "The Relationship of Ordinal Position and

Sex to Interest Patterns," *Journal of Genetic Psychology*, Vol. 119(1), Sept. 1971, pp. 29–36.

2. Lucille K. Forer, *Birth Order and Life Roles* (Springfield, Ill.: Charles C Thomas, 1969), p. 8.

3. Alfred Adler, "Reflections: Mathematics and Creativity," *The New Yorker*, Feb. 19, 1972, pp. 39–45.

4. William D. Altus, "Birth Order and Its Sequelae," *Science*, Vol. 151, January 1966, pp. 44–48.

5. William D. Bliss, "Birth Order and Creative Writers," *Journal of Individual Psychology*, Vol. 26, Nov. 1970, pp. 200–202.

6. Altus, op. cit.

7. Brian Sutton-Smith, John M. Roberts, and B. G. Rosenberg, "The Dramatic Sibling," *Perceptual and Motor Skills*, 22(3), 1966, pp. 993–994.

8. Edward H. Fischer, Carl F. Wells, and Stanley L. Cohen, "Birth Order and Expressed Interest in Becoming a College Professor," *Journal of Counseling Psychology*, 15(2), 1968, pp. 111–116.

9. Sutton-Smith et al., op. cit.

10. James M. Herrell, "Birth Order and the Military: A Review from the Adlerian Perspective," *Journal of Individual Psychology*, Vol. 28(1), May 1972, pp. 38–44.

11. Roger F. Reinhardt, "The Outstanding Jet Pilot," *American Journal of Psychiatry*, Vol. 127(6), Dec. 1970, pp. 732–736.

12. Henry Still and Betty Grissom, *Starfall* (New York: Thomas Y. Crowell Co., 1974), pp. 1–46.

Chapter 8   Women Who Achieve

1. Altus, op. cit.

2. *Life* magazine, "The Furious Young Philosopher," Feb. 7, 1972, p. 22.

3. Rhona and Robert N. Rapoport, "Early and Later Experiences as Determinants of Adult Behavior, Married Women's Family and Career Patterns," *British Journal of Sociology*, Vol. 22(1), March 1971, pp. 16–30.

4. Philip S. Very, Robert B. Goldblatt, and Vincent Monacelli, "Birth Order Personality Development and Vocational Choice of Becoming a Carmelite Nun," *Journal of Psychology*, 1973, Vol. 85, pp. 75–80.

5. Ravenna Helson, "Effects of Sibling Characteristics and Parental Values on Creative Interest and Achievement," *Journal of Personality*, Vol. 36(4), Dec. 1968, pp. 589–607.

6. *Los Angeles Times*, Oct. 5, 1970, p. 5.

7. *Los Angeles Times*, Aug. 28, 1972, p. 10.

8. Ann Fischer, "The Importance of Sibling Position in the Choice of a Career in Pediatric Nursing," *Journal of Health and Human Behavior*, Vol. 3(4), 1962, pp. 283–288.

9. Katherine K. and Richard E. Gordon, "Birth Order, Achievement and Blood Chemistry Levels Among College Nursing Students," *Nursing Research*, Vol. 16(3), 1967, pp. 234–236.

Chapter 9 Power and Politics

1. Louis Stewart, "The Politics of Birth Order," Part I, *Proceedings of the Annual Convention of the American Psychological Association*, Vol. 5, 1970, pp. 365–366.

2. Rita Dallas with Jeanira Ratcliffe, *The Kennedy Case* (New York: Popular Library, 1974), pp. 64, 122, 139.

3. Irving D. Harris, *The Promised Seed* (London: The Free Press of Glencoe, Collier-Macmillan Ltd., 1964), p. 30.

4. *Newsweek* magazine, Jan. 8, 1973, p. 17.

5. *Reader's Digest*, Dec. 1972, pp. 226–262.

6. "Fragments for a Future Nixon Biographer," Part II, *Los Angeles Times*, August 8, 1974, p. 5.

7. Winthrop Griffith, *Humphrey: A Candid Biography* (New York: William Morrow & Co., 1965), pp. 81, 82, 104.

8. Baruch, op. cit., pp. 25–66.

9. *How to Say a Few Words*, April 1971, No. 186, p. 1.

10. Georgia Babladelis, "Birth Order and Responsiveness to Social Influence," *Psychological Reports*, Vol. 30(1), Feb. 1972, pp. 99–104.

11. Gordon B. Forbes, "Birth Order of Political Success: A Study of the 1970 Illinois General Election," *Psychological Reports*, Vol. 29, 1971, pp. 1239–1242.

12. *Life* magazine, Sept 11, 1970, pp. 21–24.

Chapter 10   The Social Network

1. John M. Innes and Jean E. Sambrook, "Paired Associate Learning as Influenced by Birth Order and the Presence of Others," *Psychonomic Science*, Vol. 16(2), 1969, pp. 109–110.

2. L. S. Wrightsman, Jr., "Effects of Waiting with Others on Changes in Level of Felt Anxiety," *Journal of Abnormal Social Psychology*, Vol. 61, 1960, pp. 216–222.

3. Martin S. Greenberg, "Role Playing: An Alternative to Deception?" Part 1, *Journal of Personality and Social Psychology*, Vol. 7(2), 1967, pp. 152–157.

4. Michael F. Hoyt and Bertram H. Raven, "Birth Order and the 1971 Los Angeles Earthquake," *Journal of Personality and Social Psychology*, Vol. 28(1), 1973, pp. 123–128.

5. D.J.W. Strumpfer, "Fear and Affiliation During a Disaster," *Journal of Social Psychology*, Vol. 83, 1970, pp. 263–268.

6. J. R. Warren, "The Effects of Certain Selection Procedures in Forming a Group of Honors Students," *Special Report #8* (University of Nebraska Agricultural Experiment Station, 1966).

7. Joseph C. LaVoie, "Individual Differences in Resistance to Temptation Behavior in Adolescents," *Journal of Clinical Psychology*, Vol. 29(1), Jan. 1973, pp. 20–22.

8. *Los Angeles Times*, Aug. 8, 1973, p. 5.

9. Paul Wohlford and Marshall R. Jones, "Ordinal Position, Age, Anxiety and Defensiveness in Unwed Mothers," *Proceedings of the 75th Annual Convention of the American Psychological Association*, Vol. 2, 1967, pp. 177–178.

10. Richard E. Dimond and David C. Munz, "Ordinal Position and Self-Disclosure in High School Students," *Psychological Reports*, Vol. 21(3), 1967, pp. 829–833.

Chapter 11   Developing Sex Roles

1. Margaret Mead, *Male and Female* (New York: William Morrow & Co., 1949), p. 8.

2. William D. Altus, "Sex Role Dissatisfaction, Birth Order and Parental Favoritism," *Proceedings of the An-*

nual Convention of the American Psychological Association, Vol. 6(1), 1971, pp. 161–162.

3. Helen L. Koch, "Some Emotional Attitudes of the Young Child in Relation to Characteristics of His Sibling," *Child Development,* Vol. 27, 1956, pp. 393–426.

4. Frank H. Farley, Robert Hatch, Patrick Murphy, and Kenneth Miller, "Sibling Structure and Masculinity-Femininity in Male Adolescents," *Adolescence,* Vol. 6(24), 1971, pp. 441–450.

5. Dr. Bertram Forer in an unpublished paper, "Family Etiology of Sexual Disorders."

Chapter 12   Sexual Adequacy

1. Michael H. Kahn, Alvin R. Mahrer, and Robert Bernstein, "Male Psychosexual Development: Role of Sibling Sex and Ordinal Position," *Proceedings of the Annual Convention of the American Psychological Association,* Vol. 5(1), 1970, pp. 267–268.

2. Jan Raboch and V. Bartak, "A Contribution to the Study of Anesthetic-Frigid Syndrome in Women," *Ceskoslovenska Psychiatrie,* Vol. 64(4), 1968, pp. 230–235.

3. E. Mavis Hetherington, "Effects of Father Absence on Personality Development of Adolescent Daughters," *Developmental Psychology,* Vol. 7(3), Nov. 1972, pp. 313–326.

4. Paul Gebhard, Jan Raboch, and Hans Giese, *The Sexuality of Women,* Vol. 1 (New York: Stein & Day, 1970), p. 36.

5. Vincent Sheean, *Dorothy and Red* (Boston: Houghton Mifflin, 1963), p. 220.

Chapter 13   Marriage

1. William D. Altus, "Marriage and Order of Birth," *Proceedings of the Annual Convention of the American Psychological Association,* Vol. 5(1), 1970, pp. 361–362.

2. Walter Toman, "Large Age Differences Among Spouses and Their Family Constellation," *Psychological Reports,* Vol. 13, 1963, p. 386.

3. Peter H. Murdock, "Birth Order and Age at Mar-

riage," *British Journal of Social and Clinical Psychology*, Vol. 5(1), 1966, pp. 24–29.

4. A. P. MacDonald, Jr., "Birth Order Effects in Marriage and Parenthood: Affiliation and Socialization," *Journal of Marriage and the Family*, Vol. 29(4), 1967, pp. 656–661.

5. Theodore D. Kemper, "Mate Selection and Marital Satisfaction According to Sibling Type of Husband and Wife," *Journal of Marriage and the Family*, Aug. 1966, pp. 346–349.

6. Yi Chuang-lu, "Predicting Roles in Images," *American Journal of Sociology*, Vol. 58, 1952, pp. 51–55.

7. Everette Hall, "Ordinal Position and Success in Engagement and Marriage," *Journal of Individual Psychology*, Vol. 21(2), 1965, pp. 154–158.

Chapter 15   Parenthood: II

1. Brian Sutton-Smith and B. G. Rosenberg, "Sibling Consensus on Power Tactics," *Journal of Genetic Psychology*, Vol. 112(1), 1968, pp. 63–72.

Chapter 17   Which Birth Position Is Best?

1. Bossard, op. cit.

Chapter 18   Implications for the Future

1. Lester Brown, "Alternatives to Childbearing," *Saturday Review/World*, July 27, 1974, p. 47; excerpted from Lester Brown, *In the Human Interest* (New York: W. W. Norton & Co., 1974).

2. *Los Angeles Times*, April 19, 1974, p. 4.

3. *Los Angeles Times*, June 18, 1974, p. 10.

Bibliography

Historically, more than a thousand statistical studies have been reported linking birth order with various aspects of human behavior and personality. During the past fifteen years I have methodically collected and correlated the data gleaned from all studies available to me from throughout the world.

As may be true with any major psychological concept, it is impossible to reach unanimity of opinion. Papers and books, representing many thousands of hours of original research, contains negative as well as positive findings regarding the existence of birth-order effects. Similarly, we find both agreement and disagreement concerning which personality characteristics are vulnerable to birth order. However, the preponderance of evidence *does* support birth-order effects. This book considers only those areas in which a reasonable consensus exists *and* which are supported by my own clinical experience.

My primary thrust is integration of statistical and clinical research. The two methods are different but mutually supportive. Statistical studies reveal trends in large numbers of people, but the findings may not apply to any particular individual. At the opposite pole, clinical observation determines whether or not general findings or hypotheses pertain to a specific person. The results are as accurate as the perception of the observer. Conclusions which I have reached regarding birth order are firmly rooted in my own experience, supported by the independent research studies of hundreds of other people.

Many of these are noted by specific references, but I would like to give special credit to some which have shaped my ideas and presented evidence which is most pertinent and valuable. It is not possible to list the hundreds of researchers who have made valuable contributions, but the following are outstanding.

Anyone studying birth-order effects must give the most credit to Dr. Alfred Adler, friend, student, and later competitor of Dr. Sigmund Freud. Adler is generally conceded to be the father of research in birth-order effects on personality development. It seemed to him that the sibling relationships of men and women served an important function in determining their life styles. (Adler, so far as I know, was also the first person to use the term "life style"—a term now used rather freely.) Adler supplied me with several basic hypotheses about the influence of birth order. Like mine, his approach was clinical. His book *What Life Should Mean to You* (New York: Capricorn, 1958) is lucid and enlightening.

From 1955 to 1960 many reports were published by Dr. Helen L. Koch, now professor emeritus at the University of Chicago. In comparative studies of first- and secondborn children in two-child families, she presented fine statistical analyses of many traits differentiating firstborn from secondborn children. As she once commented when asked to summarize one of her studies for a journal:

"The findings are far too complicated to be described briefly."

Dr. Koch's studies were a rich source of information and theory for my own observations and study.

Although I do not agree with what seems to be an excessively rigid evaluation of birth-order effects presented by Dr. Walter Toman, I must accord him the respect due another psychologist who assigns birth-order effects great importance in personality development. Dr. Toman was associate professor of psychology at Brandeis University when his book *Family Constellation* (New York: Springer) was published in 1961.

A provocative presentation of differences in intellectual approach between first- and laterborn men is that by Irving D. Harris, M.D. His book *The Promised Seed: A Comparative Study of Eminent Firstborn and Later Sons* (New York: Macmillan Co., Free Press, 1964) is a rich source of information about birth-order effects on the thinking and behavior of outstanding men throughout history.

My first book, *Birth Order and Life Roles* (Springfield, Ill.: Charles C Thomas, 1969), was an organization and integration of research results as reported up to that time. I am pleased to note that many of the hypotheses which I developed in that book have been followed up by research studies.

Another major study was published in 1971 by Ezra Stotland, Stanley E. Sherman, and Kelly G. Shaver at the University of Nebraska in Lincoln. These investigators explored differences in empathy between first- and later-born children, and identified differences related both to birth position and to sex of subjects.

At the University of California in Santa Barbara, William D. Altus has explored many differences between first-and laterborn children. His article in *Science Magazine* (Vol. 151, 1965, pp. 44–49) is one of the clearest summaries of birth-order research results that has ever been written.

Published in 1956 were the results of investigations of families of six or more children, conducted by J.H.S. Bossard. One of his books is *The Large Family System: An Original Study in the Sociology of Family Behavior* (Philadelphia: University of Pennsylvania Press, 1956). This is a valuable source of information about persons coming from large families. His conceptualization of how each sibling in a large family develops a specialized role in relation to the roles already established by earlier siblings would interest any student of personality, and certainly members of large families.

Russell Eisenman of Temple University has published a number of studies on birth order and creativity, as well as esthetic preferences of individuals according to birth order.

The study of Joan K. Lasko on parent behavior toward firstborn and secondborn children (*Genetic Psychology Monographs*, Vol. 49, 1954, pp. 97–137) helped to confirm clinically observed differences between the way parents handle their first as opposed to later children.

A. P. MacDonald of West Virginia University has published a number of papers on such matters as religious affiliation, marriage, parenthood, interest in social affiliation or isolation, morality types, and attitudes toward the poor as related to birth-order effects.

An important early study was that of C. MacArthur, who published an article, "Personalities of First and Second Children" (*Psychiatry*, Vol. 19, 1956, pp. 47–54).

This is an interesting longitudinal study of birth-order effects in which observations by parents of Harvard College sophomores are related to behavior of the students.

Another influential study was carried out by Margaret B. McFarland and published in a monograph titled *Relationships between Young Sisters as Revealed in Their Overt Responses* (New York: New York Teachers College, Columbia University, 1938). Like the author of this book, Ms. McFarland concluded that rivalry is probably a part of all such relationships, and should not be a matter of concern unless it becomes exaggerated.

Good material on interest patterns and preference for ideas or social activities was published by Mark I. Oberlander of the Institute for Juvenile Research, Chicago. Excellent material on the sexuality of women was produced by Professor Jan Raboch, doctor of science at Charles University in Prague, Czechoslovakia.

Anne Roe's study of eminent scientists (*The Making of Scientist*. New York: Dodd, Mead & Co., 1953) is a model of careful social research interestingly presented, as well as a source of information about birth-order effects among eminent scientists.

A more recent book by Brian Sutton-Smith and B. G. Rosenberg, *The Sibling* (New York: Holt, Rinehart & Winston, 1971), is an excellent source of information on many of the differences between first- and laterborns. It has offered academic support to hypotheses I developed earlier on the basis of clinical experience.

The study of Marcel T. Saghir, M.D., *Male and Female Homosexuality* (Baltimore: Williams & Wilkins Co., 1973), was a rich source of information about family positions of homosexual men and women. Another valuable source on female homosexuality was that of Charlotte Wolff, M.D., *Love Between Women* (New York: Harper & Row, 1971).

The cited studies have been among the most comprehensive ones in my explorations of birth-order effects.

Index

Abortion, 186, 238
Achievement, 60-72, 129, 142, 145
  actual level of, 63
  of blacks, 110-11
  case studies of, 64-65, 67-68, 70-72, 126-27
  effect on marriage, 173, 175, 177-78, 180, 181, 182, 183
  firstborn, 60-61, 62, 63-64, 65-66, 82-83, 109, 126-27, 193, 239-40, 248
  later-middle children, 218, 219
  middleborn children, 67-69
  motivation for, 61-62
  only child, 63-65, 67
  second children, 67-69, 211, 214
  women, 87-99
  youngest child, 69-72, 219, 221
Actresses, 78

Adams, John, 103
Adams, John Quincy, 11, 103, 108
Adenauer, Konrad, 105
Adler, Alfred, 6-8, 77, 136, 145, 231
Adolescence, 22, 27-28, 88, 92, 97, 125, 138, 141, 148, 158, 209, 212, 222, 233-34
Adopted children, 31-35
Aggression, 44-45, 47, 50, 51, 55, 170, 176-77, 203
  emphasis on, 243
  of older sister of a brother, 208
  of second child, 210-11, 214
  of second child followed by others, 214-15, 216
Alcohol and alcoholics, 94, 175, 177, 221, 222
Altus, Dr. William D., 92-93, 141, 166
American Indians, 239

Anger, 83, 85, 100, 124, 129, 131, 140-41, 170, 178, 179, 203, 209, 215, 245
Anthony, Susan B., 11, 110
Anthropologists, 12
Anxiety, 120, 126-27, 145, 179, 193-94, 222
  as cause of sexual failure, 155, 156, 157
  of first child, 207, 209
  of having first baby, 201-03
  of separation, 202
Approval, need for, 116, 119, 145
Architects, 77
Artists, 75-76, 77, 78, 88
Assembly-line operators, 78
Assertiveness, 36, 44-45, 48-49, 208
Astor, Mary, 9, 78
Astronauts, firstborns as, 9, 80, 82
Athletics, 80

Baez, Joan, 11, 52, 110
Baruch, Bernard, 11, 68, 108
Beauty-shop operators, 97
Bernstein, Leonard, 11
Bible, 35
Birth Order and Life Roles (Forer), 46
Birth rate, 236
Birth-control techniques, 186, 238
Birth-order effects, achievement, 60-72
  best birth-order position, 231-34
  implications for the future, 236-49
  major patterns of, 3-14
  on marriage, 165-85
  in parenthood, 186-224

and personality patterns, 39-59
  reasons for, 15-25
  and sex-role development, 133-50
  on sexual adequacy, 151-62
  on social development, 115-32
  special circumstances in, 26-36
  using information from, 227-30
  in work, 75-111
Blacks, 110-11, 239
Bliss, William D., 77-78
Bossard, Dr. J. H. S., 28, 232-33, 238-41
Boy Scouts, 14
Brandeis University, 166
Brezhnev, Leonid, 105, 108, 178
Brontë, Charlotte, 11
Brown, Lester, 236
Buddha, 105
Bunche, Ralph T., 111
Business executives, women as, 88, 90

"Caboose baby," 28
California State University at Hayward, 109
Careers, *see* Vocations and creativity
Case Western Reserve University, 96-97
Chaplin, Charlie, 11
Chemists, 77
Chicanos, 111, 239
Child-care facilities, 244
Children, desire for, 188-90
Chromosomes, 16
Churchill, Jennie, 11, 78

Churchill, Winston, 104, 106

City University of New York, 240

Columbia University, 93

Communism, 111

Compatibility in marriage, 169-85
  least preferred, 170-71
  most preferred, 169
  paired by birth order, 172-85
  study of success and failure (1965), 171-72

Competitiveness, 10, 23, 36, 51, 125, 126, 128, 182, 213, 214-15, 217
  in families, 54, 249

Confidence, 219, 222

Conformity, 116, 122, 145

Cooperation, lack of, 6

Cornell University, 168

Crawford, Joan, 11, 78

Creativity, *see* Vocations and creativity

Da Vinci, Leonardo, 9

Dallas, Rita, 104

Davis, Angela, 11, 111

Davis, Sammy, Jr., 9

Day camps, 192

Day-care centers, 244

De Gaulle, Charles, 104

Death, 221

Defensiveness, 127

Dependency, 119, 120, 211
  of youngest child, 220-21

Depression of the 1930s, 233, 242

Disability, 29-30

Discipline, 8, 19, 22, 41, 42, 101, 192, 193, 199, 211, 222, 224, 238, 245

Disraeli, Benjamin, 11, 108

Divorce, 160, 168, 175, 176, 178, 179, 180, 181, 183, 184, 206, 217, 221
  study of (1965), 171-72

Dominance, 101-02, 188, 197, 206
  in marriage, 180, 182, 183, 184, 185
  by older children, 212-13, 214, 215-16, 219, 221

Down's syndrome, 16-17

Drugs, sensory, 243

East-West Population Center (Honolulu), 240

Education, cost of, 237

Einstein, Albert, 9

Eisenhower, Dwight, 11, 108

Engineering, 77

Ejaculation, premature, 154, 156, 157

Ethics, 122-23

Existentialism, 242

Extramarital sex, 134, 155, 168, 173-74, 230

Factors in birth-order effects, 15-25
  before birth, 16-17
  family power struggle, 22-25
  modeling and punishment, 25
  parental attitudes, 17-20
  patterns of need, 20-22

Fads, 7

Family power struggle, 22-25

Family size, future of, 236-49
  large-size family values and, 238
  with only child, 244-48

Family size, future of (*cont.*)
  small-size family values
    and, 239-44
  with two children, 248-49
Farley, Frank H., 127
Fawcett, James T., 240
Fear test, 127
Firstborn children
  achievement and, 60-61, 62,
    63-64, 65-67, 82-83, 109,
    126-27, 193, 239-40, 248
  anxiety in, 207, 209
  as astronauts, 9, 80, 82
  as brother with younger sis-
    ter, 210
  effect on women's achieve-
    ment, 99
  major patterns of, 9-10
  in marriage, 174-76, 178-80
  as older brother of a boy,
    208-09
  as older girl of two, 207-08
  as older sister of a brother,
    208
  only child as, 206-07
  parents' anxiety about, 201-
    03
  personality patterns, 41-46
  qualities as parents, 193,
    197-200
  role of parents of, 65-66,
    206-09
  self-esteem in, 209, 230,
    232, 234
  sex-role development, 138-
    39
  social development of, 43,
    121, 126-27
  vocations and creativity, 75-
    76, 77, 78-80, 81-83, 85-
    86
Fonda, Jane, 11, 78
Forbes, Gordon B., 109

Ford, Gerald, 107n.
Ford, Henry, 11, 106
Forer, Dr. Bertram, 147, 155
Franklin, Benjamin, 11, 108
Frauenfelder, Dr. Kenneth J.,
  76
Freud, Anna, 11
Freud, Sigmund, 4, 31, 52, 244
Future, implications for, 236-
  49
  large-family values and, 238
  of only-child families, 244-
    48
  small-family values and,
    239-44
  of two-child families, 248-
    49

Gallup Poll, 238
Galton, Sir Francis, 5, 6, 60
Gamov, George, 9
Gandhi, Indira, 9, 105
Gender
  effect on personality devel-
    opment, 43-46
  in predicting birth-order ef-
    fects, 12-14
Generation gap, 116
Genes, 16-17
Grissom, Virgil I. (Gus), 82
Guilt, 222
  sexual, 53, 159-60, 167

Hamilton, Alexander, 11, 106
Harris, Dr. Irving D., 105
Heath, Dr. Helen, 76
Hepburn, Katharine, 11
Hetherington, Mavis, 158
Hitler, Adolf, 104
Homosexuality, 40, 99, 137,
    143, 146-50, 154, 155-56,
    161, 205-06
  case studies of, 147-49

patterns in, 149-50
theories about causes of, 146-47
Hoover, Herbert, 11, 108
Hostility, 196, 209
Hoyt, Michael F., 120
Humphrey, Hubert, 11, 106, 107-08

Identity, search for, 128-29
Illness, case studies of, 29-30
Impotence, 156, 157, 173
Indiana State University, 127
Institute of Juvenile Research (Chicago), 76
Intelligence quotient (I.Q.), 214

Jaffe, Dr. Cabot L., 109
Jealousy, 9, 10, 13, 18, 43, 53, 192, 205, 206, 208, 222
John XXIII, Pope, 106
Johnson, Lyndon, 11, 105
Johnson, Mrs. Lyndon, 11, 108
Joiners, 121, 122

Kemper, Dr. Theodore D., 169-70
Kennedy, Edward, 11, 103-04
Kennedy, John F., 11, 103, 104
Kennedy, Joseph, 103, 104
Kennedy, Joseph, Jr., 103
Kennedy, Robert, 11, 103, 108
Kennedy, Rose, 11
Kennedy Case, The (Dallas), 104
Kennedy family, 103-04, 108
Khrushchev, Nikita, 105
Koch, Dr. Helen, 141

Large-family values, 238

Lastborn, *see* Youngest child
Later-middle children:
achievement by, 217, 218
in athletics, 80
domination by, 102
in marriage, 177-78, 180, 181-82, 182-83, 185
personality patterns, 54-55
qualities as parents, 195-96, 197-200
role of parents of, 217-19
sex-role development of, 143-45
social development of, 121, 122, 129-30
suggestions for parents in raising, 219
vocations and creativity, 77-78, 78-79, 80, 83-84
Law, firstborn in, 79
Lesbians, 40, 146, 147, 149-50, 167
case study of, 147-48
Lewis, Sinclair, 159
Life, style of, 7-8
Lindbergh, Charles, 9
Little League baseball, 14, 133
Loneliness, 9, 28, 39, 123, 124, 175, 178
in lastborn, 70, 71
of only child, 247
Losing and winning, traits for, 109-10
Love attitudes, development of, 160-62
Lying, 216

McCaghy, Charles H., 96
McCormick, Susan, 110
MacDonald, A. P., Jr., 168-69
Macmillan, Harold, 104
Mailer, Norman, 11

Marie Antoinette, Queen, 108

Marijuana, 177

Marriage, 9, 134, 165-85
  age at time of, 168-69
  case studies of, 165-66, 170-71, 172-80
  compatibility in, 169-85
  of only child, 245-46
  power in, 169-70
  study of success and failure in (1965), 171-72

Marriage counseling, 170-71

Martin, Glenn L., 64

Mary, Queen of Scots, 105

Masturbation, 153, 154, 156, 158, 204

Mathematicians, 77, 79

Mead, Dick, 12-13

Mead, Margaret, 12-13, 30, 135

Mealiea, Wallace L., 127

Medicine, career in, 79

Mental depression, 43, 52, 58-59, 178, 217, 218-19, 221, 229-30

Mental retardation, 16-17, 30

Middle children
  achievement in, 67-69
  as boy between two sisters, 215-16
  effect on women's achievement, 99
  major patterns in, 11
  personality patterns, 51-53
  as second of four children, 216-17
  sex-role development of, 142-44
  social development of, 128-29
  of three girls, 216
  See also Later-middle children

Military services, 79-80

Millet, Kate, 52, 93-94

Milliken University, 109

Mills College, 95

Modeling, 25, 40, 57, 88, 95, 100-01, 115-16, 157

Mongolism, 16-17

Monroe, Marilyn, 78

Morality, 116, 122-23, 145, 148, 193, 230

Motivation for achievement, 61-62

Multiple births, case studies of, 35-36

Murdoch, Dr. Peter H., 168

Musicians, 78

Mussolini, Benito, 104

Narcissism, 242

Need, patterns of, 20-22

Nightmares, 205

Nixon, Donald, 106, 107

Nixon, Edward, 106, 107

Nixon, Harold, 106

Nixon, Richard, 11, 30, 69, 103, 104, 106-07

Nixon, Mrs. Richard, 108

Norris, Kathleen, 52

Novelists, laterborns as, 77

Nursery schools, 192, 204

Nursing, careers in, 78, 97

Oberlander, Dr. Mark I., 76

Oedipal conflict, 124, 136, 204-05, 244

Oldest child, *see* Firstborn children

Only child
  achievement and, 63-65, 66
  effect on women's achievement, 99
  first child as, 206-07

growing percentage of, 244-48

loneliness of, 246

major patterns in, 9

in marriage, 172-79, 246

parenthood qualities of, 190-93, 197-200

personality patterns, 40-41

role of parents of, 203-06

self-esteem of, 41, 203, 247

sex-role development of, 138-39, 203

social development of, 121, 123-26

vocations and creativity, 78-79, 83

Orgasm, achieving, 154, 155, 158, 173, 174

Oxford University, 94

Pacifiers, 223

Pairing parents, 197-200

Paramedics, 218

Parenthood, 4-5, 186-224

by adoption, 31-35

as birth-order factor, 17-20

case studies of, 187-88, 190-91 194-95, 196, 204, 205, 206, 209, 210, 211, 212, 213-14, 215-19, 219-20, 221, 223

desire for children, 188-90

of firstborn, 65-66, 201-03, 206-10

general recommendations, 222-24

of later-middle children, 217-19

of only child, 203-06

pairing parents, 197-200

pyramid effect in, 187-88

quality of, by birth order, 190-96

of second child, 210-14

of second child followed by others, 214-17

of youngest child, 219-22

Parker, Bonnie, 52

Patterns, birth order, 3-14

first child followed by others, 9-11

formation of life-style and, 7-8

history of study of, 5-7

importance of gender in, 12-14

major, 8

middle children, 11

only child, 9

and parental behavior, 4-5

second child, 11

youngest child, 11-12

Patterns in sex-role development, 138-45

Peer pressure, 116, 123, 124, 126-27

Penis, 152, 154, 156

Personality patterns, 39-59, 223-24, 227

case studies of, 39-40, 42, 43-46, 48-49, 50-51, 53, 56-59

firstborn, 41-46

later-middle children, 54-55

middle child, 51-53

only child, 40-41

second of two children, 47-51

youngest child, 55-59

Phi Beta Kappa, 94

Physics, careers in, 77

Picasso, Pablo, 11

Poets, laterborns as, 77

Politics, *see* Power and politics

Pompidou, Madame, 178

Population control, 187

Power and politics, 100-11
case studies about, 100-01
political leadership, 102-08
in times of social change, 110-11
winning and losing traits for, 109-10
Power struggle, family, 22-25
Preadolescence, 209, 213
Pregnancy, 15, 17, 45
Premarital sex, 134, 158, 168
Primogeniture, 5, 6
Professors, firstborns as, 78
Prostitution, 96
Psychology, career in, 79
Puberty, 142, 144, 210
Punishment, 41, 42, 85, 211, 218, 223
as birth-order factor, 25
corporal, 207
Puritan work ethic, 232, 241
Pyramid effect, in parenthood, 187-88

Raven, Bertram H., 120
Rebellion, 48, 93, 101, 124, 196, 209, 211, 216, 221
Rejection, 28, 140, 215, 218, 220
Religious vocations, 95
Renay, Liz, 97
Responsibility, acceptance of, 56
Richmond College, 240
Riles, Wilson C., 111
Rivalry, 6, 18-19, 23-24, 34, 206
Roman Catholic Church, 106
Roosevelt, Franklin D., 9, 104
Roosevelt, Mrs. Franklin D., 105
Roosevelt, Theodore, 11, 108
Russo, Nancy, 240

Salesman, career as, 80
San Francisco State College, 103, 104
Scientists, firstborns as, 76-77, 79
Second child
achievement in, 67-69, 210, 214
aggression in, 210-11, 214, 215, 216
followed by others, 214-17
major patterns of, 11
in marriage, 176, 179, 180-85
personality patterns, 47-51
qualities as parents, 194-95, 197, 198-99, 200
role of parents of, 210-14
self-esteem in, 48, 68, 93, 213
sex-role development of, 139-42, 211
social development of, 121-22
suggestions for parents of, 214
of two boys, 213-14
work relationships, 84
as younger brother of a sister, 48, 212-13
as younger sister of a brother, 92-93, 212
as younger of two girls, 211
See also Middle children
Secretaries and stenographers, careers as, 80, 94, 217
Self-confidence, 127, 209, 212
Self-esteem, 36, 55, 145, 192, 218, 222
of first child, 209, 230, 232, 234
in marriage, 177-81, 184

of mother with first child, 201-02

of only child, 41, 203, 247

in second child, 48, 68, 92-93, 213

social development and, 116-19

in twins, 36

of women, 117-18, 145

in youngest child, 56, 69, 219

Self-sufficiency, 116, 119-20

Sex play, childhood, 160, 161

Sex-role development, 7, 25, 40, 48, 115, 133-50, 192

case studies of, 13-14, 136-37, 139-41, 142-43, 144

effects of tasteless printed material on, 243

firstborn, 138

guilt in, 53

homosexuality, 40, 99, 137, 143, 146-50, 154, 155-56, 161, 205

identifying with older siblings, 25

of later-middle children, 143-45

of middle child, 142-44

of only child, 138-39, 203

patterns in, 138-45

role formation, 135-38

of second child, 139-42, 211, 214

Sexual adequacy, 151-62

case studies of, 151-53, 155, 156-57, 159-60, 161

emphasis on, 153-54

female conflicts about, 157-58

guilt feelings and, 159-60, 167

love attitudes and, 160-62

patterns in, 155-57

seeking partners, 158-60

Sexual Politics (Millet), 52, 93

Sills, Beverly, 12

Single-child family, 244-48

case study of, 246-47

Skipper, James K., Jr., 96

Small-family values, 239-44

Social development, 115-32

case studies of, 117-19, 124-25, 126-27, 128-29, 129-30, 131-32

of firstborns, 43, 121, 125-27

of later-middle children, 122, 129-30

of middle child, 128-29

need for approval, 116, 119, 145

of only child, 121, 122-26

of second children, 121-22

self-esteem in, 116-19

of self-sufficiency, 116, 119-20

of sociability, 116, 120-22

of youngest child, 122, 131-32

Social justice, 110-11

Sociologists, 12-13, 228, 239

Sons, favoring of, 5

Spacing between siblings, 26-29, 54, 57-58

case study of, 27-28

Speech impediment, 193, 213-14

Stalin, Joseph, 104

Stanford University, 238

Stein, Gertrude, 12, 26-27

Stein, Leo, 12

Steinem, Gloria, 11

Stepchildren, 31, 33, 34, 107n., 206

Striptease performers, 96-97
Stubbornness, 216
Style of life, 7-8
Suffrage, women, 6
Suicide, 229-30
Summer camp, 215, 221
Sweet, James A., 239

Talk, learning to, 193, 203
Talkativeness, 109
Tantrums, 57, 245
Teaching careers, 76, 78, 79
Television, 204, 221, 240, 243-44
Temper, 100-01, 170, 171
Thompson, Dorothy, 159
Toastmasters' Club, 130
Toilet training, 203, 223
Toklas, Alice B., 12, 26-27
Toman, Dr. Walter, 166-67
Truman, Harry, 11, 105
Twins, case studies of, 35-36
Two-child family, 248-49
Typists, women as, 94

U.S. Army, 79
U.S. Navy, 79
U.S. State Department, 111
University of California at Los Angeles, 120
University of California in Santa Barbara, 92, 141, 166
University of Chicago, 141
University of Michigan, 240
University of Minnesota, 94
University of Montana, 77
Univeristy of Nebraska, 122
Universtiy of South Carolina, 168
University of Tennessee, 109
University of Virginia, 158

University of Wisconsin, 127, 169, 239

Values, parental, 223-24
Veterans' Administration, 70
Vietnam War, 105, 110
Violence, television, 243
Vocations and creativity, 75-86
  case studies of, 75-76, 81-82, 84-86
  choosing a vocation, 76-81
  work relationships, 81-86
  See also Women

Waiters and waitresses, careers as, 80
Walters, Barbara, 11, 78
Warner Brothers, 97
Washington, George, 11, 31, 105-06
Whittier College, 106
Wilde, Oscar, 9
Wilson, Woodrow, 11, 108
Windsor, Duchess of, 105
Winning and losing, traits of, 109-10
Women
  case studies of efforts to achieve, 87, 88-91, 93-94, 96, 98-99
  conflicts about sexual adequacy, 157-58
  conventional occupations for, 87-88, 97-99
  fighting the established order, 92-94
  higher education for, 5
  motivation to achieve, 62, 87-99
  patterns of work, 94-95

self-esteem of, 117-18, 145
society's pressures on, 95-97
suffrage, 6
working outside the home,
   238, 239, 241, 243
Women's movement, 12, 52,
   61, 64-65, 87-88, 90, 92-
   94, 236
Work relationships, 81-86
   firstborn, 81-83, 85-86
   laterborns, 83-84
   only child, 83
   secondborn, 84
   youngest children, 84-85
World War II, 104, 105, 241,
   242
Writers, laterborns as, 77
Wyatt, Frederick, 240

Xavier University, 129

Yale University, 120
Youngest child

achievement in, 69-72, 219,
   221
dependency in, 119, 211
effect on women's achievement, 99
loneliness of, 70, 71
major patterns of, 11-12
in marriage, 178-85
personality patterns, 55-59
qualities as parents, 196,
   197, 198, 199-200
role of parents of, 219-20
self-esteem in, 56, 69, 219
social development of, 122,
   131-32
suggestions for parents in
   raising, 221-22
with "two sets of parents,"
   220-21
work relationships, 84-85

Zero population growth, 236
Zola, Emile, 9

CLASSICS OF WORLD LITERATURE

_____	48793	CANDIDE & ZADIG	1.25
_____	48655	DIVINE COMEDY	1.65
_____	48540	IVANHOE	1.50
_____	48830	LES MISERABLES	1.95
_____	48803	MADAME BOVARY	1.50
_____	47191	PICTURE OF DORIAN GRAY	.75
_____	47905	TESS OF THE D'URBERVILLES	.95
_____	48813	UNCLE TOM'S CABIN	1.75

Available at bookstores everywhere, or order direct from the publisher.